NEIGHBORHOOD LAW FIRMS FOR THE POOR

NEIGHBORHOOD LAW FIRMS FOR THE POOR:

A comparative study of recent developments
in legal aid
and in the legal profession

by

BRYANT GARTH

Indiana University

SIJTHOFF & NOORDHOFF   1980
Alphen aan den Rijn, The Netherlands
Rockville, Maryland   USA

Printed in the Netherlands

for W.W.G.

TABLE OF CONTENTS

ACKNOWLEDGEMENTS

Comparative research often is closer in method to detective work than to traditional legal research. There are simply no libraries where one can obtain the various books, articles, and reports, published and unpublished, that are necessary even to keep track of legal aid reforms and how they have worked in practice. I am thus indebted to numerous persons who have helped me to compile the source material on which this study is based. I wish especially to thank: Professor Kees Schuyt of Nijmegen, who invited me to Holland and shared his vast knowledge about Dutch developments; Freek Bruinsma, now a researcher at the European University and another well-informed Dutch observer; Professors Roland Penner (Manitoba) and Larry Taman (Osgoode Hall), who helped tremendously by supplying valuable Canadian materials; Jeremy Cooper, now of the European University and formerly an activist with the Camden Law Centre; and John Goldring (Canberra) and Judd Epstein (Monash), who put me in touch with Australian sources. I also owe a great debt to Kim Economides and Paul Geerts, two researchers at the European University during my stay there. Both took an ongoing interest in my research and in the issues that this study sought to address.

Special thanks go to Mauro Cappelletti for his guidance and encouragement at all stages of the research. Indeed, without his help, I would not even have been in Florence as a researcher at the European University. I am honored to have had the privilege of working with him over the period 1975 to 1978, and to have been associated with him in the Ford Foundation-sponsored Access-to-Justice Project and the Project Seminar at the European University. I am pleased to add this study to the work already produced by the Florence Access-to-Justice Project.

I would like finally to acknowledge the material support which made this research possible. I was helped by a grant from the Katherine B. Childs Foundation administered by the American Church in Florence, and my scholarship to attend the European University was supplied by the Thyssen Foundation. I am very impressed with the generosity of a German foundation which gives a scholarship to an American to attend a university in Florence.

"This is not the first time that the winds of change have been detected: In the thirties legal education underwent a searching reexamination and young lawyers with a mission began to emerge from the law schools. The profession, however, was equal to the challenge. Legal education continues to respond to cases and doctrines, and the new breed of the thirties are the 'super-lawyers' of the sixties and seventies. Will it be different this time?"

S. Scheingold, *The Politics of Rights: Lawyers, Public Policy, and Political Change* 199 (New Haven, Yale University Press, 1974).

INTRODUCTION

Since its origins in 1965 with the "neighborhood law offices" of the "War on Poverty" in the United States, the institution of the neighborhood law firm (NLF)[1]—characterized by (1) activist, social-reform-oriented lawyers for the poor, (2) location in lower-class neighborhoods, and (3) salaries generally paid by a government (or, in a few cases, a charitable organization)—has taken on a steadily increasing importance in modern Western societies. Along with the NLFs in the United States, activist lawyers in a growing number of countries—most particularly in Australia, Belgium, Canada, England, and the Netherlands—have recently created law centers, law shops and the like which challenge the traditional roles of lawyers and the accepted methods of providing legal aid for the poor.[2]

The challenge has shaken the once firm faith (outside the United States) in "judicare" legal aid systems, according to which private attorneys are paid by the state for services to individual clients, and it has forced a debate about the role of salaried attorneys for the poor located directly in underprivileged urban areas. The final outcome of that debate, termed the "Great Debate" in legal aid by one Canadian commentator (Penner, 1977), has not yet been reached; but we can now say that the question in an increasing number of countries is no longer whether to have neighborhood lawyers for the poor but how many to have, where to place them, and what role they should play. One British law center, the South Wales Antipoverty Action Centre, is even funded by the European Economic Community's antipoverty program. The story of this major new turn towards NLFs in legal aid reform adds a vital chapter to the comparative study of legal aid (see generally Cappelletti, Gordley, and Johnson, 1975).

Beyond showing the emergence of new developments in legal aid, I am interested in exploring the "legal aid movement" as a unique case study in the role of lawyers and, more generally, of the reform of legal institutions, in effecting lasting change on behalf of the poor in modern "welfare states." The NLF movement originated in the United States as part of the "War on Poverty," and the idea has persisted that lawyers should not merely address the everyday legal problems of the poor—the so-called "symptoms of poverty"—but also should address the causes of poverty embedded in the law and the legal system. It is an ambitious objective.

In order to investigate this novel role for lawyers, which has implications much beyond the delivery of legal services to the poor, several unresolved issues and dilemmas of law in the welfare state must be sorted out. I will state some of them briefly here to provide a background for later discussion.

1. The countries studied here can all be characterized as "welfare states" in the sense that their governments are committed, among other things, to ameliorate some of the hardships and inequalities generated by the operation of their economic systems. While the countries vary in their particular programs and in the degree of hardship and inequality experienced by their populations, they are comparable in their general support of the welfare state program. How far to extend that program is of course subject to great debate, but even conservatives in these countries do not (perhaps cannot) challenge the program's general tenets.

The state—the central government—is the focal point of welfare state activity. The welfare state is built on numerous laws, many of which are designed to help the "have-nots" against the "haves." Social reform in the welfare state is advanced by government action, and the action is generally effected by new law. Many of these reform laws, however, have rarely been enforced; they have in an important sense remained merely symbolic. NLFs may be extremely useful in enforcing such laws and, if effective, could have lasting effects on the social structure; the welfare state might be forced to live up to its promises, or abandon them. On the other hand, NLFs may be the perfect form of social control, bringing disenchanted people within the complex legal system, making *some* rights effective *sometimes* (enough to make the symbols somewhat more plausible) and, in general, "disciplining" people not to protest too much or take collective action even though their social position does not really improve.

2. The legal profession, as represented in particular by its professional organizations, may be "conservative," fearing innovation in general and competition from NLFs in particular. Its interests—at least those of its most influential members—are certainly linked closely to persons and organizations that benefit from the status quo. At the same time, however, evidence that the current system of legal aid fails to reach people to make their rights effective must be taken very seriously by the professional organizations, especially those somewhat

XVIII

removed from the concerns of average practitioners. Their prestige and legitimacy depend on people's perceptions of the legal system (Tushnet, 1977; Trubek, 1972). Also, the profession's emphasis on the *independence* of lawyers serves to insulate activist NLF lawyers from political pressure, but it also tends to make them "unaccountable" to anyone but themselves. Finally, it may be that NLFs generate more business for the private bar than they take away. The bar's own interests in NLFs, therefore, point in several contradictory directions.

3. Lawyers are uniquely situated to see the failings of the legal system, and idealistic lawyers quickly see through the rhetoric of "equal justice." Legal education, in a sense, creates social critics with powers to help change the society. As Trubek notes, "law itself is a form of social criticism" (Trubek, 1977a:555). Legal training, however, also teaches "legalistic" skills which may lead well-intentioned reformers to turn social problems into "legal needs," for which the "solution" is mistakenly believed to be found only in legal strategies (e.g., Campbell, 1974). Again, translated into the NLF movement, this may result only in an advanced form of social control—domination by professionals (Illich et al., 1977).

My exploration of these dilemmas, in conjunction with a comparative history and description of the NLF movement, will be in four parts, corresponding to an idealized evolution of NLFs in a number of countries—particularly the USA, England, Canada, Australia, and the Netherlands.

Part One will examine the sociological justification for NLFs—the "unmet need" for legal services for the poor, which has been discovered in the last ten or fifteen years. One purpose will be to show the relationship of studies of unmet need to the NLF movement, suggesting that the study and the remedy cannot be separated. The limitations of these studies must therefore be traced in the history of NLFs and their approaches to legal and social reform.

Part Two will examine the establishment and development of NLFs, describing their basic organization and orientation. Beyond that, it will focus on the political history of NLFs, showing the interaction of professional legal organizations, activist lawyers and law students, and welfare state governments. This interaction has tended in the countries studied to promote the survival of publicity-funded lawyers who are at least ideologically committed to effecting social change on behalf of "have-not" groups. The chapters in this part will see what happens to the NLF "solution" when it is implemented. The method here will be to trace the history in individual countries before reaching a general comparative conclusion.

Part Three begins to explore more carefully what the tactics and strategies of NLFs are in the various settings, drawing particularly on the contrast between the United States and England. This part can begin to analyze how law centers meet the "unmet need" or seek to make rights effective, and what some of the problems and trade-offs are with the various strategies involved. The concluding chapter will contrast the types of NLFs that can be found, and outline their aims and assumptions.

Part Four then concludes the study. It asks how we ought to evaluate this movement of social change and social control, given the dilemmas I have raised. The accomplishments and limitations are discussed, along with the contribution NLFs can realistically make to a movement for change. Finally, a few general themes can be addressed, particularly the relationship of the goals of NLFs to "combined models," including institutions for vindicating rights without lawyers (see Cappelletti and Garth, 1978).

It should be noted that this study will focus mainly on developments in the United States, England, Canada, and the Netherlands, since these are the countries with the greatest experience of the type of NLF with which this study is concerned. Developments in Australia will be considered mainly because of the contrasting historical pattern, and some developments in Belgium and Norway will also be described. Brief comparative assessments of the legal aid system in Sweden as well as of the judicare systems in effect in France and Germany will also be necessary.

My own perspective, finally, should also be made clear. As an American with some experience in one U.S. NLF, my research and approach is bound to reflect my concern about what the U.S. systems can learn from other countries. To that extent, I may sometimes be guilty of being overly critical of U.S. developments.

Notes

1. This term will be used when I refer to the institution in general with the attributes noted in the text. It is also the U.S. term and it is close to the English "neighbourhood law centre." For particular countries I will use the national term or a literal translation of it.

It should be noted that my definition does not exclusively focus on whether or not lawyers are paid a *salary* by the state. It seems clear that publicly-salaried attorneys have tended to be more socially-oriented, neighborhood-oriented, and proactive (in the sense of seeking to bring certain problems to *them*) than private attorneys under judicare systems; and the debate about which method is preferable often relies on this presumed characteristic of publicly-salaried lawyers. But publicly-salaried legal aid lawyers may not fit the other requirements of my definition. Furthermore, judicare lawyers may serve as NLFs, as they do in the "law collectives" in Holland discussed in Chapter 6.

2. I will not attempt to explain systematically why NLFs developed in these modern countries and not, for example, in the Federal Republic of Germany and Italy. Obviously the matter is complicated. It can be noted, however, that the development of NLFs is made easier where there is a tradition of legal reformism, particularly one relating empirical research to such reforms. Also, the availability of substitutes will naturally affect the development of NLFs. The existence of trade union legal services, for example, has made legal aid reform seem less compelling in Germany (see, e.g., Pfennigsdorf, 1975).

Given the general similarity of Western welfare states, however, and the peculiar attractiveness of the NLF idea in those settings, it may only be a question of time before institutions analogous to NLFs develop to serve the lower classes of the population, whether they be simply the poor, national or racial minorities, or foreign workers. It may be significant that the NLF movement began in English language countries, spread to Holland, where English-language materials are accessible to the educated public, and then moved through the Flemish part of Belgium, the French-speaking area of Belgium, and most recently to France. Belgian *boutiques de droit* inspired French *boutiques de droit* set up by young lawyers and apprentice lawyers (*stagiaires*). The French *boutiques*, which may begin to have an impact on national legal aid policy in France, are discussed in only a few available works (see, e.g., *Boutiques de droit*, 1978; Dumas, 1977:243–45; Hartman, 1978).

Part One

The "Unmet Need" for Legal Services: Justifying Neighborhood Law Firms

Introduction

Why should we reform legal aid systems by creating publicly-salaried lawyers in neighborhood law firms? Is it because NLFs are capable of offering "competent" legal advice and representation at a lower cost than other legal aid systems, notably "judicare" and the "charitable system?"[1] Although some commentators have framed the issue in terms of efficiency—whether NLFs are more cost-effective in giving the representation that the poor would get if they used private attorneys (e.g., Brakel, 1977)—the proponents of NLFs have largely conducted the debate at another level. It has been argued in country after country that there is an "unmet legal need" which *requires* a new method of delivering legal services: publicly-funded NLFs.

The assumption has even been that this "need" can be objectively demonstrated and measured. For example, in *Justice for All*, the influential English Labour (Party) Lawyer pamphlet promoting NLFs in 1968, it was observed that "the extent of the unmet need should be capable of ascertainment, in round terms at least, by scientific social survey aimed at producing quantitative results based on generally acceptable criteria" (Society of Labour Lawyers, 1968:6). Inspired by this goal, considerable empirical research has been undertaken in the last ten to fifteen years, signaling an unprecedented invasion of social scientists into the "legal" policy-making domain. Studies in Australia, Canada, England, Holland, and the United States, all closely connected to the NLF movement, have sought to ascertain and measure this need, and this "objective" method continues to have powerful adherents. Roger Crampton, for example, the Chairman of the Board of Directors of the U.S. Legal Services Corporation, recently complained that "less than 15 percent of the legal needs of the poor are being met" (Crampton, 1975:1343, citing Curran, 1977), and the Dutch Secretary for Justice proclaimed his faith in sociological research into "the need for legal assistance, the way in which this need is or is not being met and the lacunae evident in this area" (Council of Europe, 1976:9).

1

Methods are still being sought to make possible a nonpolitical, objective debate about the need for NLFs, but surveys of legal need have come under increasing criticism, even by authors of these studies. One such author, Raymond Marks, now argues that "we should abandon our quest to define legal need" (Marks, 1977:204).

My own view, with some qualifications, corresponds to this conclusion, but it is useful to examine some of the approaches and findings of these surveys. They help show the important relationship between research and reform, and their conclusions do reveal insights that cannot be neglected. If we trace the evolution of legal need studies, the recent history of NLFs and some of their problems and potential can be better understood.

Chapter 1

Studies of Legal Needs and the Justification for Neighborhood Law Firms

I. From Equal Opportunity to Legal Need

The utilization of sociological research into "legal needs" depends on a basic change in the view of the legal system and legal aid. Diverse commentators have recognized and described the movement from "legal formalism" to "instrumental or technical rationality." The movement has developed as part of the welfare state. According to Unger, one "major impact of the welfare state on law is the turn from formalistic to purposive or policy-oriented styles of legal reasoning and from concerns with formal justice to an interest in procedural and substantive justice" (1976:19; see also, e.g., Luhmen, 1975:113–114; Charvet, 1976).[2] This change in the perceived role of law has had increasingly important repercussions for legal aid policy (and civil procedure generally). The framework of debate has shifted from a "traditional" to a "social welfare" approach to legal aid, and accordingly NLFs have been placed on the reform agenda.

The traditional attitude, still prevailing in much of the world, is that legal action is essentially a method for enabling individuals to enforce their property rights. A lawyer under this scheme "might be defined most succinctly as the agent of economic man," and the legal system as the "legal analogue of the market economy" (Berney and Pierce, 1975:11). Legal aid schemes within this approach arise because lawyers are recognized as a monopoly—often necessary in order to obtain a divorce, for example—and because they are seen to have a special skill which gives them a public service quality. If the poor cannot afford to purchase legal services, the solution is to *subsidize* poor individuals. This answer characterizes both the so-called "charitable" and the "judicare" systems of legal aid, the difference being that under charitable systems the legal profession provides the subsidy by taking cases for no fees, while under judicare the state pays the subsidy by compensating private attorneys. Within either of these approaches it is theoretically irrelevant whether the poor decide to utilize the system's benefits. Poor individuals, like other individuals, are presumed to know their own interests and to pursue them rationally in their own way. The legal system, to employ Donald Black's useful terminology, is "reactive," relying on citizen initiative to "mobilize" the law (Black, 1973). "Reactivity" is perfectly consistent with "formal justice," which "guarantees the maximum freedom for the interested parties to represent their formal legal interests" (Weber, 1954:228).

A reactive approach, corresponding to the market economy, may, according to Black, be contrasted to a "proactive" system, corresponding to a *"social welfare model of the law"* (Black, 1973:138). After governmental policies are set, government itself may seek to mobilize people to conform to the standards provided by a policy. The legal system, including lawyers, can be changed to fulfill particular substantive (instrumental) goals. Policy makers may not be content with reactive institutions which impede the implementation of policy decisions.

Legal need studies have become relevant to policy makers because of the ascendency of proactive mobilization. Governmental policy makers in the welfare state are now willing to entertain the notion that if people do not *choose* to further their "needs," which are invariably defined according to technical—i.e., professional —standards, it is the government's task to mobilize them. This proposition, obviously with broad implications concerning the welfare state and the idea of professionalism, has at times been accepted even by critics of NLFs. In the Conservative Party analogue to *Justice for All*, entitled *Rough Justice* and also published in 1968, the Society of Conservative Lawyers in England admitted the problem of "the failure of many people who need legal assistance to even get to a solicitor's office" (1968:19). According to this perspective, it is not enough that individuals have the economic means to obtain the services of a lawyer; the question has become whether "needy" individuals *in fact* use lawyers. This change in perspective makes the argument for NLFs not only relevant, but almost irresistable to socially-minded lawyers and welfare state governments, particularly liberal or labor ones.

II. The Legal Needs of the Poor: A Diagnosis and a Remedy

Reflecting this new welfare state approach, the landmark sociological study by Carlin and Howard in 1965 concluded that "lack of economic resources"—the unequal opportunity to retain a lawyer— is not the principal barrier to access for the poor.[3] Citing other studies showing that "about two-thirds of lower-class families have *never*

4

employed a lawyer, compared to about one-third of upper-class families" (1965:382), they argued in an oft-quoted passage that lack of economic resources

> represents only one element in a complex social process leading an individual to seek out and obtain legal representation. At least four steps are involved: (1) awareness or recognition of a problem as a legal problem; (2) willingness to take legal action for solution of the problem; (3) getting to a lawyer; and (4) actually hiring a lawyer (1965:423).

This analysis is striking when contrasted to the traditional model of lawyers. It focuses the attention of the state on the perceptions of the poor, and encourages positive, proactive measures to make the poor more "willing" to take legal action. The legal needs of the poor could not be met unless "those providing legal services take the initiative in 'going to the people'" (Carlin and Howard, 1965:423). It was found, not surprisingly, that existing voluntary, charitable programs did not satisfy their test. (Indeed, they were never meant to.)

The poor *needed* lawyers for other reasons as well. The law was "unbalanced"; the inability of the poor to assert their own interests through legal strategies had resulted in "class justice." In a number of areas where the poor had legal problems—in particular, in criminal law, landlord–tenant law, civil rights, consumer law, welfare law, mental health law, and family law—the law was unfair and had to be changed (see also Carlin, Howard, and Messinger, 1966; Wald, 1965).

> It is crucial that the legal problems of the poor be dealt with at an institutional level. This would include: (1) bringing about changes in the routine practices of landlords, finance companies, and local merchants, that tend to weaken or violate existing legal rights; and (2) reforming administrative regulations and official procedures (within welfare agencies, certain courts, police departments) that are inconsistent with or violate standards of due process (Carlin and Howard, 1965:431).

We thus find a mixing of legal needs with what might be termed the "sociolegal" or "politicolegal" needs of the poor, but still the focus is on *legal* strategies and new approaches by *lawyers*: "Lawyers serving the poor must be capable of exercising as high a level of technical skill and ingenuity as lawyers serving the wealthy individual or large corporation" (Carlin and Howard, 1965:431).

Other U.S. studies, also connected with the NLF movement, bolstered the conclusions of Carlin and Howard by focusing more specifically on the types of legal problems experienced by the poor. The poor, it was found, were likely to see the "legal" dimensions of problems mainly, or even exclusively, when they concerned domestic relations matters, criminal charges, personal injury claims, and debt

5

inform the poor of their rights and "proactively" enforce them; (3) and to be able to utilize legal strategies positively (*"dans un sens positif"*) to challenge laws and practices against the interests of the poor. The consistency of the diagnosis and the cure are such that one skeptical English commentator observed, with some justification, that legal aid reforms have been treated as a *"deus ex machina*, which, if only correctly assembled, will restore equality to the legal system" (Alcock, 1976:162).

III. Another Diagnosis and an Expanded Cure

This legal need justification for NLFs, however, has been undermined somewhat by another series of empirical studies beginning in 1969 and utilizing a slightly different theoretical framework. Mayhew and Reiss, studying the use of lawyers among the general population in Detroit, Michigan, began to shift attention from objectively measure-able "legal needs" to the *organization* of the legal profession and how it serves or inhibits certain types of claims (Mayhew and Reiss, 1969). Going beyond studies of the legal needs of the poor, they emphasized that individuals in general, not just the poor, could not make use of lawyers in nontraditional areas of law. As Mayhew wrote in a more recent article explicitly setting out his critique:

> In all these traditions of thought and work, the emphasis has been on whether legal services available to the well-to-do are or should be also available to the poor, not on the more fundamental question of whether the legal system is adequately organized to represent any claims at all. *There may be a whole range of claims that are not well protected for anyone* [emphasis added] (Mayhew, 1975:401).

The point is that the categories of rich and poor are inadequate for diagnosis or cure. Certain types of problems "surrounding such daily matters as the citizen's relation to merchants or public authority" are not brought to lawyers (or, more generally, the legal system) since "the institution of legal advocacy is not organized to handle these problems on a routine basis" (Mayhew and Reiss, 1969:317). These conclusions are also supported by important recent studies both inside and outside of the United States.[7]

The best example outside of the United States is the 1976 Dutch survey financed by the Dutch Ministry of Justice and undertaken by Schuyt, Groenendijk, and Sloot. It explicitly corroborates Mayhew's insights. The authors found that "the problems of people in the lower social classes are significantly related to social welfare law, labor law, rent and housing, and criminal law. But these areas of the law are, with the exception of criminal law, precisely the areas that are not

8

served well by the legal profession" (Schuyt et al., 1977:111). Further, nonpoor individuals with social welfare problems faced the same basic problems (although somewhat less often) in enforcing their rights in nontraditional legal areas: "Lawyers serve individuals mostly in divorce cases; they do not to any great extent serve individuals in their conflicts with governments or organizations. On the contrary, lawyers serve corporate bodies and large organizations" (Schuyt et al., 1977:112).

We thus have two apparently different analyses of why the "needs" of the poor (and individuals) are not met by the traditional methods of delivering legal services, including judicare legal aid systems. The first focuses more on the inability of the poor to recognize and pursue their legal needs, while the second addresses the failure of the legal system to mobilize individuals in general. The second thus has the advantage of expanding the inquiry to consider the organization of the profession in general, not just the peculiarities of the poor, and it also forces one to consider whether, given the evident organizational deficiencies of lawyers, there are other possible institutions which can meet the need just as well or better. Mayhew suggested, in fact, that every legal institution, whether by relying passively on an informal network of contacts and referrals, or by utilizing proactive strategies, creates "both channels of access and barriers to access" (Mayhew, 1975:404).

Nevertheless, these more sophisticated legal need studies (despite the fact that they call attention to the plight of middle-class individuals) are quite similar in many ways to the other studies. They merely expand on our knowledge about unmet needs. They too are used to show "objectively" that proactive NLFs and their analogues for the middle class are the most effective methods of getting people to vindicate their new welfare state rights in landlord–tenant matters, consumer matters, and social welfare disputes (see Griffiths, 1977:268). Again, therefore, we find an "objective," technical reason for this new method of delivering legal services.[8]

IV. Some Problems with the Technical Solution

These apparently objective methods of justifying NLFs have consider-able appeal, and the themes of "unmet need" and "making new legislation effective" recur throughout the discussion of NLFs. It is certainly true, for example, that since the Second World War, in England and more recently in the United States, a huge array of welfare state legislation has been created to improve the position of the "have-nots" either through government benefits or by changing

9

number of countries. The studies may even make respectable the adoption of legal strategies aimed at change on behalf of the poor as a class. The hard questions of politics, effectiveness, and accountability, however, are avoided by professional diagnoses and cures. These questions and attempts to resolve them must be considered in subsequent chapters examining NLFs in practice. It must not be forgotten, however, that a movement for change has sparked the legal needs studies. A question that will underlie subsequent chapters, therefore, is whether idealistic NLF lawyers are capable, politically or personally, of adopting strategies which overcome the limits implied in the approach taken in legal need studies.

Notes

1. Judicare means that private attorneys are compensated for the services they provide to persons unable to pay the fees. The "charitable system" is where lawyers have an honorific duty to provide services at no charge to poor persons who need legal advice or assistance (for a comparative analysis of these systems, see Cappelletti, Gordley, and Johnson, 1975).

2. In Luhman's words:

> "the pace of change in law has accelerated so much that the mutations of law can no longer be controlled by means of the hitherto existing dogmatic methods. At the same time political requirements, as far as input and output are concerned, have grown considerably: democracy, which refers to input functions, and the welfare state, which refers to output functions, are today, with us, political concepts without opponents, and in both ideas is inherent a tendency to dissolve formalistic legality and skill in handling definitions" (1976:113–14).

3. Significantly, these legal need studies helped to build a coherent, policy-oriented legal sociology movement in the United States. The first article of the first issue of the *Law and Society Review* was an expanded legal need study by Carlin, Howard, and Messinger (1966).

4. Typical is the following statement in a symposium on "The Legal Needs of the Poor."

> "What is required is the scholarly analysis of social and economic forces, the identification of suitable pressure points, and, then, by inspired and vigorous advocacy, the application of legal doctrine in the fashioning of remedies that will deter future misconduct and effect change—in short, the skills of a lawyer" (Levi, 1966:285).

5. The Commission of Inquiry into Poverty was set up in 1972 by the Liberal–National Coalition and expanded in early 1973 by the Labour Party to include "law and poverty" (see Sackville, 1975).

12

6. The link between diagnosis and solution was not merely academic. Jerome Carlin, for example, became the first director of the San Francisco Neighborhood Legal Assistance Foundation. The Ford Foundation became active in funding NLF experiments in the United States, and the Nuffield Foundation did likewise in England.

7. The recent American Bar Association survey of the legal needs of the public carefully refrains from policy conclusions, but the data are completely consistent with the Mayhew and Reiss findings. For example, they show that a lawyer will be consulted in 40 out of 100 real property acquisition disputes, 77 out of 100 divorce actions, and 70 out of 100 disputes on alimony or support, compared to 7 out of 100 "serious disputes" on major consumer purchases, 15 out of 100 serious difficulties with a federal agency, and 10 out of 100 infringements of constitutional rights (Curran, 1976:161).

8. The difference, however, is that one might be somewhat hesitant about favoring NLFs if the middle class is victimized just as much by the current organization of legal services. There is no longer an objective reason to favor only the poor. Griffith's review of the Schuyt et al. study is in fact very critical of the Mayhew approach for obscuring the effects of wealth (or income) on access (1977:280–81). The point here is only that each approach tends to seek a solution in changes in the profession, such as NLFs and—for Mayhew—group and prepaid services (Mayhew, 1975:421).

give a general picture of the present state of NLFs in modern societies. And, fourth, it will seek to discuss these developments from a somewhat different perspective than that usually employed by partisans or opponents of NLFs. The movement is often portrayed as liberal, or even radical, versus conservative, left versus right. It is better to examine the positions of the various interest groups, which do not line up along a left–right dichotomy. In particular, close attention must be paid, where possible, to the policies and politics of the welfare state governments, to the interests and ideology of the legal profession, with its various components and divisions, and to the activities and aims of the NLF lawyers and their constituencies. The following six chapters, especially the concluding comparative one, will seek to highlight the roles of these groups and show how they have interacted in response to the NLF challenge.

Chapter 2

The United States

I. Origins of the Neighborhood Law Firm Movement

The NLF movement in the United States began officially in 1965 as
part of President Lyndon Johnson's "War on Poverty." Its origins,
however, can be traced at least back to the early 20th century. Three
historical developments provided the inspiration for the movement as
it finally emerged. The first was the traditional American legal aid
movement (for civil cases). Legal aid had been organized primarily
under the auspices of local bar associations in urban legal aid offices
with full-time, salaried attorneys. The second historical root consisted
of the development of litigation techniques, in particular the "test
case," as methods of changing the law and promoting social reform,
and the third was the awakening of interest in poverty and strategies
for eliminating it, particularly that of "community action."

A. The U.S. Legal Aid Movement

Most commentators trace the origins of the legal aid movement in the
United States back to 1876, when the first "legal aid society" was set
up in New York City to help German immigrants (the *Deutscher
Rechtsschutz Verein*) (e.g., Auerbach, 1976). The idea of such legal aid
societies, as a supplement to the honorific duty of lawyers (only in
criminal cases) to provide some aid to the needy, spread slowly to
help immigrants and other especially needy groups. By 1900, there
were six such societies, and the institution was beginning to be
established as a goal of reformers throughout the country.

Legal aid societies then began to proliferate, aided no doubt by a
desire to help assimilate the wave of immigrants from southern and
eastern Europe who were concentrating in the major urban areas.
The plea of the director of the New York office, Arthur von Briesen,
was that, given legal aid, "a weak and helpless person ... is very apt to
become a staunch supporter of the social organization of that
community and a very poor listener to the preachers of discord and

discontent" (Auerbach, 1976:55), and this plea struck an increasingly responsive chord. By 1910 there were fifteen U.S. legal aid societies, including for the first time one sponsored by a local bar association; and by 1920 there were forty-one U.S. legal aid societies.

The legal aid movement had clearly begun, but it then received an important boost through the publication of Reginald Heber Smith's *Justice and the Poor* in 1919. Smith's study, funded by the Carnegie Foundation, exhaustively described the state of legal aid in the United States. He found forty-one cities with some sort of legal aid organization, employing sixty-one full-time and 113 part-time (one-half to one-third of the working day) attorneys. This situation, he concluded, was woefully inadequate and left the lower classes unable to use the law. Thus, "Differences in the ability of classes to use the machinery of the law, if permitted to remain, lead inevitably to disparity between the rights of classes. ... And when the law enforces a distinction between classes, revolution ensues or democracy is at an end" (Johnson, 1974:6).

While many bar leaders, including the President of the New York Bar, resisted Smith's pleas, Smith's essentially conservative appeal did make a strong impression on several leaders of the American Bar Association (ABA), including Charles Evans Hughes. Hughes, a former candidate for President of the United States and a future Chief Justice of the U.S. Supreme Court, persuaded the organizers of the Annual Convention of the ABA in 1920 to set up a panel on legal aid, with Smith as a member. This was a turning point in the legal aid movement; the ABA began to assume a much greater interest in legal aid reform. For example, a Special Committee on Legal Aid under the chairmanship of Hughes was created at the 1920 Convention, and in 1923 the National Association of Legal Aid Organizations (later the National Legal Aid and Defender Association—NLADA) was set up with close ties to the ABA (Johnson, 1974:7–8).

Legal aid societies became an important expressed concern of the bar, and their number increased by thirty in the 1920s. The method increasingly was to set them up under the auspices of local bar associations, since it soon became evident that such support was indispensible to a society's success. Local bar associations, however, were never as enthusiastic about legal aid reform as the national bar which, removed from the immediate concerns of urban lawyers and, not unimportantly, often composed of prestigious, elite corporate lawyers, tends to serve as the conscience of the profession. For example, Harrison Tweed, a Wall Street corporate lawyer and the NLADA president, stated somewhat patronizingly that "local bar associations do not always rally to a man in a fight to the finish for the establishment of adequate service to the poor" (Johnson, 1974:8). This local bar/national bar cleavage, as will be seen, recurs often in the history of legal aid.

The legal aid movement, characterized by local bar reticence and national bar support, stagnated through the depression of the 1930s and the war years of the 1940s. Other problems became more pressing. In an ABA-supported study published in 1951, Emery Brownell of the NLADA found only seventy legal aid society offices in operation (Brownell, 1951).

It is interesting, nevertheless, to note that the depression—and a combination of the need for legal business and the desire to do good— did provoke some new thought and experimentation with "neighborhood law offices." Under the influence of the National Lawyers' Guild, founded in the mid-1930s, and Professor Karl Llewellyn of Yale (Llewellyn, 1938:104), new "neighborhood law offices" aimed at aiding middle- and low-income persons were created in Chicago and Philadelphia (Auerbach, 1976:207; Abrahams, 1949). Set up against the wishes of the organized bar, they were placed in poor residential areas where they charged very low fees for their services. While these neighborhood law offices were not ultimately very influential, they were notable efforts to move into the poor neighborhoods to provide them with the benefits of the law. In addition, they are interesting historically because they challenged, to some extent, the profession's way of meeting the needs not just of the poor, but also of some middle-class individuals. The Philadelphia system survived at least into the 1960s (Abrahams, 1964).

In the 1950s legal aid societies proliferated much more rapidly; there were 249 by 1963. Much of the inspiration for this increase came from England, sparked by the passage of the Legal Aid and Advice Act of 1949. The British system of private attorneys compensated by the national government was not regarded with enthusiasm by any but the most liberal of U.S. lawyers. To American individualists, government payment appeared to constitute the first step to "socialism." Thus, as stated by the leading historian of the legal aid movement (and former director of the OEO legal services program), Earl Johnson, Jr., "Suddenly the legal aid movement [through private legal aid societies] was America's savior from 'socialization of the legal profession'" (Johnson, 1974:18). Legal aid societies received new impetus as the fear of socialism inspired otherwise reticent local and state bar associations to act. While lawyers or bar associations provided only 8.5 percent of the funds for these programs in 1950, the figure rose to 12 percent in 1960 (Council for Public Interest Law, 1976:23).

By the mid-1960s, therefore, the system of legal aid by salaried attorneys, financed by charities and local bar associations and under the supervision and control of those bar associations, was entrenched, as was the ABA's national role as principal proponent of legal aid.

This is not to say that these legal aid societies were very effective. They were notoriously understaffed and overworked. The combined annual budget, for example, was only $4 million in 1962 for 236 legal aid offices (Johnson, 1974:9). Further, eligibility standards were very strict; they were controlled by boards dominated by conservative local attorneys; and the lawyer's role remained a very narrow one: "Legal aid emphasized service to individuals exclusively; there was no law reform or class action litigation; only a minimal effort was made to uncover problems of the poor and sensitize society to legal needs. ... [The offices] avoided community education or publicity so that their work schedules would remain tolerable" (Handler et al., 1978). What is important at this point, however, is simply to emphasize (1) the bar's established concern with legal aid, however it developed and whatever its motives, and (2) the existing model of staff attorneys for the poor. These became instrumental in the design and implementation of the OEO program.

B. Legal Reform Through the Courts

A second development vital to the emergence of the NLF movement in the late 1960s was the increasing utilization of "test case" litigation to achieve social reform. Under the U.S. system of a written constitution and judicial review (coupled with the stare decisis doctrine), the courts—especially the Supreme Court—had always been important in American law-making. Still, only in the beginning of this century did social reform groups seek systematically to promote change through litigation.

The two principal examples of these groups were the National Association for the Advancement of Colored People (NAACP), founded in 1909, and the American Civil Liberties Union (ACLU), founded in its present form in 1920. Both were nationally-known models of "social advocacy" through test cases and class actions.[1] The NAACP—the more important of the two—began its legal attack on racial discrimination with victories in the U.S. Supreme Court in 1915 against certain voting restrictions, in 1917 against housing segregation, and in 1923 against the exclusion of Blacks from juries in criminal cases. In 1939, the NAACP established a special organization, the Legal Defense and Educational Fund, Inc. (the "Inc. Fund"), which continued the extraordinary litigation record of the

20

NAACP. By 1952, the Inc. Fund had won thirty-four of the thirty-eight cases it had argued before the Supreme Court, and two years later the Fund finally succeeded in overturning de jure school segregation in the celebrated case of *Brown v. Board of Education*, 347 U.S. 483 (1954) (see Handler et al., 1978:22–23). *Brown* in turn provided a precedent in the 1950s and 1960s to challenge successfully, on behalf of large groups or classes of black persons, segregation in "buses, golf courses, bathhouses, courtrooms, voting, marriage, public accommodations, housing, as well as other state activities" (Handler et al., 1978:22). It was an extraordinary record and a testament to the unique possibilities of social change through the courts in the United States.

The importance of this approach to social reform as a model for the NLF movement in America can scarcely be exaggerated. As Handler, Hollingsworth, and Erlanger point out:

> Supreme Court victories had an enormous appeal. At the stroke of the judicial pen, so it seemed, legal rights and legitimacy were given to disadvantaged groups. The executive and legislative branches of the government, thought to be hostile and indifferent to the claims of blacks and other minorities, appeared to be circumvented. The style and location of the litigation were very important in influencing lawyer recruits. Young, elite, motivated lawyers would work with the leaders of the organization, and their legal work would be in the prestigious Federal courts, often at the appellate level. The legal training of young lawyers and the law school conception of the role of law and lawyers in social reform concentrated on appellate court litigation. The Warren Court and the NAACP litigation seemed to be the perfect example of what law, lawyers, and legal education were all about (1978:23).

In the early 1960s, when the attack on racial discrimination was stepped up under the Kennedy and Johnson administrations, the NAACP test-case model spread to other civil rights organizations as well. It was clearly—and in fact may still be—the model for social change through law in America (e.g., Council For Public Interest Law, 1976:36–38).

C. Legal Strategies and the Emergence of the War on Poverty

The extent and seriousness of poverty in America were "uncovered" in the early 1960s, and the liberal Democratic administrations sought to enact programs to attack the problem.[2] They did not propose to redistribute wealth, but rather to enable people to "break the cycle of poverty" through other means. NLFs were enlisted to help break the poverty cycle.[3] The Legal Services Program shared a common analysis of poverty in the 1960s with the other programs of the War on

Poverty's Office of Economic Opportunity (OEO), especially that of "community action agencies." While the approach cannot be examined here in detail, it should be noted that it rested on these assumptions: that there was a "cycle of poverty" that prevented the poor from helping themselves or taking advantage of many social services or educational opportunities; that professionals, including teachers, social workers, and ultimately lawyers, could assume leadership of the disadvantaged to help them "proactively" to take advantage of social services and educational opportunities in order to enable them to overcome their cultural handicaps; and that to avoid the vices of bureaucratization which prevented existing social service programs from reaching the poor effectively, it would be necessary to create new institutions and to "involve" the poor in their operation. While the point is not essential here, it should be noted that "involvement" of the poor did not mean "control" by the poor (Marris and Rein, 1972:59–84; Yale Law Journal, 1966:602–10). Too often NLFs and community action are thought to stem from different diagnoses of poverty and the role of professionals. In fact, the "democratic," nonprofessional character of community action is often exaggerated. Community action and the NLFs both developed from the same approach.

The approach implied that neither massive funds nor basic changes in political power were necessary. In common with the " legal need" studies produced around this time, it rested on a "social engineering" model of reform.[4] However incomplete this perspective may be in practice, as was pointed out before, it had great appeal to socially-oriented professionals and to a welfare state government. It is a perspective particularly attractive also to charitable foundations like the Ford Foundation, who seek to solve political problems with new programs that do not imply major political changes.

Two particular experiments—one in New Haven and one in New York City—helped produce the institutional structure of the "War on Poverty," including the legal services component (and community action). Both were closely linked to the Ford Foundation's "grey areas" program of the late 1950s and early 1960s (Marris and Rein, 1972:37–44), which sought "to experiment with new ways of improving social conditions in the central cities and of opening up new opportunities for those now living in these urban 'grey areas'" (Handler et al., 1978:29).

The first legal program to be considered is Community Progress, Incorporated (CPI), of New Haven, Connecticut. The original proposal for CPI suggested that "a plan be worked out, with the cooperation of the New Haven County Bar Association, to provide legal assistance at the community schools. Lawyers would look at all the legal problems of the family, would provide legal advice on simple matters, and would make referrals on more complex cases" (Marris and Rein, 1972:220). The lawyer's role was to be part of a "multiservice" professional approach, including use of social workers and others, in order to "diagnose, refer, and to coordinate" legal problems. The legal office began operating on 2 January 1963, with two staff attorneys under the employ of CPI (Johnson, 1974:22).

Jean Cahn, one of the two lawyers, took a broader view of her role than that originally anticipated. Contrary to the wishes of the executive director of CPI, she sought to pursue cases even if they were controversial or against governmental agencies (Murphy, 1971:116). This soon involved CPI in a major crisis. She assumed the legal defense of a young black man accused of raping a white woman, and by doing so aroused considerable public hostility. CPI in turn feared the public controversy, and she was asked to withdraw as defense attorney. She refused, was forced to resign, and the existing legal services program was terminated. (It was later set up independently as the New Haven Legal Assistance Association.)

Jean Cahn and her husband, Edgar Cahn, then a Yale law student, proceeded to draw some conclusions from the New Haven experience that greatly influenced the subsequent NLF movement. The article they wrote entitled "The War on Poverty: A Civilian Perspective," was widely circulated in Washington, D.C. prior to its publication in July 1964 in the *Yale Law Journal*. It has had a lasting influence in the United States and elsewhere. The Cahns perceptively noted the weaknesses in the "community action" program developed by the Ford Foundation and later implemented on a much larger scale as part of the War on Poverty. They recognized that the strategy there was to have a war "fought by professionals on behalf of the citizenry through service programs" (1964:1320). Further, they saw that the role of the poor was to be more "acquiescence" than "participation." They accurately foresaw that the emphasis on technical issues to be settled by experts would cause the program to avoid political problems and controversy in order to seek broad alliances. The result, they argued, would be that the "civilian perspective necessary to make the program responsive and to let the poor express 'dissent and criticism' will be lost" (1964:1331).

Accepting as given that the "community action program" was incapable of adopting the "civilian perspective," the Cahns suggested that one solution might be an *independent* "neighborhood law firm" to serve as an aggressive advocate for the poor—"providing representation to individuals and groups in cases which have broad institutional implications and widespread ramifications" (1964:1346). While sensitive to the limits of their proposal, it is especially noteworthy that, while they lost faith in other professionals to define the poor's needs and meet them, they retained the hope that the civilian perspective could be implemented through lawyers and legal strategies.[5] Unlike some others disenchanted with nonpolitical community action, they did not call for a shift to political strategies for organizing the poor (Marris and Rein, 1972:225–30): "it may take less time and effort to 'import' a lawyer to articulate a concern than to press the same demand by organizing citizen groups" (Cahn and Cahn, 1964:1335).[6] Anticipating the legal need studies to some extent, they observed that "the potential of extended legal services, including legal representation, legal education, and preventive counseling for the poor is only now coming to be appreciated" (1964:1336). The Cahns thus made the classic appeal to set up neighborhood law firms for the poor. While dynamic and forward looking, this new legal approach retained the same commitment to and faith in the technical skills of the professional lawyer that was seen in the legal need studies.

The Cahns' proposal, reflecting their evaluation of the New Haven experience, captures the major themes drawn from the pre-OEO experiments. The New York City Mobilization for Youth (MFY) program, however, also merits attention. Funded by the President's Committee on Juvenile Delinquency and Youth Crime, as well as by the Ford Foundation, Mobilization for Youth opened a "storefront service center" in 1962 on New York's Lower East Side. It soon became a center of fairly aggressive organizational activity on behalf of the neighborhood. Because of its activities, it "became the victim of a sustained and powerful prosecution which all but destroyed it" (Marris and Rein, 1972:227).

The employment of two full-time lawyers in 1963, followed by two more in 1964, must be seen as part of its aggressiveness (Piven and Cloward, 1972:292–93). Thus, in late 1964 when legal services became a formal division within MFY, funded by a specific grant of $50,000 from the President's Committee and set up in cooperation with Columbia University, its explicit aim was to use legal strategies to effect social change. Edward Sparer, the director, had been influenced by civil rights lawyers, and he implemented this new commitment with the strategy of test case litigation in welfare, housing, consumer, and criminal law.

The test case strategy quickly led to a dispute not unlike that which took place in New Haven. According to Johnson's account, the first series of test cases filed against the New York Welfare Department

24

raised the issue of to whom the legal unit was accountable (Johnson, 1974:23–25). Sparer argued for the independence of the legal unit, citing the Canons of Ethics regulating the lawyer–client relationship, while the chairman of MFY's Committee on Direct Operations, Henry Cohn, insisted that "the type of cooperative effort envisioned in the original MFY proposal required that all professions and disciplines participating in the program subordinate their professional standards to the common interest" (Johnson, 1974:24–25). The issue was then put to Judge Florence Kelley, brought in by the city to consider the matter, and, not surprisingly, she supported the lawyers. The MFY Committee then went along with her decision. The legal division was given the independence thought to be consistent with legal professionalism.

These experiments were not evaluated systematically, but they pointed to an appealing new approach to legal aid, which could take place in the context of the War on Poverty declared "unconditionally" by President Johnson in early 1964, but which would remain independent of community action agencies (Handler et al., 1978).[7] The consensus was not in favor of a truly "civilian perspective," although the "involvement" of the poor clearly was sought, but rather toward a new type of proactive legal professionalism borrowed in large part from the civil rights movement. This role and approach, as has been noted, was reflected also in the "legal need" studies, and it was not at this point inconsistent with the assumptions and diagnoses underlying the War on Poverty.

The NLF model was brought to the attention of policy makers, most notably by the Cahns, at that time working for the government, and finally by a Washington, D.C., National Conference on Law and Poverty held in November 1964 and sponsored by the U.S. Department of Health, Education and Welfare.[8] Indeed, it appears that despite the fact that no mention of legal services was made in the Equal Opportunity Act of 1964 (Public Law No. 88–452), the idea of a nationally-funded legal services program was already under serious consideration. Sargent Shriver, the Director of the Office of Economic Opportunity (OEO)—the basic "war on poverty" agency —was very receptive to the ideas being pushed by the Cahns and others. Edgar Cahn thus was able to announce at the Washington Conference that OEO had decided to develop a national legal services program within the OEO's Community Action Program and that Jean Cahn would be in charge of coordinating it. By the end of the year, indeed, OEO funded a new demonstration project in Washington, D.C., and the Mobilization for Youth law program in New York. It also approved grants for new neighborhood law offices

in Oakland and Detroit (Pious, 1972:419). The system of decentralized, government-salaried and socially active lawyers for the
poor was initiated.

*D. The Role of the Bar in the Establishment and Early Operation of the OEO
Legal Services Program*

The national legal services program was initiated without the
involvement of the organized bar; it was based on a number of
experiments and the initiative of the Ford Foundation and reformers
such as the Cahns and Edward Sparer. The role of the two hundred
existing legal aid societies and the national and local bar associations,
however, as the reformers recognized, had to be determined, and the
beginning was not too promising (see Pious, 1971:369–74; Johnson,
1974:43–49).

In December 1964, just after Edgar Cahn's announcement, the
NLADA Executive Committee passed a resolution stating that "The
creation of separate, duplicating agencies to offer legal services under
Economic Opportunity programs will be more costly and less
effective than will the proper use of existing facilities, and serious
ethical questions will be raised where nonlawyers attempt to practice
law" (see Johnson, 1974:309).

The situation changed very quickly, however, as the ABA and
subsequently the NLADA saw their interests in a new program. Key
figures in the ABA establishment, including President-elect Lewis
Powell (now a Supreme Court Justice), and William McCalpin, met
with the Cahns in January 1965, and it was agreed, inter alia, that a
National Advisory Council would be formed to provide bar leaders
with a means of influencing OEO legal services policy. With the
support of key bar figures, the ABA House of Delegates formally
endorsed the new program on 8 February 1965.

The "true" motives of these bar leaders cannot of course be known.
One element to recognize is that this endorsement continued the
tradition of the bar elite's concern about legal aid for the poor.
Perhaps the bar leaders saw an opportunity to capitalize on the
momentum generated by the War on Poverty to overcome problems
with the existing legal aid societies. A good legal aid system, needless
to say, makes the ABA more respected, and the existing system was
being criticized pretty severely. In addition, however, one detects a
defensiveness in the bar's position. As Johnson writes, "Powell was
aware of the fate of the AMA [American Medical Association] for
resisting Medicare and realized the OEO Legal Services Program
presented problems for the legal profession much like those that

26

Medicaid had posed for the medical profession" (Johnson, 1974:57; see also Powell, 1965). William McCalpin, citing with admiration the position of the English Law Society (in control of their legal aid program), stated, "Whether we shall enjoy the obviously more favorable position of the English bar remains to be seen. It is up to us. There is every reason to believe that by acting boldly now we can guide and shape the external forces prodding us to move forward" (McCalpin, 1965:551).[9]

The ABA did in fact "guide and shape" the OEO legal services program. The gradual increase in its influence in the first months has been well-documented by Richard Pious, who wrote, "In sum, between 1964 and 1966 the Legal Services Program was created within the CAP [Community Action Program] of OEO and passed into a coalition of bar leaders and their nominees to the OEO. The National Advisory Council (set up as part of the agreement to obtain the ABA's support) became a forum to work out disagreements, educate bar leaders, and publicize bar support for the program" (Pious, 1972:422). Jean Cahn was fired as coordinator, and the subsequently-created position of director of the program was filled at the end of the summer of 1965 by Clinton Bamberger, appointed "with the explicit endorsement of the American Bar Association, and the National Legal Aid and Defender Association" (Pious, 1972:421, see also Johnson, 1974:66).

The ABA's guidance in the formative months of the program obviously had serious and lasting consequences on the implementation of NLFs. We can here enumerate the most important of those consequences as the exploration begins of what happens to the NLF idea in practice.

1. The first consequence was that, *consistent* with the aims of the Cahns and others, the legal services component of the War on Poverty was increasingly removed from the Community Action Program (CAP) (Johnson, 1974:42). This result was not inevitable in the absence of bar involvement. Indeed, in March 1965 "Shriver removed the Cahns from control and appointed officials from CAP and the General Counsel's Office to administer the program" (Pious, 1972:421; see also Pious, 1971:371). CAP officials wished to keep neighborhood legal services as part of a coordinated local service effort under the auspices of community action agencies, and they had a strong early influence on Shriver. The bar leaders, however, subsequently persuaded Shriver to take the program from direct CAP control and appoint Bamberger as director. While CAP efforts to control the national program or its local offices persisted, the program henceforth maintained an important degree of independence (Yale Law Journal, 1971:236, n. 15).

2. The OEO legislation's formal requirement that there be the "maximum feasible participation" of the poor in OEO programs, of which NLFs were one, may have been given less emphasis. For example, Shriver assured the ABA in the summer of 1965 that, "Our statute requires maximum feasible participation of the poor in all aspects of antipoverty programs. We intend to carry out the mandate of Congress on this. But to do so does not require the imposition of inflexible and arbitrary quotas" (Shriver, 1965:1065; see also Johnson, 1974:108–12). Nevertheless, as I have noted, the participation of the poor in other OEO programs should not be exaggerated. Further, the bar's influence here was not inconsistent with the NLF reformers. As Johnson stated with respect to the governing boards which were in charge of local legal services projects, "Board membership for the client community was not a central tenet of the neighborhood lawyer ideology" (Johnson, 1974:112).

3. Related to the reduced emphasis on the participation of the poor was an increased concern with "lawyer control" of the governing boards of NLFs. This was essentially the policy adopted by Bamberger from the beginning, and he announced it officially in June 1966: "Our rule might be stated to be as follows: we require a majority of lawyers on the board unless we are persuaded that it would be impossible to obtain such a majority ..." (speech cited in Johnson, 1974:327).

4. The role of the local bar associations and their generally affiliated legal aid societies was greatly strengthened. This had extremely important repercussions, especially in the early years. The ABA leaders successfully urged, for example, that OEO "utilize to the maximum extent deemed feasible the experience and facilities of the organized bar such as legal aid" (Bamberger, 1966b:849), and the statutory authorization of the program in 1966 even required local bar consultation (Public Law No. 89-794, §222a). Of course, it is quite understandable that existing resources should not have been overlooked in building the legal services program, particularly given the need to build the program quickly; but the reliance on local bars and existing programs was still extraordinary. About "half of the early grants went to existing legal aid societies and most of the first legal services budget was allotted to local bar associations or bar-sponsored groups of lawyers" (Bamberger, 1966b:849).[10] Furthermore, according to Handler, Hollingsworth, and Erlanger, "Although the ultimate question of whether a local bar association had a veto was never fully resolved, it was generally agreed that some kind of bar endorsement was necessary for federal support" (1978:32).[11]

28

5. One effect of this reliance on local bars was, as will be explained in more detail below, to weaken considerably at the outset the emphasis of the program on social change through law, as opposed to a more traditional "service" orientation. One commentator thus reported in 1969 that, "In legal services circles an oft-heard explanation for the heavy emphasis which most programs place on the service function is the allegation that the local bars have thwarted attempts to implement the Cahns' suggestions" (Hannon, 1969a:242; see Pious, 1971:378–86).

6. The social change approach, in addition, was being played down somewhat at the national level under the influence of the ABA alliance. On the one hand, the Director, E. Clinton Bamberger, proclaimed that legal services were to attack poverty, while, on the other hand, he emphasized that programs would "be locally planned, locally generated, locally staffed, and locally administered" (Bamberger, 1966a:225). It was clear that this emphasis, reflected also in the amendment requiring consultation with local bar associations, could be interpreted as giving the local bar the right to give their own, inevitably more conservative, orientation to the program. Significantly, in the spring of 1966, the President-elect of the ABA, Orison Marden, also a member of the National Advisory Committee of the OEO Legal Service Program, stated that after "careful study" of the plans for legal services, he and other bar leaders had concluded that they "would merely involve financial assistance to local communities for more and better legal aid" (Marden, 1966:845).

Without denying the commitment of the OEO leadership to aggressive NLFs along the lines suggested in the Cahns' proposal in the *Yale Law Journal*, it is nevertheless true that, as observed by Philip Hannon, "in the beginning it was not made clear to the rank and file members of the Bar what the ultimate purpose of these programs was to be. And it is also clear that these men had company in high places in the professions" (Hannon, 1969a:245; see also Hannon, 1969b). The immediate result of this confusion was that many new programs were funded which, under the influence of local bar associations, did not share the reformist perspective of the OEO leadership.

7. The benefit gained from all these apparent compromises, however, was the support of the ABA, one of the most powerful political pressure groups in the United States, and this support played a crucial role in the program's survival, including the survival of its "social change" components.

II. The OEO Legal Services Program is Implemented

A. The NLF Model and the Expansion of the Program

The price of ABA support was undeniably some attenuation of the NLF idea as implemented in practice, especially because of the reliance on local bar associations and the ambiguity of "local control." Nevertheless, the program was initiated with idealistic pronouncements such as the following clarion call by Bamberger to the National Conference of Bar Presidents in February 1966:

> We cannot be content with the creation of systems of rendering free legal assistance to all the people who need but cannot afford a lawyer's advice. This program must contribute to the success of the War on Poverty. Our responsibility is to marshal the forces of law and the strength of lawyers to combat the causes and effects of poverty, remodel the systems which generate the cycle of poverty and design new social, legal and political tools and vehicles to move poor people from deprivation, depression, and despair to opportunity, hope, and ambition (speech quoted by Johnson, 1974:119–20; see also Shriver, 1965:1064).

Further, despite some ambiguity in earlier drafts (Pye, 1966:227–30), the official *Guidelines for Legal Services*, published by OEO in February 1966, proclaimed the importance of "group representation" and "law reform" and reiterated that at least some form of meaningful client participation would be required of all the recipients of OEO funds. They also announced goals which were not unlike those suggested by legal need studies, particularly that of Carlin and Howard. One goal was to "accumulate empirical knowledge" to find the best method "to bring the aid of the law and the assistance of lawyers to the economically disadvantaged people of this nation," and another was to "finance programs to teach the poor and those who work with the poor to recognize problems which can be resolved best by law and lawyers" (OEO, 1966:2–3). An OEO pamphlet published in 1967 entitled *Legal Services in Action* described in greater detail the appropriate activities of NLFs. The pamphlet emphasized welfare issues, consumer law, housing law, and juvenile law, and even included descriptions of efforts to organize action groups and represent neighborhood interests.

The cluster of novel social reform and other proactive strategies which characterize NLFs became part of the OEO Legal Services Program (LSP). These activities will be discussed in some detail in Part Three, but it is important to recognize here that "law reform" was singled out in early 1967 by the second Director, Earl Johnson, Jr., as the primary goal of the LSP and the standard by which individual projects were to be evaluated for funding purposes (Johnson, 1974:132–33; how the strategy affected funding is discussed in Hannon, 1970). The test case and class action approach of the civil rights lawyers was to be put at the service of the poor.

The focus on this strategy was not surprising, given the program's orientation toward lawyer-initiated change, the experience of the civil rights movement, and the strategies developed in MFY, an OEO prototype discussed earlier. In fact, OEO took over the bulk of the funding of the Center for Social Welfare Policy and Law at Columbia University, which grew out of the Mobilization for Youth project, and this Center became the first of thirteen national "back-up centers" specializing in developing strategies for reforming the substantive law on behalf of the poor (Johnson, 1974:181). Neighborhood law firms undertook a number of other reformist activities which were probably less traditional than test cases and class actions, but law reform through the courts became the most widely-known and discussed. The following sections will examine how the aggressive activities of OEO lawyers, particularly in regard to law reform, fared once they were implemented at the local level. We must go a step further in seeing how the "NLF solution" to the problem of the legal needs of the poor is battered and twisted in confrontation with its opponents (and supporters) in practice.

A few details about the remarkable scope of the legal services program being implemented should first be provided. There were twenty-seven local projects in existence by the end of 1965 (Pye, 1966:230); about 200 projects in 1967, involving some 850 neighborhood offices and 1200 lawyers; and the OEO's LSP peaked in 1972 (prior to the recent revival of legal services) with over 2700 lawyers and 265 projects (Hollingsworth, 1977:301). Federal funding of neighborhood law firms went from $27 million in fiscal year 1966—to be compared to the $4 million spent by charitable legal aid societies on civil legal aid prior to OEO—to a pre-Legal Services Corporation high of $71.5 million in fiscal year 1971 (Handler et al., 1978:19). The number of clients seen by NLFs went from 350,000 in 1967 to 1,200,000 in 1971 (Hollingsworth, 1977:303).

B. NLFs, Local Bars, and Governing Boards

The local bar associations, as noted, were generally deferred to in setting up NLFs and given a prominent, if not controlling, representation on the governing board of the local projects. Deference to local bars did not, however, necessarily lead to enthusiasm about the new federal legal aid programs. Again the pattern was ABA enthusiasm coupled with local bar and local attorney indifference or even hostility, at least at the outset. Some local bars simply refused to allow the new programs. Tactics of local attorneys opposed to OEO included antitrust lawsuits, cases challenging the legality of the program, and threatened complaints before grievance committees (see Harvard Law Review, 1967:843–45). If a program was nevertheless set up, such local pressures could make it difficult for the lawyers to act in any way likely to arouse local bar antagonisms (see Girth, 1976:55).

To understand this local bar attitude, which has recurred throughout the legal aid movement, the nature of the local bar must be explored in more detail. At least outside of the larger cities, local bars tend to have many "solo practitioners" and lawyers in small, noncorporate law firms, and these lawyers are very different from the prestigious corporate lawyers who comprise the ABA leadership. The American legal profession is highly stratified, and those at the top—in earnings, prestige, and power within the profession—tend to be with the large corporate firms. They have nothing to fear from the economic competition of legal aid, and they tend, as already noted, to serve generally as the "conscience" of the profession. The "solo" and small firm lawyers, on the other hand, supply the principal opposition to staff legal aid. They may worry that the community (and their clients) will be disrupted by legal aid lawsuits, or they may simply not feel a new system is necessary; but it is also quite clear that these are the attorneys who most fear a loss of income as their clients go to free legal aid offices (see Pye and Garraty, 1966:865; Harvard Law Review, 1967:843–45).[12]

Attitudes, however, were far from uniform, and many local bars supported the new legal aid program (if not, as will be seen below, necessarily an activist program). It may be, as Harry Stumpf suggested, that the broad ABA–local bar cleavage—which he termed plaintiff vs. defense but could also by small vs. "large" firm—is repeated at a smaller scale at the local level (Stumpf, 1975:247–48). He drew attention to one local bar association president's successful speech advocating the program, and this speech was not unlike what might have occurred at the national level. Noting that "altruism" could be useful, the local bar president suggested that, "through this public relations gimmick, we can build our own image and in the long run people will begin to think of going to a lawyer in the same way they do to a doctor" (Stumpf, 1975:203). The elites of the profession are less concerned with competition and more concerned with image, legitimacy.

Some recent studies of local bar associations and NLFs help show

32

how attitudes changed once the programs became established. The program seems to have gained the *general* support of the legal profession at all levels, and local hostility similarly subsided (Champagne, 1975–76:861). Anthony Champagne, for example, reviewed surveys completed in 1971 and felt that 85 percent of a cross-section of the legal community found that the poor were in "substantial" need of individual "legal representation," and 60 percent believed that there was a similar need for "law reform" (1975–76:865). Support was much lower, however, from personal injury lawyers who stood to lose some of their contingent fee business. Data obtained from a 1969 New Jersey study by Marjorie Girth support this finding: 96.1 percent of the private bar members interviewed reported that OEO had not affected their incomes (and 1.5 percent said their income had been raised), but 45 percent of solo practitioners admitted to the bar between 1925 and 1934 said their incomes had suffered. Presumably the age of these lawyers limited their ability to adapt to a different type of legal practice (Girth, 1976:82).

At least among some members of the bar, therefore, economic motives may lead them to oppose the legal aid program and its extension, and they may be right. The number who are in fact hurt, however, is very small, and it is understandable that, once programs are started and have little real effect on the business of the vast majority of lawyers, the opposition is greatly reduced.

A major source of influence of the local bar was through the projects' boards of directors—numerically dominated by lawyers and influenced very strongly by local bar associations (see Yale Law Journal, 1971:244, n. 43; Champagne, 1974). Corresponding to the decline in concern about local projects once they were established, most local boards did not interfere appreciably with staff lawyers. As stated by Handler, Erlanger, and Hollingsworth, "After programs had been in operation several years, it ... became fairly clear that governing boards (sometimes highly responsive to bar associations) for the most part had only formal roles and inputs. It was the program director and the staff who ran the program, with some input from client representatives" (Handler et al., 1978:64; see also Champagne, 1975–76:866).

When Boards did intervene, and when local bars did put pressure on NLFs, it was generally in the direction of encouraging more individual legal aid and less law reform (see, e.g., Girth, 1976:55–56; Johnson, 1974:172; Yale Law Journal, 1971:247–48; Stumpf, 1975:257). A 1971 study of 201 legal service projects thus found:

Board[s] of directors which play an active role in determining policy, usually reflect a conservative local bar association. Since most boards are numerically as well as psychologically dominated by attorneys and since most boards have the power to veto the project's handling of particular cases, some bars have in effect been able to restrict LSPs [Legal Services Programs] caseloads to individual services (Auerbach Corp., 1971, quoted in Champagne, 1975–76:866).

Similarly, the interviews of legal services lawyers by Handler, Erlanger, and Hollingsworth produced the following data:

In 1967 most lawyers said that the local bar associations were either helpful (59.4 percent) or indifferent (25.5 percent), rather than hindering (15.5 percent). In 1972 there was somewhat of a shift: bar associations were said to be less helpful (down to 40.2 percent) and more hindering (19.5 percent), but the biggest increase came with indifference—from 25.5 percent to 40.3 percent. The greater the time a program spent on service work [individual cases], the more likely lawyers were to say that the local bar was helpful. Also, in the offices that were rated high by the regional directors there were more negative feelings about local bar association attitudes (Handler et al., 1978:64).

Local bar pressures, therefore, continued against the kind of law reform favored by LSP officials in Washington, D.C. As suggested by Stumpf, "The private attorney ... appears to act primarily as a surrogate for the interests he represents, and these interests are those which reflect established community values. If this is so, it is politically naive to expect the private attorney to share and further the goals of OEO legal services" (Stumpf, 1975:246). These local pressures did not, however, to any great extent affect the local NLFs' autonomy. As the preceding quotation from Handler, Erlanger, and Hollingsworth shows, those who felt the most pressure were the ones who resisted it most effectively by taking the aggressive approach favored by OEO headquarters. Clearly the local bar did inhibit the implementation of social change strategies, as opposed to traditional service work, especially through local bar control of governing boards, but evidently the pressure diminished over time and allowed other pressures to outweigh the local bar's influence. While, as will be seen, the precise amount of law reform work undertaken cannot be measured with certainty, it does appear that the amount increased over the years as the national headquarters emphasized law reform and a new breed of lawyers replaced the lawyers of the traditional legal aid societies. (Handler et al., 1978; Hollingsworth, 1977:307–08; see Chapter 9 below). Indeed, as demonstrated by the research of Ted Finman, "local interests may have little power to alter the course of action set by a program's own ideology" (Finman, 1971:1078).

One further dimension to the local bar's approach to NLFs should

34

be explored—the issue of "judicare." While the OEO program was being put into effect, practicing lawyers began increasingly to see the virtues of the judicare system as a local alternative. While the appeal of judicare should not be considered only in economic terms, it is clear that the strong earlier opposition to the English-style plan had been overcome once federal money really became available (Stumpf, 1975: 250; articles praising the English system included those of Pelletier (1967) and Fendler (1971)). In addition, as has been noted, judicare plans tend to be more passive than OEO staff programs were, relying on individuals to seek legal services in traditional matters instead of affirmatively utilizing legal strategies to further the interests of the poor as a class. Once judicare was seen as an alternative, its "gospel" was repeated increasingly by local bar associations, not to mention others opposed to the law reform component of OEO (Stumpf, 1975:232–37, 245–46). By early 1966, in fact, as judicare applications for funds began to come into OEO headquarters, it was clear to Bamberger that, "we won't see anything but 'Judicare' [applications] ever again unless we do something about it" (Johnson, 1974:118).

Three experiments were accordingly funded, chiefly in order to "contain" judicare, and Bamberger announced that there would be no more judicare until these experiments had been "assessed." Bamberger's well-known speech, quoted at length earlier, in which he emphasized the social change orientation of the program, was a speech directed against the "English System": "It clearly can achieve no other goal than the mere resolution of controversies. The Legal Services Program of the Office of Economic Opportunity and the Legal Aid Movement have far greater ambitions" (Johnson, 1974:119–20). Significantly, Bamberger had the support of ABA leaders for this policy. The ABA had chosen to back the OEO program and would stick by its commitment. Bar leaders already were giving speeches praising "law reform" (e.g., Voorhees, 1967; see Johnson, 1974:326; Pious, 1971:376). Further, as Johnson points out, the cleavages in the U.S. legal profession were again vital; many "ABA leaders harbored a low regard for the calibre and motives of the practitioners most likely to represent the poor under such a system. They envisioned an unseemly scramble for the judicare dollar among thousands of marginal lawyers, a spectacle that could inflict untold damage on the profession" (Johnson, 1974:119). With this help from the ABA, judicare was contained, but its virtues have certainly not been forgotten. Indeed, as will be seen, judicare is now more than ever before being examined seriously in the United States.

C. The OEO Legal Services Program, the National Bar, and Federal and State Governments

The initial national political problem of the legal services program, as noted before, was to become as independent as possible from the Community Action Program (CAP). Although there continued to be friction between community action officials, who still had some say in the funding and administration of legal services programs, the bar (working very closely with LSP officials through the National Advisory Council) did succeed for the most part in keeping legal services distinct from CAP at the national, regional, and local levels. ABA lobbyists, for example, helped by the lack of adverse pressure against program activities in the first year of operation, were able to overcome the opposition of community action officials (and the Bureau of the Budget) and persuade the members of Congress (about three hundred of whom were lawyers) to give the program a statutory basis for receiving grants directly from Congress—bypassing CAP (Public Law No. 89-794, §211-1(b)). In 1969 the ABA succeeded finally in making the legal services program completely independent of CAP by order of the Director of OEO (Cornell Law Review, 1974:964 n. 22; Pious, 1972:439). One begins to see the power of the ABA, arguing on the grounds of the lawyer's independence, to pressure a Congress composed mainly of lawyers (see, e.g., Robb, 1971b).

Further political threats against the legal services program at the national level began in 1967, arising initially out of the aggressive law reform activities of California Rural Legal Assistance (CRLA) (see Falk and Pollack, 1973; Karabian, 1973). As has been documented in detail elsewhere, CRLA—one of the largest recipients of OEO funds and, interestingly, unaffiliated with any local bar associations—was successfully prosecuting a whole series of cases against the state of California requiring, inter alia, the provision of higher medical aid benefits to indigents, the implementation of new food stamp programs, and the enfranchisement of California's 80,000 Spanish speaking residents. These activities enraged the very conservative governor of California, Ronald Reagan, and he prevailed upon a U.S. Senator from California to act. Senator George Murphy, a conservative Republican from California, offered a federal amendment to the LSP appropriation in late 1967 which would have provided that, "no project ... may grant assistance to bring any action against any public agency of the United States, any State, or any political subdivision thereof" (113 Cong. Rec. 27, 155 (1967)). The national attack on the LSP had begun. The Murphy amendment, which would have crippled the program, lost in the Senate by a vote of 52–36, and ABA leaders feared a similar, more sophisticated attempt in the relatively conservative House of Representatives. Displaying their skepticism about local bar associations, ABA lobbyists were even on guard against the possibility of an amendment "giving state and/or local bar associations some veto power over the activities of Legal Services Programs," because "such an amendment would accomplish the result sought by Murphy" (Pious, 1972:428). The national bar, further, moved specifically to defend the law reform and test case approach of CRLA, emphasizing that the lawyer's independence and ability to represent his clients must not be restricted. John Robb, for example, testified as follows before Congress as Chairman of the ABA's Committee on Legal Aid:

> A legal service program without law reform will never get to the place where it is intended. It will never bring equal rights for people, it will never stand out, it will never bring dissidents into our system in feeling they have some stake here, and that problems can be solved within the system (Johnson, 1974:169).

This reasoning and an extremely powerful lobbying campaign were so successful that the major negative amendments never even reached a vote (see Pious, 1972:428–29).

Controversy continued to mount, however, as the law reform activities of LSP became more well known and widespread. The Congressional challenge was especially serious in 1969—the next time OEO came up for a two-year renewal—when Senator Murphy proposed that the state governors be given a veto, subject to override only by the President, over the funding or refunding of all or any part of local LSP projects (115 Cong. Rec. 27, 894–97 (1969)). Despite the opposition of ABA leaders, the amendment passed the Senate 45–40. Again, however, the ABA leaders stepped up their lobbying campaign: "Within sixty days of adoption of the amendment by the Senate, the American Bar Association, the National Bar Association, The American Trial Lawyers Association, the National Legal Aid and Defender Association, the Judicial Conference of the United States, more than fifty state and local bar associations, eighty-five law school deans, and eleven thousand students and law professors joined to fight the Murphy amendment" (Robb, 1970:331). The newly inaugurated Nixon Administration even opposed the restrictive amendment, if not with great enthusiasm, and the House rejected it and refused to allow the final compromised House–Senate law to contain it. The great power of the organized bar had saved the program, and particularly its test case and law reform components.[13]

Political attacks on the program, however, did not abate. There were numerous problems, for example, at the state level, where governors possessed the power to veto any OEO project, subject only to the override of the OEO Director. Governor Reagan of California used this power twice, in 1970 and in 1971, to veto funding of CRLA. The veto was overridden, but it was conditioned on the making of a competing $2.5 million grant to an experimental judicare program. Programs in Arizona, Connecticut, Florida, Louisiana, Missouri, and North Dakota also suffered vetoes (see Parker, 1974:526–27; Yale Law Journal, 1971:260; Pearson, 1971:648). These vetoes, too, were overridden at the national level, but OEO often was pressured into compromises to obtain state support. These attacks did not succeed in altering the program substantially, but they helped create pressure for further national efforts to weaken it. The Nixon Administration, which initially had caused few problems for the LSP—indeed had approved a budget increase from $42 million in 1969 to $58 million in fiscal year 1970—began to turn against the program.

In 1970 the new OEO leadership appointed by the Nixon Administration sought to "regionalize" or "decentralize" legal services administration, with the aim of putting much of the control of the legal services program in the hands of regional directors (see Girth, 1976:96–99; Sullivan, 1971:25–26; Cornell Law Review, 1974:981; George, 1976:688–89). Such directors at that time would have tended to be tied to OEO Community Action personnel and reluctant to challenge the political status quo. Both plans were quickly dropped because of political pressure from, above all, the ABA, again emphasizing the required independence of lawyers. Surviving this challenge, however, was still nothing compared to struggles that took place one year later when the forces opposed to the LSP could focus on legislation, by now already proposed by the ABA, aimed at setting up a more or less independent legal services corporation able to avoid the political pressures which had plagued the OEO program.

D. The Legal Services Program—The Struggle for Independence

As early as 1968, bar leaders in the National Advisory Council, legal services officials, and others had begun to consider finding a new place, outside of OEO, for the LSP (Robb, 1971a:558). A number of studies of this possibility were undertaken in 1970, accelerated by the growing pressures placed on LSP. While LSP attorneys increasingly feared interference from the Nixon Administration, the Administration itself—embarrassed by its handling of the CRLA funding veto and the battles with the ABA over decentralization—

was looking with favor on the idea of separating itself from the program. The Administration was not immune to the program's virtues, particularly its more conservative ones, and it perhaps sought an opportunity to "draw the fire provoked by legal services for the poor and insulate the Administration itself from political attack" (Cornell Law Review, 1974:190).[14]

By 1971 both sides supported the concept of an independent corporation (see generally Pious, 1972:441–42). They differed considerably, however, about details. Two bills were introduced in Congress—one by the Administration and the other a bipartisan bill based on recommendations of the National Advisory Council. The divergent bills, it should be noted, signaled the final break over legal services policy between the ABA—expressed by the National Advisory Council—and the Nixon Administration.

The bipartisan bill placed essentially no limits on activities of legal services lawyers, except for a prohibition of representation in criminal cases. It would have authorized $140 million in general revenues in the first year of operation and $170 million the following year. The legal services corporation it proposed would have been governed by a nineteen-member board, composed of five members selected by the President; one chosen by the Chief Justice of the U.S. Supreme Court; three by a Client's Advisory Council; three by a Project Attorney Advisory Council; six ex-officio members, including the President and President-elect of the ABA, the President of the NLADA, the President of the National Bar Association (a Black lawyer organization), the President of the American Trial Lawyers Association, and the President of the American Association of Law Schools; and a chairman of the board and executive director appointed by the other members.

The Administration bill, prepared without consulting the National Advisory Council or even the newly-appointed (February 1971) director of the LSP, was somewhat more restrictive. In addition to proposing a funding level of only $67.5 million the first year, it would have explicitly forbidden representation in criminal cases and "duplicative and frivolous appeals," and it would have permitted legislative lobbying only at the invitation of the legislature. The corporation would also have been forbidden to make grants to "organizations which spend more than three-fourths of their funds on collective litigation on behalf of the poor." Finally, and most significantly, the corporation would have been governed by an eleven-member board and chairman designated by the President and approved by the Senate. Despite this potential political control by the President and the proposed limits on the corporation's activities, it is notable that this bill, and its sponsors, still emphasized "professional independence" which, it was recognized, would legitimately lead to law reform and even lobbying.

The basic conflict between the bills was over the manner of appointing the board, which, of course, in turn could determine the basic orientation of the program. It was clear that President Nixon at this point had in mind a more conservative type of program than had existed under OEO.

Demonstrating again the power of the ABA, the bipartisan bill passed the Senate with the help of a significant number of Republicans, and with some amendments it passed the House as well (see Pious, 1972:443–44). The compromise version ultimately enacted by both Houses in late 1971 attempted to placate the President by giving him more control over the board than was originally anticipated. It would have provided for a seventeen-member board, six of whom were to be named by the President and the rest chosen from lists provided by the interest groups named in the original bipartisan bill. Nevertheless, despite the strong support of the ABA and members of both political parties, the President in December 1971 vetoed the act containing the corporation proposal. He announced that "the restrictions which the Congress has imposed upon the President in the selection of directors of a Corporation is … an affront to the principle of accountability to the American people as a whole [sic]" (quoted in Pious, 1972:445). Showing that "accountability" and "law reform" were at this point closely related, he asked Congress to work on creating an agency "which placed the needs of low-income clients first, before the political concerns of either legal services attorneys or elected officials" (quoted in Agnew, 1972:930). An attempt to override the veto was defeated.[15]

Having failed to secure a legal services corporation which presidential appointments would dominate, the Administration began specifically to attack the law reform efforts in the OEO program. Vice President Agnew spoke out in early 1972 against suits challenging governmental activities, and he published an article in October condemning the program as "a systematic effort to redistribute societal advantages and disadvantages, penalties and rewards, rights and resources" (1972:930). He suggested that more national control, particularly of "law reform" and other "political" activities, could make the program more "responsible and accountable to the public" (1972:932). Agnew's attack was vigorously challenged by ABA leaders on the grounds that: (1) most programs did not do much law reform; (2) law reform was essential in many instances; and, above all, (3) Agnew was proposing an infringement of the OEO attorneys'

40

independence by suggesting measures to control lawyers' activities (e.g., Klaus, 1972). At this time, however, the bar's influence with the Administration was at a low point, and when Nixon was re-elected by a landslide vote in November, the Administration was emboldened to take still harsher measures against OEO in general—which it had also been criticizing—and against the legal services program.

Nixon appointed Howard Phillips, an extreme conservative, to dismantle OEO, and the legal services program was apparently meant to be included (see Arnold, 1973). Agnew, for example, sent a memorandum to Phillips stating that, "of all the OEO programs legal services is the one most capable of fundamentally altering America. For that alone, it should be the first eliminated" (quoted in Ehrlich, 1976:64). Phillips himself was quoted as saying that the program is "rotten and it will be destroyed" (119 Cong. Rec. 20, 696 (1973)), and he fired the LSP Director, abolished the National Advisory Council, and eliminated law reform as an acceptable goal of legal services. A successful lawsuit on behalf of OEO in general stopped Phillips—whose name, for political reasons, was never submitted for confirmation by the Senate—from implementing his decrees, but considerable damage was nevertheless done, and OEO never did recover (see George, 1976:715; Hannon, 1976:645).

Nixon, however, did revive the legal services program, thanks largely to the ABA lobbying pressures which continued after the demise of the National Advisory Council (see George, 1976:696–97). In May 1973, he submitted a new legal services corporation bill to Congress, which, with several amendments, finally did become law. The proposed bill, similar to that which he he had proposed in 1971, was surprisingly unrestrictive in view of the attacks on law reform activities that had just taken place. It contained the prohibition on criminal representation, a ban on lobbying, and the restriction on funding public interest lawyers. Despite the fact that the eleven-member board would be appointed only by the President, with the consent of the Senate, the bar and the legal services community now favored the bill. They had obviously lowered their sights in view of the difficulties that their original bill had encountered. The new bill, however, was still subjected to numerous attacks by political conservatives in the House and Senate. Legal services was more controversial than ever.

In the House of Representatives, in what became known as the "Thursday night massacre" of 21 June 1973, twenty-four restrictions were placed on legal services lawyers by congressional amendments aimed at curbing controversial activities (Drinan, 1976; Cornell Law Journal, 1974:985–86). Restrictions were perceived as so damaging that some liberal House members even refused to back the amended bill. Several similar amendments were also placed on the bill that passed the Senate, but none were so severe.

The most important of the House-imposed limitations, both substantively and symbolically, concerned the funding of the so-called "back-up centers"—specialized institutions playing a key role in law reform efforts. The Green amendments, adopted narrowly in the House, sought to prohibit completely the funding of these centers, and this provision became the major source of contention in the House–Senate conference to adopt a compromise bill to send to the President. The House conferees, prodded by ABA lobbyists, yielded on this issue; and when the bill was returned to the House to vote on the conference bill, an effort to restore the Green amendment was narrowly defeated (George, 1976:717–18). Both legislative bodies thus supported the bill continuing the funding of back-up centers.

The legislative story, however, was not quite over; the bill became the subject of "impeachment politics" in Nixon's final weeks in office (George, 1976:717–18). While Nixon (and Agnew) had earlier supported the back-up centers, the quest for anti-impeachment votes apparently led him to try especially hard to please conservative Congressmen. He threatened to veto the bill unless the controversial Green amendment was reinstated, and he succeeded in his threat; proponents of the program were simply unwilling to give up the bill still another time. Nixon then signed the final bill on 25 July 1974 (just prior to his resignation) (Public Law No. 93–355, 42 U.S.C. §2996).

The struggle had taken almost four years. During that time the LSP was thoroughly enmeshed in controversy and unable to obtain any increased funding at all above the figure of $71.5 million. Because of inflation, the LSP had been forced to cut services drastically. The number of legal services attorneys had dropped from 2500 to 2100, and the number of NLFs dropped 41 percent to 638 (Breger, 1976:424). Finally, there was the opportunity to begin again, somewhat freed from the crippling political pressures that had involved legal services in a fight "with just about everyone and everything" (Klaus, 1976:132). The new opportunity, however, was circumscribed by the provisions of the new law and dependent on the appointees made to the new Board.

III. The Legal Services Corporation

A. The Legal Services Corporation Act of 1974

The basic structure of the OEO's Legal Services Program has remained intact under the Corporation. Legal aid is still delivered primarily by quasi-independent, local NLF projects funded by and in some sense accountable to the national administration in Washington, D.C. The primary aim of the 1974 law was to remove the program from political influence, except for Congressional control over the amount budgeted and Presidential appointment of the members of the newly-created governing board. Consistent with this removal from politics is the requirement that the board be bipartisan and the removal of any threat of veto by state governors over the funding of legal services projects (42 U.S.C. §2996f (f)). Further, the emphasis on "professionalism"—decision-making by lawyers over basic policies at both the national and local levels—was retained and enshrined in the new law. Aside from the obvious requirement that individual attorneys abide by the Code of Professional Responsibility established by the ABA (42 U.S.C. §2996e(b)(3)), the law provided that the relevant governing boards must be lawyer-dominated: 60 percent of the local governing body must be lawyers (42 U.S.C. §2996f(c)), and lawyers must also comprise a majority of both the state advisory councils (42 U.S.C. §2996c(f)) and the eleven-member national board of directors (42 U.S.C. §2996c(a)). (The Board appoints the LSC President, a position analogous to the OEO position of Director.)

In addition, the 1974 legal services law (as implemented by regulations of the Legal Services Corporation—LSC) provided that employees of the LSC or individual projects may not engage in a wide range of "political" activities, including organizing groups or participating in public demonstrations, picketing, boycotts, strikes, or various illegal activities.[16] Lobbying activities not pursuant to representation of a qualified client or at the request of the appropriate legislative body were also proscribed (42 U.S.C. §2996f(a)(5)). While some of these general restrictions could be important, their effect is probably minimal. There are exceptions within the statute, especially the broad protection provided to lawyers by the Code of Professional Responsibility, and in any event they are not really inconsistent with the activities that were pursued by the OEO attorneys (see Part Three below).

Particular controls on legal representation are also serious but probably not very important taken as a whole. Controls provided by the 1974 law included relatively insignificant methods for program directors to supervise the bringing of class actions or appeals, and prohibitions, subject to some exceptions, on criminal and juvenile representation and on the taking of "fee-generating cases" (42 U.S.C. §2996f(b)(1)). The latter provision, consistent with prior OEO practice, was designed to minimize competition with local attorneys who, because of the contigent fee system, might still earn a fee from an indigent client. More important, as a result of the "Thursday night massacre," Congress composed a laundry list of unpopular lawsuits that legal services lawyers were instructed not to bring: suits for the desegregation of elementary or secondary schools, suits to obtain a nontherapeutic abortion, and cases involving Selective Service violations or military desertion.

Finally, restrictions on grants to "back-up centers" should be mentioned. In retrospect, this issue can be seen to have been given an exaggerated significance. It is clear at this point that the law has had some effect, but it has been more to cause inconvenience than permanent harm.[17] The law did not prohibit the law reform activities of back-up centers, and those are continuing. The law prohibited grants to centers engaged in "research and support functions" unrelated to particular litigation, but these too have not been terminated. Rather, research and support functions have had to be brought within the LSC rather than funded by grants. This entailed making a sometimes difficult distinction between research for specific litigation on behalf of a client, which can be done at back-up (now called support) centers, and general research, which cannot, but the distinction has been made. According to one of the members of the first Board of Directors of the LSC, "In the main, these research efforts have been continued 'in-house' by the Corporation—in many cases by the same personnel who had previously worked on them" (Breger, 1977:11). The Green amendment has not had the impact its supporters hoped or its opponents feared (see Johnson, 1977:320–21).

Aside from these prohibitions, one affirmative obligation of the LSC should be considered—the requirement to study "alternative and supplemental methods of delivery ... including judicare, vouchers, prepaid legal insurance, and contracts with law firms" (42 U.S.C. §2996f(c)). The pro-judicare forces, arising from local bar associations and opponents of the activism of neighborhood lawyers, had to be placated. Judicare and other systems must now be studied seriously, with the results reported to Congress. As of early 1978, sixteen experimental judicare programs were being funded at a total cost of over $1.5 million (Legal Services Corporation, 1977b; Legal

Services Corporation, 1978). It is too early, however, to tell whether these experiments will lead to any major changes.

B. *Implementing the Legal Services Corporation Act*

It should be clear from the foregoing summary that the statute itself cannot determine the orientation of the program beyond very general terms. Not only is the statute brief, but also it is vague and often even self-contradictory. Its provisions did not *mandate* any major changes in how attorneys choose to serve the client community. Much has continued to depend on how individual lawyers and programs function and how policy is set. These matters will be considered in Part Three of this study, but it is important here to recognize that while the rhetoric of the War on Poverty is gone, the proactive, reformist orientation of poverty lawyers, developed within that war, may not be. In asking what that orientation is under the new corporation, it is appropriate to begin by examining the Board of Directors appointed by President Ford (who replaced Nixon).

President Ford was no great supporter of the program's more controversial aspects. He tried to appoint some Board members unsympathetic or even hostile to the program, including one of the leaders of the attack on CRLA in California, William Knecht, and Edith Green, the sponsor of the House amendment against the back-up centers (Arnold, 1975). The ABA and other legal services supporters put up such a fight against these nominees that two of the most controversial, including Green, withdrew, and Knecht was refused confirmation by the Senate. Ford ultimately appointed a Board composed essentially of supporters of the legal services program (Arnold, 1975:36). The all-attorney Board, containing only four of the original eleven nominees, was confirmed on 9 July 1975. This Board then appointed Thomas Ehrlich, at that time Dean of Stanford Law School, to serve as the first President. And Ehrlich, with the approval of the Board, underlined the program's continuity by designating Clinton Bamberger, the first director of the OEO Legal Services Program, as his Executive Vice President (the second highest administrative position).

There is no doubt that, under this first Board, the program in general has been somewhat less oriented toward social change. One reason, however, is simply that the political climate has changed in the United States. According to one member of the LSC staff,

> During the 1960s and early 1970s, legal services projects often could not avoid the larger social questions that affected their clients. These questions were largely formulated by outside persons and organizations within the poor

community who pushed legal services programs to respond to their needs. This external pressure has been reduced in recent years and, as a result, many legal services programs no longer address the underlying political questions that affect their clients (Trister, 1978).

Nevertheless, as the concern expressed by the author of that statement shows, the "social change goal" is still important. Moreover, it is clear that the strategy of "law reform" is still very much a part of the program. This has been recognized in the preservation of the functions of back-up centers and in the statements of legal services leaders. All Board members, the President, and his staff emphasize that staff lawyers must not concentrate solely on individual clients (e.g., Crampton (the Chairman), 1975; Crampton, 1976; Thurman, 1976; Breger, 1976). Clinton Bamberger, for example, made the following remarks recently:

> Legal aid in the United States has three characteristics that I consider fundamental, essentially immutable, and affecting the rational purposes of legal aid. These characteristics are substantial public funding, reform of the law for the benefit of the poor, and full-time salaried lawyers specializing in the law of the poor (Bamberger, 1977:207).

The impetus for law reform admittedly no longer comes from the top. The approach under the Corporation has been to require that "each local program ... establish its own set of priorities for caseload control and resource management" (Ehrlich, 1976–77:165; 45 CFR Part 1620).[18] Those who were active in law reform before, however, are no doubt still active. As another member of the first Board, Marshal Breger, suggested, "it is unlikely that the changed rhetoric has, in fact, affected the day-to-day activities of operating programs" (Breger, 1977:23).

My point here, however, is not to provide detailed information on the current operation of the program (see Bellow, 1977; Katz, 1978; Francis, 1977), nor to imply that law reform has emerged as the paramount goal of the Corporation. Indeed, there is some evidence that law reform has not prospered as much as has individual service work.[19] Legal services in the United States is still in flux, only beginning to come to grips with its future now that its basic political and financial crisis is over. This first Board can be seen as a transitional one, as the LSC found its institutional form and secured stable funding. A long overdue discussion on the goals of the program is beginning to take place (Legal Services Corporation, 1978b), and it is by no means clear that the strategies and methods of the past ought to or will be continued in the future.

What is important here, however, is that while many questions are

46

left open, the institutional *framework* is still favorable to a proactive, social-reform-oriented program with lawyers who are expressly allowed to seek social change on behalf of the poor. There was tremendous political pressure to stop such activities, particularly "law reform," and the new law puts some limits on legal services attorneys, but the basic NLF idea survived conservative opposition and has even begun to prosper. The LSC has made great strides in gaining increased funding from Congress. From $71.5 million annually in 1971–1975, the amount climbed to $92.3 million in 1976 (the first year the request was made by the LSC itself) to $125 million in 1977 and to $205 million in 1978. The number of legal services programs has already increased from 258 in 1975 to 320 in 1977, employing about 3,700 lawyers.[20]

In late 1977, in addition, the Legal Services Corporation Act was amended in several ways favorable to the program's goals. The law provides now that clients of legal services programs must be represented on the Corporation's national board of directors, and make up one-third of the governing boards of local programs (Public Law No. 95-222, 42 U.S.C. §2996c). The ban on representing juveniles was lifted, the ban on grants to back-up centers was relaxed considerably, and the wording was loosened slightly on the prohibition against organizing groups. The Legal Services Corporation's new prosperity owes something, of course, to the advent of the more liberal Carter Administration, but it is clear that controversy had already died down and prosperity was on the way.[21] As Carter's appointees to the LSC Board assume power in 1978 and 1979, the LSC may move further toward developing its social reform potential.

In concluding this chapter, it is instructive to consider the fate of the Community Action Program (CAP), the other very controversial OEO program. Both grew out of a rather technical "end of ideology" approach to the "cycle of poverty," emphasizing the need to make social programs work better, while neglecting the political problems that an attack on poverty and the status quo would necessarily imply. The technical, nonpolitical approach proved to be an illusion, but the responses to it were different. CAP became embroiled in political struggles which led ultimately to its demise, while the legal services component—no less controversial—took ideological shelter behind the ethic of professional independence and practical shelter behind the lobbying power of the ABA, and it thereby managed to survive. In very general terms, which can be made more meaningful through comparative analyses later in this Part, a liberal government, inspired by young activist lawyers, implemented the NLF program as part of its low-cost, technical "war on poverty." The bar leaders—the bar elite—chose to support and control the program rather than to fight it, and when controversy arose—as it must when government funds are used to disrupt the status quo—the bar defended the program in all its aspects and was powerful enough to enable it to survive without substantial change and to become somewhat freed from political pressures. The only problem, which must be considered in Part Three, is that while the bar has pushed the program in the direction it was initially going, it may have prevented the program from developing a more creative and effective approach.

Notes

1. "Social advocacy" is the term of Philip Selznick (1976). For other discussions of these developments, see Rabin (1976); Council for Public Interest Law (1976:30–40); and Handler et al. (1978).

2. The most important book in this rediscovery was Michael Harrington's *The Other America: Poverty in the United States* (1962) (see generally Haveman, 1977). One must recognize that poverty overlaps considerably with race in America, and the growing number of urban Blacks were generally the focus of programs.

3. According to Lawrence Friedman: "Broadly speaking, there were *three* paths that might be taken—transfer payments, changing the poor, and changing society. The first was too expensive, the third too revolutionary. This last had been a stimulus for the program, and it rumbled on, but the second became the dominant theme when the law was actually drafted" (Friedman, 1977:36). This quotation suggests that only this "middle course" is, in fact, available to welfare state governments short of funds and wary of basic social change. This dilemma of reform is analyzed by Marris and Rein (1972:29–84).

4. This was the era in America of the "end of ideology," in which many assumed that a basic consensus existed in society such that social problems were matters of technique, with remedies designed by experts, rather than developed through conflict and politics. The most famous book of the genre is D. Bell, *The End of Ideology* (1961). According to Bottomore, a critic of that approach,

> "Ever since the war the notions of 'policy sciences' and 'social engineering' have steadily gained ground, and in spite of much recent criticism the main line of development in research is still (and in some countries increasingly) toward quantitative, policy-oriented studies which are intended to provide technical solutions to social problems" (1976:190).

5. The Cahns recognized the problem of choosing cases and strategies, stating that, "In the final analysis, the decision to take or refuse a case will be a matter of intuition, empathy, and hunch" (1964:1346).

6. This is not to imply that organizational strategies would necessarily have been "desirable" at that time. As Marris and Rein point out, "It seems unlikely that any programme of community action, so dependent upon a consensus of established

leadership and public funds, could be at the same time an effective champion of radical democracy" (1972:233). The point here is that the Cahns' proposal was, as they recognized, rooted in legal professionalism and thus subject to a number of limitations and dangers. (*See* Chapters 10 and 11 below for a discussion of NLFs and "professionalism.")

7. Johnson suggested that at this point "three schools of thought could be isolated: the 'social rescue' theory embodied in the 1964 New Haven proposal [made after Jean Cahn left], the law reform strategy pioneered by Wickenden and Sparer [for MFY] and the Cahns' 'Civilian Perspective'" (1974:34). While this division may have been evident, the important point is that, as Johnson states, "All three did share a commitment to a fundamental social and economic goal—the reduction of poverty" (1974:35).

It should be noted also that the lessons of the experiments were brought together in coherent form in the Washington, D.C., Neighborhood Legal Services Project, funded by the Ford Foundation (Johnson, 1974:27–32; see Pye, 1966:231–43). This office received one of the first OEO legal services grants.

8. The Department of Health, Education, and Welfare, published the *Proceedings* later that year. Some quotations from the *Proceedings* are quite instructive. Charles Grissen from MFY stated, for example, that "the existence of unmet needs, of numbers of unserved eligible recipients is a mandate to seek new organizational forms by which to provide service" (H.E.W., 1964:77). Another Washington, D.C., speaker, making arguments very similar to those of Carlin and Howard's legal need article, criticized existing legal aid societies because "they have waited for clients to come to them ..." (H.E.W., 1964:94). NLFs were seen as the answer to these problems.

9. It may also be that the bar was defensive because the U.S. Supreme Court had begun to question the bar's traditional restrictions on innovative legal services programs, in particular group legal services (e.g., Schwartz, 1965).

10. Pious quoted a memorandum to the effect that by 1 July 1966, "the organized bar at the local level had sponsored 74 applications and participated in drafting 42 others. It was not involved in 14 applications and opposed only six" (1972:422). A number of existing legal aid societies, however, did not, for various reasons, obtain federal support (Johnson, 1974:319). In 1974, Charles Parker wrote that "Sixty traditional legal aid organizations appear to have accepted OEO grant offers as the major source of their funding and thirty-eight of these organizations still rely almost entirely on non-federal money. The remaining fifty seem to have disappeared ..." (Parker, 1974:518–19).

11. The most notable exception was in San Francisco, where the program that was set up was an alternative to that favored by the bar, and accordingly the bar had little influence over its actions (see Stanford Law Review, 1967; Johnson, 1974:89, 123).

12. A recent article by Gary Bellow on the current controversy within the profession about advertising provides a very interesting comparison. Large firm lawyers, he argues, are now willing to allow advertising because it will have little effect on them and because "it would be foolish to risk the influence and prestige of the profession by continuing its inaccessibility to so many people." "Small lawyers," on the other hand, fear that advertising will lure away their clients to larger and more

efficient legal offices (Bellow, 1976:3–4). Again the theme is image consciousness at the upper levels versus bread and butter concerns among the legal rank and file.

13. According to Pious, "The result was not inevitable, however; had Shriver not given bar leaders control of the LSP an entirely different outcome would likely have resulted" (1972:431). Under President Nixon the bar's control continued until some time in 1970. By that time the ABA's support of the LSP was well established and the bar sought to preserve the program as it was.

14. President Nixon's awareness of the program's conservative virtues is evident from his subsequent message introducing the 1971 bill. He said that "legal service has reaffirmed faith in our government of laws" and given the poor "a new reason to believe they are part of the system." In addition, however, Nixon also defended the program's actions against government. He urged that "the legal problems are of sufficient scope that we should not restrict the right of these attorneys to bring any type of civil suit" (Presidential Message to Congress, 5 May 1971).

15. Another bill was enacted by the Congress in July 1972, but it contained similar restrictions on the President and, when faced with a veto threat, was ultimately dropped in a House–Senate conference. According to Professor Johnson, an effort was made in the Conference Committee to rewrite the bill, and the rewritten version would have been acceptable to the President. Supporters of legal services, however, preferred no bill at all to that one. In retrospect their decision was a bad one, because after the 1972 election they could only succeed in obtaining a bill even worse than the one they once rejected (information from Earl Johnson, Jr., Florence, Italy, 6 June 1978).

16. The prohibited political activities are set out in the regulations published at 45 CFR Parts 1608 and 1610, which became effective on 23 July 1976. Of particular interest in the statute is the ban on the organization of groups:

> "No funds made available by the Corporation under this subchapter, either by grant or contract, may be used ... to organize, to assist to organize, or to encourage to organize, or to plan for the creation or formation of, or the structuring of, any organization, association, coalition, alliance, federation, confederation, or any similar entity, except for the provision of legal assistance to eligible clients in accordance with guidelines promulgated by the Corporation" (42 U.S.C. §2996f(b)(6)).

The wording of this ban was relaxed slightly by the amendments of 1977. Public Law No. 95–222, 28 December 1977, 91 Stat. 1619. The language (42 U.S.C. §2996f(b)(7)) now prohibits legal services personnel from acting "to initiate the formation, or act as an organizer, of any association, federation, or similar entity, except that this paragraph shall not be construed to prohibit the provision of legal assistance to eligible clients ...."

17. The back-up centers are now called "support centers" and must do "direct counseling and representational activities, professional responsibility activities in accordance with the Code of Professional Responsibility of the American Bar Association and such 'housekeeping' activities as are normally carried on by law offices." 41 Federal Register 17977, 29 April 1976. For a current description of support centers, see Council for Public Interest Law (1976:100–05).

18. Under the regulations (45 CFR Part 1620), the following factors shall be

50

among those considered in establishing priorities:

(1) the resources of the recipient;
(2) the population of eligible clients in the geographic area served by the recipient;
(3) the availability of another source of free or low-cost legal assistance in a particular category of cases or matters;
(4) the urgency of particular legal problems of the clients of the recipient; and
(5) the general effect of the resolution of a particular category of cases or matters on persons least able to afford legal assistance in the community served.

19. In particular, the Corporation's approach to fund-raising has emphasized providing two lawyers for every 10,000 poor persons and $7 per poor person. This formula is based on an idea of "legal needs" which emphasizes individual service. (See Chapter 8 below.) In addition, the formula implies that increased funding be utilized to set up new programs to cover as much of the population as possible and that funding be spread out evenly among programs. Those programs which were in areas where over $7 was spent per poor person—e.g., California—have not received relative increases in funding; yet these were often the programs most active in law reform. According to Professor Johnson, these problems are being addressed with a view toward making the funding formula flexible enough to encourage activist programs (information from Professor Earl Johnson, Jr., Florence, Italy, 6 June, 1978).

20. The 320 projects are divided into some 700 offices. Data from late 1976 show that the projects varied in size from one having more than 300 employees to a project having one attorney and two support staff. The median project employed nineteen staff members of whom six were staff attorneys, two were managing attorneys, five were secretaries or clerks, and four were "paralegals" (Legal Services Corporation, 1977b:12–13).

21. Prior to the election of Carter, for example, nine Democratic senators from the Senate Labor and Public Welfare Committee joined with five Republican members to recommend a $140 million budget for fiscal year 1977. As Earl Johnson noted, "It is doubtful that many antipoverty programs could enlist such a broad array of powerful senators in support of a doubling of its budget during the midst of a recession" (Johnson, 1977:319). Congress in 1975 gave $88 million to the Corporation despite President Nixon's recommendation for $80 million. Similarly, the 1978 budget was raised from $175 million to $205 million. Controversy has not, however, been completely eliminated as exemplified by the statements of conservative members of the House in 124 *Congressional Record* 5533-46 (1978).

Chapter 3

England and Wales[1]

It would not be difficult to explain the absence—if that were the case—of NLFs in England (or the rest of the world outside of the United States) (e.g., Green and Green, 1970). While test case, law reform litigation has a strong tradition in the United States, England lacks a written constitution, has a stronger attachment to the doctrine of precedent, and the tradition of Parliamentary supremacy precludes courts from overruling legislative acts. Courts are not utilized to promote change in the same way as in the United States (e.g., Morrison, 1973; Friedman, 1975:212–13). The legal profession, in addition, has not been concerned with the types of problems characteristic of the welfare state. The work of English solicitors concerns mainly divorce proceedings and the conveyancing of real property, not with new laws and legal and social developments (Abel-Smith and Stevens, 1967:209–10), and barristers are perhaps even more removed from social reform movements. Further, since 1949 England has been in possession of the most celebrated "judicare" legal aid scheme in the world (e.g., Dworkin, 1965), to which private practitioners are strongly attached, both symbolically and at times financially. Finally, many other advice organizations, particularly the now over 700 Citizens' Advice Bureaus, complement and supplement the 1949 scheme (Brooke, 1976; National Consumer Council, 1977).

While some leading commentators have continued to emphasize these factors in denying the need for OEO-like neighborhood law centers in England (e.g., Pollock, 1975), history has passed them by. The twenty-five to thirty neighborhood law centers are now considered, for example, by the prestigious and influential Lord Chancellor's Advisory Committee, to be "an integral and essential branch of legal services"—"the public sector in legal services"—and they are not going to disappear. Attention must thus shift to the developments that have established NLFs in England and made them survive in this apparently very different legal environment.

52

I. Origins of the NLF Idea in England and the Early Role of the Law Society

While the basic idea of NLFs and the impetus for reform came from the United States, it should be noted that there were some precedents both for activist lawyers on behalf of the poor and for a staff system of legal aid as opposed to the judicare system. Particularly interesting were the so-called "poor man's lawyers" linked to the charitable "settlement house" movement in England at the end of the 19th and beginning of the 20th centuries. The settlement houses, according to a detailed study by Diane Leat, were set up to "catalyse" social change on behalf of the poor, and, as one part of that effort, they sought to use the law through mechanisms such as "legal advice centres" and Tenants Protection Committees, both staffed by full-time lawyers (Leat, 1975).

A study of poor man's lawyers connected to one of these settlement houses, Toynbee Hall in East London, shows that they not only gave legal advice, but also undertook litigation on behalf of both individuals and groups. The legal strategies, moreover, were selected to complement the attack on poverty being waged by the settlement houses. This evidently sophisticated and innovative approach to legal services thus has many resemblances to the current NLF movement. The fervor of this early movement, however, soon died out. All that survived were the organizational forms that it created (Abel-Smith and Stevens, 1967:148–49; Legal Action Group, 1972).

Settlement houses still exist in England, and there are now numerous legal advice centers—over sixty in London alone (e.g., Legal Action Group, 1977a). While some of these centers employ one or two full-time solicitors, and while not all are limited to just giving legal advice, it appears that most of them are merely means by which private solicitors can contribute a share of their time to advising the poor (Abel-Smith et al., 1973:29–36, 101–06; Bridges et al., 1975).

These advice centers are nevertheless important, partly because they provide a form of accessible legal advice which has long supplemented and aided the judicare scheme. Moreover, according to a study made in 1972, there was an "explosion" in these agencies after 1968 (Legal Action Group, 1972), and the fact of this proliferation was important for several reasons. First, it helped to reveal that the judicare scheme was not reaching a large number of individuals: "so inadequate are the statutory schemes that advice centres which are little more than variations on the old PML [poor man's lawyer] theme are springing up to fill the gaps" (Legal Action Group, 1972:7). Further, those involved in advice centers were recep-

53

tive to the idea of going beyond part-time advice toward full-time solicitors able to handle cases from start to finish (e.g., Partington, 1977).

A third antecedent worth mentioning is the network of legal advice centers which were to be set up under the English judicare scheme adopted in 1949 (Legal Aid and Advice Act 1949,c.51).[2] Following the recommendations of the Law Society and the Rushcliffe Committee, the statute provided for "legal advice centres" in the tradition of those descending from the poor man's lawyers, and these centers were to be staffed by lawyers paid a salary by the Law Society. The about 100 staff lawyers contemplated under the scheme were to work full-time in area offices set up to administer the scheme or in branches of the area offices, except when the population in the area was too small to support a full-time solicitor (Abel-Smith and Stevens, 1967:322; Pollock, 1975:30). Shortly after the scheme was enacted in July of 1949, however, the Labour government announced that, "owing to the general economic situation, the scheme would in the first instance only be implemented with respect to the High Court and Court of Appeal, and for cases remitted to the County Courts" (Abel-Smith and Stevens, 1967:328). Thus, the legal advice provisions were not implemented then, and, in fact, never have been as originally envisioned.[3]

These centers, however, as well as the legal advice centers financed by charities, were never meant to do much more than provide legal advice, supplementing the various voluntary and local-authority-financed advice agencies, particularly the Citizens' Advice Bureaus which have proliferated since the Second World War. As noted recently by the Council of the Law Society, "The establishment of law centres was not, as might have been expected, a progression from 'poor man's lawyers', centres such as Toynbee Hall, but from the experience gained in the United States with neighbourhood law centres [NLFs] ..." (Law Society, 1977:203).

The recognition of the U.S. influence, however, is not meant to suggest that deeper reasons, rooted in the social forces found in the modern welfare state, were not also crucial in making possible the NLF movement in England. As in the United States, poverty was rediscovered by policy makers in England in the 1960s (e.g., Abel-Smith and Townsend, 1965), and many of the same pressures for a technical, inexpensive "abolition" of poverty were felt at least as strongly in England.[4] Nevertheless, the "idea" for NLFs was imported from across the Atlantic (see also Zander, 1979:401, n.23; Partington, 1977; Jackson, 1977:553–54).

The call for NLFs in England began in 1966 and 1967 with the publication of several articles praising the virtues of the OEO Legal

54

Services Program and emphasizing the inadequacies of the English legal aid and advice system (Zander, 1966; Lill, 1967).[5] The reform banner was picked up by the Society of Labour Lawyers, who in 1968 held a conference and drafted and circulated their own call for neighborhood law firms. Their influential pamphlet, entitled *Justice for All* (published in final form in late 1968) discussed the "unmet need for professional legal services" and the sociological reasons for that "unmet need," and it concluded by recommending experimentation with three or four "local legal centres" to solve the problem. The study proposed that the experimental centers be located in poor neighborhoods; undertake a wide variety of services, excluding conveyancing, representation in criminal cases beyond mere advice, divorce litigation, and personal injury cases; litigate only in exceptional cases, such as when the case could have a large community impact or serve as a "test case"; and that the management "include some persons who could speak for the clients themselves" (Society of Labour Lawyers, 1968:46, 61–62). While certainly proposing a less "social change"-oriented model of NLFs than those thought to be operating in the United States (Byles and Morris, 1977:55), this proposal did move far toward the American model, which it described in detail in an appendix. The publication of this pamphlet placed NLFs at the center of the legal aid debate.

Furthermore, as shown by the contemporaneous pamphlet by the Society of Conservative Lawyers, entitled *Rough Justice* (1968), the terms of the debate had shifted. Conservative lawyers agreed that the judicare system must "reach out" to the poor in order to remedy "the failure of many people who need legal advice ever to get to a solicitor's office" (Society of Conservative Lawyers, 1968:19). The concept of "legal need," and the requirement of a program to satisfy the "unmet need" was embraced by both pamphlets, and this political consensus necessarily put the Law Society on the defensive.

The initial reaction of the Law Society, supported by the influential Lord Chancellor's Advisory Committee, was quite different than that of the American Bar Association in the United States. The Law Society elected to fight rather than join the NLF movement. Law Society leaders and the Lord Chancellor's Advisory Committee denied the usefulness of the American model in the English setting. The Advisory Committee, for example, stated that the adoption of NLFs would be a "radical and expensive alteration in the legal advice scheme" (Lord Chancellor's Office, 1966:51–52; see also Lord Chancellor's Office, 1967:para. 32). The Law Society argued, in a memorandum of February 1968, that NLFs would "exercise a divisive social influence," would be expensive, and would be "based upon notions of indigency and charity constituting a step backwards" (Law Society, 1968). The new President of the Law Society made a speech in October 1968 strongly condemning any proposal along the lines of OEO Legal Services: "Such a plan would be the thin edge of the wedge. It would mean a loss of the independence of the profession and could lead to a totally nationalised legal service" (cited in Society of Labour Lawyers, 1968:51).

It was not enough, however, to criticize the NLF model. As observed by Seton Pollock, then administrator of the judicare scheme, "though the economic clouds were still dark, the urgent need to move forward had been emphasized by a more widespread knowledge of the advances being made in America under their Legal Services Program" (Pollock, 1975:71). It may be that this new climate inspired reformers within the Law Society to act, hopeful that they could capitalize on the momentum already generated. But it is also true—and I think more important—that new proposals by the Law Society were necessary to stave off criticism of the Society and the scheme with which its members had been basically content. Something clearly needed to be done to solve the newly discovered problem of the unmet need for legal services.

The Law Society's February 1968 memorandum made several substantive proposals, but it rejected any role for publicly-salaried staff attorneys. The pressure of events, however, moved them away from that position. Increasing concern and publicity in 1969 about unmet legal needs, coupled with the fear that the Labour Party would win the June 1970 election and implement a competing legal aid scheme administered by some new institution, brought a slight but important change in the Law Society position (see Zander, 1973:370). The revised proposals were then given the semi-official support of the Lord Chancellor's Advisory Committee in the *Report of the Advisory Committee on the Better Provision of Legal Advice and Assistance*, published in January 1970 (see also Law Society, 1969).

The basic proposal, called the "£25 Scheme," was designed in essence to allow up to £25 worth of legal advice without the client going through the formal process of applying for legal aid. The Law Society suggested that much of the need for legal services would be met by this scheme. Legal advice would be more accessible to the poor and more attractive to lawyers, and the new scheme might even induce private solicitors to move into deprived areas. Here then was a way *private* solicitors could meet the unmet need.

The second proposal was to create an "Advisory Liaison Service," involving three types of activities: (1) liaison officers were to be appointed by the Law Society to give assistance to Citizens' Advice

Bureaus and their clients and to refer to a suitable solicitor, when appropriate; (2) "advisory centres," limited to "all the work done by solicitors under the £25 scheme," were to be set up in "areas where solicitors in ordinary practice are unable to meet the demand for legal advice and assistance"; and (3) "legal centres" offering the full legal-aid-covered services were to be created in areas where solicitors cannot "meet the demand for legal advice and assistance and legal aid."

This salaried component was clearly intended to be very limited, but the notion of salaried attorneys now had more legitimacy. The Advisory Committee, however, while recommending immediate implementation of the first proposal, recommended only limited experimentation with the second. They felt that the need for the "law centres" should first be seen by experimentation and sociological research. In effect, they were suggesting that they wait to see how much of the unmet need could be taken care of by private practitioners under the £25 scheme.

These proposals—the first response of the Law Society to the NLF challenge—were enacted into law with the Legal Advice and Assistance Act of 1972 (Legal Advice and Assistance Act, 1972, c.50, rewritten and consolidated in the Legal Aid Act 1974,c. 4), despite a change from a Labour to a Conservative government. Part I of the new law, covering the £25 scheme, was then implemented in April 1973, but Part II, covering the Advisory Liaison Service and what have been termed "Part II" (or "Section 16" as included in the Legal Aid Act 1974) law centers, has yet to be implemented. A reason for initial delay may have been the desire to first see the £25 scheme in action, but another, probably more important reason for further delay was that "neighbourhood law centres" began to develop in response to *independent* initiatives inspired by writings such as *Justice for All.*

II. The North Kensington Neighbourhood Law Centre

In July 1970, the North Kensington Neighbourhood Law Centre opened its doors in a very poor area of London, becoming the first such center in England and, for nearly three years, the only one. This very conspicuous prototype, therefore, taught a number of important lessons to both supporters and opponents of this type of legal aid system, and the problems it faced have been recurring ones in the English NLF movement. It is thus helpful to give its history some attention here. Moreover, while the literature on the law center movement is still relatively small, there is available an excellent recent study of the North Kensington Law Centre by Anthea Byles and Pauline Morris, entitled *Unmet Need: the Case of the Neighbourhood Law Centre* (1977).

England's first neighborhood law center opened at a very propitious moment. The Law Society, as noted, had just moved to a position where it admitted the necessity of experimentation with the NLFs in areas ill-served by solicitors, such as North Kensington, and accordingly the Society gave its full support to this experiment once other forces had taken the initiative.

The "prime movers" in North Kensington were a solicitor, Peter Kandler, and a number of "community workers already involved in the area" (Byles and Morris, 1977:19). The founders were strongly influenced by the conference held in August of 1968 by the Labour Lawyers, and Kandler, already involved in giving some legal advice in North Kensington, "was becoming increasingly frustrated by the limitations imposed on a service which could offer only advice" (Byles and Morris, 1977:9). The proposal to set up the law center suggested that "the service provided at such a centre would be analogous to that provided by the traditional family doctor. Thus the lawyers by working there would become accepted as part of the community ..." (Byles and Morris, 1977:9). This idea sounded much tamer than the OEO-type of NLF, with no emphasis here placed on "social change" through law as opposed to merely curing the community's legal problems. One should not, however, overemphasize a proposal clearly tailored to obtain the support of charitable institutions and the local and national Law Society.

"The task of 'selling' was not an easy one, but the organizers were helped by the presence of a number of 'establishment' figures on the working party" (Byles and Morris, 1977:10). Grants obtained from two foundations provided the rather small sum of £9000 for three years. When combined with projected revenues from the legal aid scheme and a subsidy in the form of a reduced rent charged by the local government authority, however, the grants enabled the center to open, although barely. The West End Law Society supported the proposal and the Law Society in Chancery Lane—the national Law Society—provided a "waiver" permitting the center to advertise and to handle free of charge cases not falling within the legal aid scheme. Prominent members of both the Labour and Conservative parties were present at the center's opening, and the President of the Law Society made a speech there praising the initiative and the "spirit of cooperation" that produced it (Wegg-Prosser, 1970; see also Zander, 1978:76–77).

Despite this highly publicized and apparently auspicious beginning, the center had a very difficult time. The most immediate problem was funding, a problem "which dogged its every step" (Byles and Morris, 1977:23). The limited funding provided by the charities forced the center to operate on a "shoe-string budget," and it severely inhibited the center's efforts to provide an effective service. Problems in obtaining funding to supplement the sum provided for the initial three-year period and to enable survival after that period in turn exacerbated other conflicts which unavoidably surfaced once the center began to become a force in the community.

The effort to find supplementary resources revealed the less than enthusiastic attitude of the local governing authority. In both 1971 and 1972, the center sought funds from the Home Office under the "Urban Aid Programme"—a program not unlike "community action" under OEO—but the applications failed. The necessary local government support was apparently not forthcoming because of the center's "somewhat tenuous relationship with the local authority" (Byles and Morris, 1977:25). Hostility became open, even notorious in the summer of 1973, when the center's funds became so low that it appeared that it would have to close down on December 1. The center staff in desperation requested £17,500 from the local authority, the Kensington and Chelsea Council (by this time several new law centers had received such local authority financing and there appeared no place else to turn).

Some Council members praised the Center's work, but the overall reaction was negative. After some delay, finally in late 1973 the leader of the Council, a Conservative, said that perhaps a loan could be made, but it would be conditioned on the resignation of Peter Kandler and two of his colleagues. Sir Malby Crofton then went on to assail the law center as "a Centre for the dissemination of vicious propaganda" ("Tom Thumb," 1973). While this reaction was extreme, it shows how the inevitably "political" role of the center was creating some enemies. The center came close to its end, but, fortunately, the favorable publicity generated from this attack led to some "crisis" funds from a few charities and, early in 1974, to individual donations of £3,000 and £10,000 from anonymous members of the public (North Kensington Law Centre, 1974:1–3). The center was not exactly prospering, but it survived.

Relations with local solicitors were generally very good at the outset, and they would have stayed good except for the vicissitudes of national legal aid politics and the center's funding problems. Observers noted, for example, that through referrals and the need for other solicitors to respond to the center's lawsuits, the center's presence actually "generated business for solicitors in private prac-

59

tice" (Freeman, 1974:173). The funding problems, however, forced the center to handle more criminal work than it otherwise would have. The center needed the legal aid funds that can be obtained for criminal defense. Thus, "some solicitors practising criminal law felt that the Centre was taking on too much criminal work of the kind that the private profession was well able to do ..." (Wegg-Prosser, 1974). This attitude caused a substantial deterioration of relations, expressed strongly by the local Law Society representative at meetings of the center's management committee (Byles and Morris, 1977:28).

This local level problem was exacerbated further by the growing hostility of the Law Society in Chancery Lane to the law centers that had been set up. This hostility, reflected in the increasing difficulty for new centers and center staff to obtain waivers from the Society, related to the establishment of a number of other law centers in 1973. These new centers, as noted by Byles and Morris, undermined the Society's "wish to set up centres of its own under the Legal Advice and Assistance Act" of 1972 (Byles and Morris, 1977:28).

The North Kensington Neighbourhood Law Centre itself became completely bogged down in individual cases in its early years of operation. It was unable to develop a strategy to reduce the caseload and set priorities. This paralysis stemmed from the center's financial problems, which greatly inhibited experimentation, and from basic differences of opinion within both the staff and the management committee about what other strategies to adopt. The problem was well summarized by Byles and Morris:

> [M]any of the staff, and some of the Management Committee, felt that to concentrate exclusively on casework was to perform only a very limited function and they sought ways of extending the role of the Centre. This proved yet another source of debate, some of the Management Committee fearing what they interpreted as "political" activity on the part of the Centre. Thus any extension of community-oriented work in such areas as housing, immigration, community relations or the enforcement of rights, was interpreted as a potential area of conflict with government, and as such, a threat to the "nonpolitical" role which it was felt proper for a lawyer to maintain in his professional capacity. These fears were very much to the fore amongst certain members of the local Law Society, and caused some friction between staff and representatives of that Society on the Management Committee who were anxious about the "correct" role of the Centre (Byles and Morris, 1977: 62; see also id., 14–20).

The kinds of activities that made NLFs in the United States into a movement for social change, therefore, were not yet undertaken in any systematic way.

Nevertheless, North Kensingtons's caseload dramatized and added plausibility to the "unmet need" argument, and its experience contributed greatly to the debate about what such centers should do. The basic dilemmas were discovered first-hand and the NLF movement in England and Wales learned some valuable lessons.

III. The NLF Movement Expands and Gains Support

Between January 1973 and May 1974, the number of "neighbourhood law centres"[6] in England and Wales increased from one to fifteen (Zander and Russell, 1976), with ten of them located in various parts of London (Leach, 1974). The "unmet need" revealed by North Kensington's early experience apparently helped persuade a number of local governments—more sympathetic than was that in North Kensington—to provide financial support for the local initiatives of activist lawyers and reform groups to finance new law centers. In addition, central government funding from the Home Office's Urban Aid-Community Development Program supplemented the local government funding, and, finally, the Nuffield Foundation, which by now had formed its Legal Advice Research Unit, began to support two "experimental" law centers, one in London—the Newham Rights Centre—and one in Wales—the Adamsdown Community Law and Advice Centre.[7] Before tracing some of the basic themes in the common experience of these law centers and those twelve or so centers which have since been formed, it is appropriate to trace the developments at the national level which created the environment in which these law centers operated.

With the establishment of a significant number of law centers, the law center movement became more than just a series of legal aid experiments (cf. University of Birmingham Institute for Judicial Administration, 1974). The great client demand for the resources of the law centers made it clear that a useful social service had been created which went beyond the services provided by private practitioners under the legal aid scheme. Beginning in early 1973, in addition, the existing law centers began to organize into what became the "Law Centres Working Group," giving them the possibility of speaking with a collective voice on issues of national concern (initially on the question of waivers to law centers). This informal organization added to the efforts of the Legal Action Group (LAG) founded in late 1971 and funded by the Nuffield Foundation. LAG's reformist lawyers had been from the outset very much in favor of legal aid changes along the lines proposed in *Justice for All*. These factors, combined with the increasing recognition by governmental policy makers that the Law Society's position was mainly to protect its own narrowly-defined interests, caused an important shift in the attitude of the Lord Chancellor's Advisory Committee. Further, in early 1974 the Labour Party again took power. This meant a new Lord Chancellor and a government more sympathetic to novel welfare state programs.

The change in approach by the Lord Chancellor's Advisory Committee is especially dramatic, given that the Committee (which does not change substantially from year to year) had in the past always been in agreement with the Law Society (Zander, 1979:393–94). In the Committee's report for the year 1971–72, it recognized that the new "voluntary centres" are "supplying a needed service," but it lamented the fact that "some voluntary centres have received finance out of central funds under the *Urban Programme*" (Lord Chancellor's Office, 1972:36).

> We find it anomalous that Government funds should be provided to extend legal aid in a way which is not consistent with the policy followed over the years for the provision of legal aid. There is a danger that if this form of subvention continues to be supplied it will have the effect of encouraging two competing schemes of legal aid which will undermine the present unity of the whole Legal Aid Scheme (Lord Chancellor's Office, 1972:39).

The Committee urged some experimentation with the "Part II" or "Section 16" legal centers authorized by the 1972 law, but such centers, if implemented, would be part of the existing schemes administered by the Law Society. Such centers, it was hoped, would eliminate the need to support the independent centers.

The Report of the following year shows a remarkable change. It goes into some detail into the problem of unmet need from the perspective of the law centers: "There are many people whose legal rights are, for a variety of reasons, going by default; ... some of these are unaware even that they possess such rights; others realise it but either do not know how to obtain help in enforcing them or lack the money or the ability, or both, to do so ..." (Lord Chancellor's Office, 1973:36). With this statement of the problem came the recognition that the existing neighborhood law centers, not legal centers to be created under the 1972 act, may be the model for the future: " They represent examples of a new approach to the provision of legal services which in our opinion will need to be taken into account when any improvements are made to the statutory schemes" (Lord Chancellor's Office, 1973:37).

The Labour Lord Chancellor appointed in February 1974, Lord Elwyn-Jones, quoted the Advisory Committee's words about "rights in default" in his first address to the House of Lords on 21 March 1974

(Hansard, House of Lords, vol. 350, cols. 380–83, 1974). He gave particular emphasis to the need to expand law centers in their existing form. Several months later he announced that he would seek £50,000 in emergency funds from Parliament to help law centers that were threatening to shut down (Hansard, House of Lords, vol. 351, cols. 1079–89, 1974). This meant, according to Zander, "that the Lord Chancellor's Office had for the first time taken a position between the Law Society and the law centres movement" (Zander, 1976:396). This affirmative support, both political and monetary, reflected the government's recognition that the promotion of neighborhood law centers was an important welfare state policy, not simply a question of how to organize legal aid.

The consistent support of law centers by the Lord Chancellor's Office has given a very important spur to the movement. It may also have made the Home Office, which consults with the Lord Chancellor, more willing to support law centers under the Urban Program (cf. Law Society, 1977:218). The result has been a new growth in the absolute number, and an increasing reliance on central government funds. Accordingly, of the twenty-four law centers in England and Wales existing in late 1976, five were wholly or partly financed by grants from the Lord Chancellor's fund, which was set at £100,000 for 1976 and £150,000 for 1977. In addition, a further ten centers were financed in whole or in part by the Home Office Urban Program (under which, in general, the central government provides 75 percent of the funding and the local government authority 25 percent). Total central government funding went from £69,530 in 1974–75 to £149,530 the following year, then to £380,410 and up to £527,350 in 1977–78 (Hansard, House of Commons, written answers, 17 January 1978, col. 141).

The number of law centers in England and Wales has now reached twenty-seven, with a further twenty reported to be in the advanced planning stages.[8] Most of the existing centers employ two to five lawyers and have a full-time staff of five to fifteen. The total budget for them for 1977–78 is estimated at £2 million (Lord Chancellor's Office, 1978:95). This figure is only a small fraction of the U.S. commitment to NLFs, and the individual NLFs in England are smaller than their U.S. counterparts, but a very substantial beginning has been made to add NLFs to the well-established and well-funded (£44 million civil and £41 million criminal) English judicare system (Lord Chancellor's Office, 1978:95).

IV. Implementing the NLF Model

A. *The Adoption of a Social Change Orientation*

In the United States OEO lawyers were from the beginning supposed to provide more than just individual legal services. They were expected to be part of the "War on Poverty," and national policy encouraged the adoption of strategies to help the poor as a class, especially the strategy of "law reform." In England the situation was different. While the approach of American lawyers was described and to some extent promoted in writings such as *Justice for All*, there clearly was no single articulated national policy to unite the independent law centers in an activist direction. For various reasons, in fact, the North Kensington Neighbourhood Law Centre concerned itself in its first years almost exclusively with individual casework.

With the proliferation of law centers, building in part on the North Kensington experience, new strategies were adopted, leading toward the adoption of a more social reformist orientation. Without discussing the strategies of law centers at length, one can trace the general movement away from the existing North Kensington model of individual casework. This movement had two origins: first, it developed from new models of neighborhood advocacy with origins similar to that of the OEO program in the United States; and second, the movement evolved from the inevitable disenchantment with individual casework that came to lawyers concerned with helping the poor better their position.

In 1973 and 1974 at least three new law centers sought to provide an alternative model to the purely individual casework approach. This alternative emphasized social reform in general, not unlike NLFs in the U.S.; but they also emphasized particularly "group work" and "community development and control," in contrast somewhat to the situation in the United States.

In the English legal environment, as will be seen in Chapter 9, much less emphasis was placed by activist lawyers on "law reform"—especially test case litigation—as a mechanism for social change. Several historical reasons for this very important difference might be adduced: (1) the substantive law was already far more advanced in England in terms, for example, of welfare, consumer, and tenant rights, particularly when compared to U.S. law in 1965; (2) at this point (in 1973 and 1974), there was already some disenchantment with test cases in the U.S. movement, and the English were able to draw on that critical literature; (3) without a Supreme Court, a written Constitution, and the doctrine of judicial review, test cases understandably never could be as important in England as they were in the United States, particularly the United States in the Warren Court era; and (4) it appears that in England lawyers were inspired by a more "political" stance than that taken by most of their American counterparts. This made them more wary of law reform and more receptive to strategies designed to give power to the disadvantaged.

One of these alternative law centers, the Newham Rights Centre in London, was financed entirely by the Nuffield Foundation (at £20,000 per annum for three years) (Newham Rights Centre, 1975). A second was the Adamsdown Community Law and Advice Centre in Cardiff, Wales, financed partly by the Nuffield Foundation (£6,000 per annum) and partly by the Urban Program set up in 1969 (£14,000 initial grant plus £8,000 per annum) (Adamsdown Community Trust, 1978; Brooke, 1977:15–18; Local Government Grants (Social) Act 1969,c.2), and a third, the Brent Community Law Centre in London, was financed by the Urban Program (£12,000 per annum for five years) (Brent Community Law Centre, 1975). It is instructive that these centers avoided local funding and instead developed from national social reform programs reminiscent of the Ford Foundation and OEO in the United States.

Both of the sources of funding for these new English experiments were aimed—at least originally—at addressing the "needs" of the poor considered broadly. The Nuffield Foundation "hoped to provide an opportunity for lawyers, social workers and community workers to share their knowledge and experience, and to involve the local community at grassroots levels, not through any advisory board or committee, but through active involvement. In practical terms it was felt that this multidisciplinary aim could most appropriately be achieved by working with and through local groups, rather than dealing with individual cases" (Byles and Morris, 1977:65).[9]

The approach of Brent—rooted in the philosophy of the Urban Program—was similar in emphasizing groups:

> The Centre was to ensure that the actual needs and aspirations of people within the deprived areas rather than the established and perceived needs should be harnessed to determine the course of our own and public policies aimed at meeting those needs. Our work necessarily involved helping those people to organise themselves and generally to help them to help themselves. This approach was much the same as that of the Urban Programme as a whole (Brent Community Law Centre, 1975:16).

The Urban Aid Program, mentioned before, has many similarities in aim to community action in the United States. A sister Home

Office program, which funded a number of Community Development Projects (CDP) in deprived areas—including several projects for NLF legal aid—was even closer in orientation to U.S.-style community action. As stated by Marris and Rein:

> The Home Office Community Development Projects follow explicitly, on a much smaller scale, the American [community action] experiment. ... In twelve selected areas, a team of social workers is to be specially assigned to coordinate services, stimulate community organization and encourage the people of deprived neighbourhoods to initiate their own scheme (1972:17; see also Hill, 1974:37, Partington, 1975).

Further, the ambiguities revealed in the American experience with law and community action also existed in England. Community action became either political action or ineffective action, and the former created numerous difficulties with local authorities and national sponsors (Home Office CDP, 1977; Hill, 1974:117). Again, it appears that the most durable of the controversial CDP projects will be the essentially independent law centers that it created.[10] The CDP closed in August 1977 but the Home Office Urban Program continues to support a number of law centers set up under the program.[11]

The parallel between the United States and England is intriguing, and it gives further insight into the role of reformist foundations—like Ford and Nuffield—and central government policies in developing NLFs. It should not be suggested, however, that NLFs developed only from the schemes of social planners. The NLF models of Brent and Newham, for example, were not imposed on the rest of the law centers. A number of law centers continued and still continue to emphasize such case work, most notably the Paddington Neighbourhood Law Centre, which is funded primarily by the local authority and combined with a Citizens' Advice Bureau (Paddington Neighbourhood Advice Bureau and Law Centre, 1976; see also Hackney Advice Bureau and Law Centre, 1977). Moreover, virtually all the law centers have increasingly *chosen* to emphasize group work, partly because of their conclusion that individual work was simply not effective enough. The problems of the neighborhoods required a broader approach.

In *Towards Equal Justice*, the first collective statement by the Law Centres Working Group, published in September 1974, the desire to go beyond the early North Kensington efforts toward something like the U.S. model was clearly evident: "It is significant that experience has driven the various law centres towards a broadly similar approach and, although it was reached independently, that this approach in turn is remarkably similar to that of the OEO and Law

Centre type organizations in North America" (Community Law Centres, 1974:1). The paper went on to emphasize the NLF strategies of group work and community development. The centers thus began to form a consensus away from merely individual casework and towards a particular type of NLF model.

The trend toward group work and other reformist strategies has continued and become even more pronounced. The most recent statement of the Law Centres Working Group, published in February 1978, makes this quite clear. While admitting the ongoing importance of "casework," the Working Group suggested, "we would be content to see much of this [individual case] work go into the private sector thus liberating Law Centres' limited resources to do what we consider to be the most important tasks described ... under the headings of group work and education work" (Law Centres Working Group, 1978:34). It is now clear that the law centers see their role as mobilizing the community to assert and extend their rights and developing the legal and political strength of the underprivileged. The aim is to improve the position of deprived groups as a whole, not just of aided individuals. While there are important differences in tactics between NLFs in England and the United States, their basic articulated aim is the same.

B. Law Centers and Management Committees

"Management Committees" in England play a very important role both practically and symbolically. These committees are empowered to "decide the policy of the Law Centres," including the "determination of priorities and, consequently, the selection of the appropriate combination of work methods" (Law Centres Working Group, 1978:47). This is a broad mandate, and it appears that it is taken very seriously (see Zander and Russell, 1976:214).

Management committees in England, according to the available data, are much more significant and less lawyer-dominated than their American counterparts, the "governing boards of neighborhood law firms." At least four reasons can be suggested initially to account for this difference: (1) The English law centers have as a rule grown more out of voluntary activities in local communities and thus have more ties to local residents. American NLFs were created to a great extent by national initiatives and were linked to local bar associations more than voluntary groups; (2) The lesser emphasis on test case litigation and greater emphasis on "group work" in England makes the centers' activities more comprehensible to lay people; (3) While the American NLFs were accountable ultimately to policy makers in Washington

67

who handed out the funds, thus making local control somewhat of a fiction (at least until the recent emphasis on locally set priorities), the management committees in England have been given the power to set local strategies; (4) While in the United States the organized bar has emphasized that professional independence requires "lawyer control" over NLF governing boards and this is now required by law, the Law Society in England has taken a different view. Whatever the reasons, instead of objecting to lay management committees "as being in some way a threat to the independence of lawyers ... the Law Society and the Lord Chancellor's Office appear rather to have welcomed the concept of local committees [even if not controlled by lawyers] as a bulwark for the lawyers against domination by the local funding agency" (Zander, 1979:403).

Management committees nearly always contain at least two official Law Society representatives, one national and one local, representatives from the local council, and representatives from various "helping organizations" (e.g., Citizens' Advice Bureaus, Voluntary Social Services), but the majority of the twelve to twenty-five member committees are local residents who may be elected but tend especially to represent local organizations such as tenants' unions (see Zander and Russell, 1976:214; Brooke, 1977:9; Balham Neighbourhood Law Centre, 1977; Hillingdon Community Law Centre, 1976; Paddington Neighbourhood Advice Bureau and Law Centre, 1976; Newham Rights Centre, 1977).[12] For the Adamsdown Law Centre, for example, a Committee is elected primarily from an individual membership open to all those within its ward boundaries, with some additional "coopted members who have some special experience or professional skills to contribute" (Adamsdown Community Trust, 1978:6).

Management committees, as already seen in the discussion of the North Kensington Law Centre, may limit the activities of the center to individual casework. This type of role is not so far from that of the few bar-controlled governing boards in America that were active. In England, however, the conservatism of many committees has not prevented the law center movement from seeing a much more creative role and assigning priority to working towards this role. Peter Kandler, the first solicitor of the North Kensington Law Centre, emphasized in 1974 that "control of these organizations belongs to the local community and does not belong to the lawyers because if it does then the whole idea of Law Centres begins to fail" (University of Birmingham Institute of Judicial Administration, 1974:67). The Law Centres Working Group stated specifically that "[t]he truly effective Management Committee serves as a constant check that the Law Centre is remaining responsive to local need and not getting bogged down in rigid work structures as professionals left to their own devices have an inclination to do" (Law Centres Working Group, 1978:47; see also Adamsdown Community Trust, 1978:45; Newham Rights Centre, 1977:4).

We lack objective studies on how many committees are fulfilling this function effectively, and the Law Centres Working Group even states that "[f]inding the best way to set up a Management Committee to fulfill these functions has, it must be admitted, been something of a problem in the early days of the Law Centre movement" (Law Centres Working Group, 1978:47). The vital importance of these committees, however, must be recognized. Lay-controlled committees have become a basic component of the law center movement in England, and they are accepted by all the major interest groups involved. The Law Society and the Law Centers Working Group have even agreed that "a majority of the voting members of the Management Committee of a salaried service should normally be able to represent the interests of the recipients of the service" ("Waivers of the Solicitors Practice Rules," 1977). And the Lord Chancellor in 1978 (prior to the Conservative victory, however), emphasized that, "There is, to my mind, a continuing place in the law centre movement for local control" (Speech at Garratt Lane Law Centre Annual Meeting, November 15, 1978, at 2).

C. Law Centers' Relations with Local Government

Most of the law centers get some funding from the relevant "local authority," although, as North Kensington and a few other examples show, such funding is not necessarily stable or forthcoming in every case, particularly from Conservative local governments (e.g., Saltley Action Centre, 1978; Wegg-Prosser, 1978), and the centers agree that long-term national funding would be more desirable (Law Centres Working Group, 1978). For law centers who do obtain such funding, it appears that relations tend generally to be cordial, despite some ups and downs, with the work of the law centers gaining increasing respect and even appreciation by local councillors. The major source of local friction has been in housing (e.g., Zander and Russell, 1976:214; Home Office CDP, 1977:19–24). Local authorities are heavily involved in housing regulation and in providing local housing, and law centers most frequently confront them on these vital matters. The Newham Rights Centre's recent report thus states: "in housing matters the relationship is appalling" (Newham Rights Centre, 1977:15). This basic conflict, however, has not prevented the development of a decent working relationship.

A 1977 study undertaken by the Local Government Group of the Law Society, based on inquiries sent to "the chief solicitors of all twenty-three local authorities in whose areas law centres operate," makes it possible to explore the development of this relationship in more detail. The local authorities who were canvassed clearly appreciated that "most law centres ... [are] fulfilling a definite need and doing it well" and recommended increased support from the central government (Local Government Group, 1977:330). One respondent stated, for example, "There are cases where the law centre comes into conflict with the Council, but I find it much better that people thinking they have suffered a raw deal at the hands of the Council should have access to professional advice and representation." It is evidently recognized that law centers can prevent violent and other forms of disruptive protest, and this undeniable function of law centers is no doubt appreciated at the local level.

Law centers may also, however, stir up trouble by engaging in "crusades," "general campaigns," and "being associated with the activities or causes of certain politically-inspired groups, generally labelled as 'extremists'." Thus, "independence of action should not be abused by extending the legal assistance rightly given in individual cases to the organisation of community or quasi-political action, which can find expression through private organisations specifically so motivated" (Local Government Group, 1977:338).

The local authorities, in sum, favor neighborhood law centers. They would prefer to orient centers toward individual cases and away from more political work, particularly the organization of dissenting groups, but their general orientation tends to support the present law centers despite those centers' efforts to concentrate on "group work." Law centers are highly visible to local authorities, and this makes local funding especially precarious; a particular heated controversy can provoke a quick and emotional attack on the center. It also appears, however, that the stabilizing function of law centers is sufficiently recognized to create an overall positive assessment.

D. Law Centers' Relations with Local Solicitors

The detailed study of the North Kensington experience showed that local representatives of the Law Society could be concerned about law centers maintaining a "nonpolitical" stance. In part, however, this conservatism resulted from the newness of the NLF approach in England. In more recent years, the principal issues of concern among local solicitors, the local Law Society, and the law centers have involved the questions of referrals and criminal legal aid cases. Once law centers have been set up, as in the United States, the more ideological problems have tended to fade into the background. At this point, according to the Law Centres Working Group, "apart from one or two isolated instances of friction, relations at a practical level between law centers and solicitors are good" (Law Centres Working Group, 1978: App. II at 6; see also Zander, 1978:87–88; Law Society 1977:215).

Law centers clearly generate a substantial amount of new work for local solicitors in England and Wales. First, lawsuits brought by law centers create work for defense lawyers. As Peter Kandler observed, "Because the tenants came to me, their landlords had to get solicitors to defend the cases" (Freeman, 1974:173). Second, as solicitors recognize, law centers clearly attract a large number of persons who would not otherwise consult solicitors, and law centers cannot and will not take all the cases (Law Society, 1977:216). Increasingly, in fact, the centers have sought to limit their individual caseloads to concentrate on actions affecting larger segments of the community. Clients that qualify for legal aid are very often referred to a private solicitor willing to take the case under the judicare scheme. The Camden Community Law Centre thus wrote in 1976: "This year again we referred nearly seven hundred clients to private solicitors. It seems clear that besides being able to take up individual cases, the Centre performs an important brokerage function in relation to legal need in the community, encouraging local people to seek advice and assistance and providing a referral service" (Camden Community Law Centre, 1976:3). Other law centers report the same experience.[13] According to the Law Society, law centers have generated enough legal aid business so that, "at least one office has been established in each case in the vicinity of the North Kensington, Manchester, and West Hampstead centres, while no less than four offices each have been established near the Camden and Islington Centres" (Law Society, 1977:216).

Friction between local solicitors and law centers may similarly relate to pocketbook issues. Although, for obvious reasons, not discussed in the law centers' reports, there is sometimes a tendency, seen already in North Kensington, to look to legal aid when center funds become short. Legal aid cases, particularly criminal cases— "the profitable side of legal aid" (Newham Rights Centre, 1977:43)—can be taken in increased numbers to bolster center revenues. Several law centers—of those not opposed in principle to handling a substantial number of individual cases—do apparently undertake a notable amount of criminal work,[14] and it can be argued that private solicitors would be willing and able to do that work themselves. This "duplication" of services can undermine local solicitor support and, in fact, has been a key concern of the national Law Society and local societies throughout the history of law centers (e.g., Law Society, 1977:204).

E. Relations among Law Centers, the National Law Society, and the Lord Chancellor's Office—The Waivers Controversy

The Law Society in England, in contrast to the ABA in the United States, pushed aggressively on behalf of the interests of local practitioners who feared competition from legal aid clients. A reason may be that Law Society leaders are somewhat closer to the "average solicitors" in England; certainly the American legal profession is much more stratified than the English one, which still seems to be relatively homogeneous in class background and prestige, and England does not really have "elite" corporate law firms to the degree they exist in such cities as Washington, D.C., and New York (Abel-Smith and Stevens, 1967:403–04, 435–37). These elite lawyers in America are those farthest removed from typical local practitioners, and they tend to dominate the ABA leadership. These ABA leaders supported NLFs even when opposed by many, if not most, local practitioners, and provided crucial support to the U.S. NLF program.

A second, more tangible reason for different attitudes may simply be that in England many private solicitors already receive substantial legal aid income on behalf of poor clients. The fear of loss of income by solicitors in private practice is more widespread and pronounced in England than in the USA, where the fear of loss was much more speculative. Poor people may indeed go to English law centers instead of to private solicitors. The Law Society has fought hard to defend solicitors from this potential rival for business.

The Law Society's concern with competition was clear in its 1970 proposal for what are now called "Section 16 Legal Centres" (they still have not been created); they were to be implemented only when the needs of the residents demonstrably could not be met by private local solicitors. The most important manifestation of the Law Society's strong anticompetition position has been with respect to the debate on "waivers." This debate, in addition, illustrates the basic roles of law centers, the Law Society, and the Lord Chancellor's Office in the law centers' move toward acceptance.

The Law Society, which administers the Solicitors Practice Rules, has the power to grant waivers of particular rules, and such waivers are necessary for solicitors in law centers to advertise their services

72

and in general to seek clients affirmatively.[15] This power gave the Law Society substantial leverage over law centers. Considerable conflict has been generated as the national Law Society, often bolstered by a local Law Society, has sought to use its power "to devise means to ensure that waivers would not be used to the unfair disadvantage of practitioners" (statement of Seton Pollock, for the Law Society, in Zander and Russell, 1976:213; see also Law Society, 1977:204).

The national battle over waivers, which finally came to a truce in July 1977, commenced in early 1973, when the Law Society began to impose very strong conditions for waivers on new law centers (see generally Zander, 1977:1236–39; Zander, 1978:88–94). The Society's aim was to insure that law centers were not established in areas where they might compete with private solicitors and that, when established, they would be under the control of the local Law Society and refrain from work that private solicitors would do. Waivers would be "revocable at will" by the Law Society if centers overstepped their role. These conditions were strongly opposed by the Law Centers Working Group and the Legal Action Group.

In July 1974 these groups were joined by the Lord Chancellor, Lord Elwyn-Jones, who had just taken a public position favoring law centers to reduce the "unmet need" for legal services. The result of his intervention was a preliminary agreement under which parties seeking waivers and encountering difficulties could report to the Lord Chancellor, who then would advise the Law Society of his view on the matter. Reasonable conditions to prevent unfair competition and to monitor compliance with that requirement were accepted under that agreement.

This agreement was made subject to the development of a permanent document from negotiations among the Lord Chancellor's Office, the Law Society, the Law Centres Working Group, and other interested organizations. The ensuing negotiations lasted three years and were apparently quite heated. Before their conclusion, however, many of the pivotal issues had to be confronted explicitly. This confrontation was necessitated by the proposed Hillingdon Law Center's request for waivers in late 1975.

Hillingdon (a borough of London) had the first local authority in a "relatively affluent area" to agree to fund a law center. Since there were already numerous private solicitors available, the local and national Law Societies argued that there was "no established need for the Centre" (Hillingdon Law Centre, 1976:7). Despite support of the center from all the local advice and "helping agencies" in the area, in March 1976 the Law Society for the first time simply refused to grant waivers. A national controversy arose with the Law Society portrayed in a rather bad light; it was seen as looking out for its own selfish interests, not the public interest. In May the Lord Chancellor "advised" the Law Society to grant the waivers, and the Society complied.

The Lord Chancellor now recognized that the Law Society could not be left to determine the "need" for a law center. He informed the Law Society that need,

> ... is a matter for the funding agency, and if the agency decides to establish a law centre in a particular case ... it is not for the Law Society ... to concern itself with whether or not a law centre is needed at that place. What the Law Society does have to satisfy itself about is that the centre is properly constituted and independent, and that its services will not duplicate those normally provided by private practitioners to such a substantial extent as to amount to unfair competition. As long as the centre binds itself as to the kinds of work it will undertake, ... this latter condition should be regarded as satisfied" (Lord Chancellor's Office, 1976:71).

The Lord Chancellor suggested further that conditions for waivers be spelled out precisely; this became the basis for final negotiations, ending in August 1977.

The final agreement, published in the *Law Society's Gazette* (1977) recognizes the right of funding agencies to determine need. It also requires law centers to have "a management committee which is independent of the funding agency." Most important, the management committee of a law center must declare that, apart from situations such as emergencies or where private practitioners are unavailable, salaried solicitors will not provide more than "initial advice and assistance" in cases involving (1) conveyancing; (2) commercial matters; (3) divorce proceedings; (4) probate matters except personal applications in small estates; or (5) criminal matters where the accused is twenty-one years of age or older. This last condition, which makes it more difficult for law centers to obtain legal aid funds, "almost caused the collapse of the negotiations" (Zander, 1977:1238), but the need for agreement caused the law centers to concede.

Under the agreement, the Law Society may consider "revocation of waivers" if the number of "exceptional" cases in the above proscribed areas "is so disproportionate to the total number of cases undertaken by the centre that the services normally provided by solicitors in private practice are being unnecessarily duplicated." Disputes about waivers and revocation are again subject to the "advice" of the Lord Chancellor.

This compromise agreement goes very far to mollify private

74

solicitors; it is not surprising that the Law Centres Working Group is openly critical of it (Law Centres Working Group, 1978:31–32). Nevertheless, it is also a victory for law centers, aided by the Lord Chancellor, since they can continue to operate essentially as before (with perhaps fewer criminal cases), and more centers can open regardless of the opinion of the Law Society.

The Law Society no longer will try to treat law centers as it would have "Section 16" legal centers foreseen by the 1972 legal aid reform—i.e., by limiting them to areas where an absolute lack of solicitors is available to handle legal aid work. It recognizes officially that law centers are *entitled* to handle "certain specialized fields such as housing and welfare law" (Law Society, 1977:204). A division of labor has de facto been accepted with respect to individual matters. In the words of the Law Society statement, "There is now, and may well be for some time to come, a need to supplement the legal services provided by traditional methods" ("Waivers of the Solicitors Practice Rules," 1977:338).

In addition, the Law Society has now endorsed some of the methods of the law centers, particularly that of "community control." The severity of this change can be seen by comparing two policy statements. In 1974 the Law Society's report to the Lord Chancellor contained this passage:

> The concept of responsibility to the local community is superficially attractive but is riddled with problems. The lawyer in his function of lawyer is responsible to serve the lawful interests of his client in accordance with the law laid down. The service of a particular community or any section of it is a matter of general social concern and falls into the realm of politics, law reform and administrative action (Lord Chancellor's Office, 1974:40).

This passage was part of a strong defense of the proposed Part II (Section 16) centers as the *only* ones necessary to supplement the judicare legal aid scheme. In contrast, in the Law Society's Evidence to the Royal Commission, dated April 1977, the Society criticized Section 16 centers as *inadequate* because, inter alia, "There is no means of involving local organisations or other representatives of the community in the management of a law centre ... or of delegating powers to such a Management Committee" (Law Society, 1977:205). As noted before, the waiver agreement itself refers to control by independent management committees, of which, "it is considered that a majority of the voting members ... should normally be able to represent the interests of the recipients of the service."

Finally, a related theme of the waiver controversy is that of control over the law centers. The Law Society now recognizes that control should be left primarily with the centers' management committees. The current position can be compared to the Society's insistence in 1974 that *it* should control both the salaried and the private components of the scheme: "The [Law Society's] Council would view with deep concern any developments at this juncture that would lead towards two legal aid schemes operating in the same general field. They believe this would precipitate serious problems of coordination of effort which can best be avoided by a unified scheme administered by the Law Society under the guidance of your Lordship" (Lord Chancellor's Office, 1974:40). The Law Society still favors "coordination," but it has given up the idea of being policymaker and administrator of the entire system.

As illustrated by the waiver struggle and its resolution, the Law Society, pushed by the Lord Chancellor and forced to face the reality of the existing, apparently successful law centers, has changed its position substantially. While certainly not giving up on its interests, it has taken a much more flexible view of those interests and how they can best be preserved. One should not forget that one of its interests is to appear to represent the public interest, rather than merely that of a narrow guild.

F. Law Centers' Recurring Funding Difficulties

The problem of funding for law centers relates to the previous discussion but deserves some separate attention. First, it is worth underlining that the present more or less ad hoc system has led to a permanent funding crisis: "funding for individual centres has been inadequate, inconsistent, and irregular. Most centres have had to live from hand-to-mouth on an annual basis, having to devote disproportionate amounts of effort to securing next year's funds merely to maintain existing levels of service" (Law Centres Working Group, 1978:50). Funds have increasingly been supplied from the Lord Chancellor's office on an emergency basis, but this is not conducive to long-term planning or expansion. Moreover, the need to justify the activities to the funding agency *each* year exacerbates the problem of obtaining public funds for potentially controversial actions. This is especially true for those receiving funds from local authorities. It is less of a problem for those with longer duration grants from the Home Office Urban Program.[16] Those relying on the Lord Chancellor's fund for law centers, however, must justify each one year grant. The Newham Rights Centre, for example, has reported pressure from the Lord Chancellor's Office to increase the amount of individual work which can be covered under the Legal Aid Scheme (Newham Rights Centre, 1977:14).

76

The present funding system is unsatisfactory, not only because of a general shortage of funds, affecting all social services and felt most strongly at the local level, but also because ad hoc funding has prevented a national policy on law centers from developing. Such a national policy, including stable funding for law centers, may emerge from the recommendations of the Royal Commission on Legal Services.

V. The Royal Commission on Legal Services: Unresolved Issues and the Future of Legal Aid in England and Wales

A number of critical issues remain unresolved in the development of neighborhood law centers in England. First is the question of how much resources should be available to law centers, and whether these should be existing ones, new independent ones, or the not yet implemented Section 16 centers. At present, as noted before, about £2 million goes to the twenty-seven or so existing law centers, while some £85 million goes to civil (£44 million) and criminal (£41 million) legal aid and advice. Law centers are funded from several different sources, and there is still the possibility of setting up Section 16 legal centers if the Lord Chancellor so decides.

Second is the question of how the systems should be coordinated, and by whom. This problem is compounded because presently the Law Society (under the supervision of the Lord Chancellor) administers the civil scheme while the Home Office handles criminal legal aid. A partial response to this coordination problem is the waiver document discussed earlier, but obviously the administration of that agreement will not be without further conflict.

A third question is whether some control over the *quality* of law centers is necessary or desirable and, if so, to whom should responsibility be entrusted. The Lord Chancellor's Advisory Committee emphasized this problem in 1976: "We are increasingly concerned about the lack of any uniform code of minimum standards for law centres or, if there were one, any uniform means of enforcing it (as opposed to individual action by the funding agent)" (Lord Chancellor's Office, 1976:72).

It appears at present that the Lord Chancellor's Office, aided by the Advisory Committee, is already concerned with these problems and heavily involved in the funding and coordination of law centers. Examples of this involvement have been seen, and another should here be mentioned. In June 1976 the Lord Chancellor announced that legal aid would no longer be available for the hearing of un-defended divorces, thus saving, according to his estimates, about £6 million. (The change was implemented in April 1977.) He stated then that the savings could be used partly to help law centers with their financial problems. The important role of the Lord Chancellor is undeniable, but it is thus far still rather vague and unsystematic. No comprehensive public policy has been enacted through statutes or even proclaimed in any detailed public statement. The Lord Chancellor is part of the government, but his duties with respect to law centers reflect no clear governmental policy. Further, it may be desirable to create new institutions to oversee the entire legal aid system. These problems are at present in limbo, due to the creation in mid-1976 of the Royal Commission on Legal Services. Significant new policy developments will, for obvious reasons, have to wait for that Commission's report, which is expected late in 1979.

The Royal Commission is composed of fifteen persons, of whom five are lawyers.[17] The terms of reference are very broad: "To inquire into the law and practice relating to the provision of legal services in England, Wales, and Northern Ireland and to consider whether any, and if so what, changes are desirable in the public interest…" (Royal Commission on Legal Services, 1977:1). The commission must consider such issues as the monopoly possessed by solicitors on conveyancing, advertising by solicitors, the divided profession (solicitors and barristers), and, of course, the future of legal aid.

In considering the future of legal aid in England and Wales, therefore, it may be instructive to compare the evidence submitted to the Royal Commission by several of the principal actors involved, particularly the Law Society, the Law Centres Working Group (LCWG), the Legal Action Group (LAG), the Society of Labour Lawyers, and the Lord Chancellor's Advisory Committee. Four basic issues will be considered here—national coordination, the role of and control over the present law centers (and future ones of the same type), the place for Section 16 legal centers, and the role of other advice centers, particularly the Citizens' Advice Bureaus.

All the principal groups recognize serious problems with existing coordination machinery. The LCWG (1978: App.1), the Legal Action Group (1977:15–24), and the Society of Labour Lawyers (1978:23) propose that a "Legal Services Commission" be created to administer and oversee the entire legal aid system, including that part now under the Law Society (see also Haldane Society of Socialist Lawyers, 1977). The LAG evidence refers specifically to the experience of the U.S. Legal Services Corporation and the Quebec *Commission des services juridiques*. In contrast to the U.S. Legal Services Corporation, however, all three groups proposed that the Commission should include *a majority of nonlawyers* along with repre-

78

sentatives of the Law Society, the Bar Council, and the National Association of Citizens' Advice Bureaus. Members, at least according to LAG, would be selected by the Lord Chancellor. The others leave this issue open. According to LAG's evidence, in addition, the Commission would appoint Area Legal Services Councils (again with a majority of laymen) to administer and coordinate the schemes locally.

The Law Society and the Lord Chancellor's Advisory Committee's proposals both reject the need for a Legal Services Commission (Law Society, 1977:171–73; Lord Chancellor's Office, 1978:98–99).[18] They suggest that the Lord Chancellor oversee the entire system, including law centers and civil and criminal legal aid. The Law Society's further concrete proposal is that *it* create Area Legal Services Committees composed of interested lawyers and, for the first time, nonlawyers (Law Society, 1977:217; Lord Chancellor's Office, 1978:101–02).[19] This suggestion, if implemented, would require a statutory change in the existing scheme, since the new institutions would be subcommittees of the fourteen legal aid Area Committees which must by law be composed of lawyers. The Area Legal Service Committees, according to the Law Society, "would have a primary responsibility for the coordination and provision of adequate legal services in its area and would be serviced by one or more liaison officers. It would be in an ideal position to decide where legal services need supplementing, and by what means" (Law Society, 1977:217). Policy decisions would be made by the Lord Chancellor, advised by his own Committee and these new decentralized ones. The Lord Chancellor's Advisory Committee favors a similar solution, although it emphasizes that the Lord Chancellor should obtain reports directly from the new committees, rather than through the Law Society. It also suggests that it expand its own ambit to cover criminal legal aid policy, as well as civil legal aid.[20]

The proposals made to the Royal Commission regarding the establishment and monitoring of law centers are in line with the above framework. The Law Society and Lord Chancellor's Advisory Group want all funding decisions to be made ultimately by the Lord Chancellor, perhaps according to "need" as established by the new local committees. Since the Area Legal Service Committees would presumably be appointed by the Law Society, there probably would be a bias against new law centers patterned after the existing ones. Subsidized private solicitors or other favored alternatives might be chosen instead. The Law Society, in particular, continues to urge that consideration be given to strengthening Citizens' Advice Bureaus— including by means of adding law centers affiliated with them—and setting up Section 16 Centers as reformed along the lines already mentioned. It strongly "rejects the view that [the present] law centres are the only or, in many places, the best way of providing legal services in deprived areas" (Law Society, 1977:217). Control of the law centers (except Section 16 ones controlled by the Law Society) would remain primarily with local management committees with some oversight by the new local organizations and the Lord Chancellor.

The Legal Action Group, the Society of Labour Lawyers and the Law Centers Working Group proposals are similar in form, except for the potentially crucial difference that the Law Society and to an extent even the Lord Chancellor would be given less influence over the establishment, maintenance, and control of law centers; the quasi-independent Legal Services Commission would handle these matters. In addition, they naturally place a much greater emphasis on law centers. According to LAG, for example, "it seems inevitable that public funds will be concentrated on expanding the salaried sector of the profession..." (1977:23; see also Law Centres Working Group, 1978:19,24; Society of Labour Lawyers, 1978:18). LAG envisions not only the "establishment of more law centres on the present model," but also the "[d]irect employment of salaried solicitors in centres run by the Legal Services Commission" (1977:23).

The LCWG evidence also deals at some length with interim proposals in the absence of a new Legal Services Commission. Three suggestions merit particular attention. The first is for a "Standing Committee on Public Legal Services," to be composed of "a membership drawn from organisations actually practicing in the field," such as the LCWG, the Law Society and the National Association of Citizens' Advice Bureaus (Law Centres Working Group, 1978:App. I at 4). This Committee would "have the job of advising the responsible ministers directly on each individual application for funds and on the principles to be applied to applications." Thus the present system of funding by the Lord Chancellor's office, the Home Office, local governments, and others would be coordinated through a new advisory group.

The second proposal is for a "Support and Development Unit" to be operated by the LCWG. Its role would be to encourage and advise existing law centers and proposed ones, provide some training, and initiate "a continuing service of education about changes in the law and administrative procedures" (Law Centres Working Group, 1978:App. I at 7). In this way the existing and proposed centers would develop stronger ties and provide greater mutual support.

The third proposal is a direct response to the concern for standards

80

expressed by such bodies as the Lord Chancellor's Advisory Committee. The LCWG is adamant in its opposition to the imposition of "uniform standards of action on all Law Centres, in blatant disregard of all that has been said about community responsiveness" (Law Centres Working Group, 1978:50). It suggests instead that a statute should create an independent Registrar to undertake the registration of public legal service projects (Law Centres Working Group, 1978:App. I at 9–10). The Registrar would satisfy himself that the following conditions are met: (1) at least two full-time lawyers are employed; (2) the services are to a "deprived community" in a "defined geographical area"; (3) at least half the budget is from public funds or charities; (4) a constitution guarantees the project's independence, and "persons able to represent the interests of consumers of the service should have a majority control as its management body"; (5) the project is nonprofit; and (6) it is adequately insured against professional negligence. Registration would then give the project an entitlement to receive the various waivers and statuses necessary to operate. This is a device designed to protect the existing law centers and ensure their independence from the Law Society and other existing central government bodies, but at the same time not neglect the need for some minimum standard to insure law center quality.

At the time of this writing the Royal Commission has not yet reported, but indications are that only minor changes in the status quo will be proposed. According to *The Economist* (9 June 1979, p. 22), the report as drafted,

> gives a cautious go-ahead to increasing the 30 or so law centres because these have given many people access to the law for the first time. None the less, some members of the commission were worried that the centres were too left-wing, siding too much with the underdog—say, the tenant and not the landlord.

Law centers still generate controversy, but we can expect that the report will provide further confirmation of the importance of law centers and their unique role in the emerging combined system of legal aid in England and Wales.

How the important issues of detail will be resolved by the report, however, remains to be seen. In particular, the Law Centres Working Group has expressed fears, based on rumors of the report's contents, that the commission will not support the practice of local control by management committees (Law Centres News, 1979:1). If the rumors are true, the report may push for the creation of new law centers accountable only to national funding agencies. That would probably not affect the operation of the existing centers, but it obviously would affect the direction of the movement. It appears, however, that the local control approach is too important to the English law center movement for the central government—even a Conservative one—to neglect. Certainly we can expect the commission to recommend a greater central government involvement in policing all the law centers; the proposals of the Law Centres Working Group obviously asked too much. But the law centers are now well-organized and appear strong enough to maintain the novel approach that they have developed to date. They had a difficult struggle, particularly against the Law Society, but with the crucial support of the Lord Chancellor's Office they were able to survive and expand their numbers. There are still open issues, and the Commission's report will no doubt stimulate a wide open debate, but the prognosis is most likely for a further expansion of the present breed of law centers.

Notes

1. I refer to England and Wales, since they represent one legal jurisdiction of the United Kingdom. For shorthand, however, I will often refer only to England, since that is where most of these developments have taken place. It should also be noted that there are law centers in at least Belfast, Northern Ireland, and Glasgow, Scotland. The former belongs to the Law Centres Working Group.

2. For background on this law, see Abel-Smith and Stevens (1967:315–48) and Pollock (1975:27–64). The legal aid scheme followed the *Report of the Committee on Legal Aid and Legal Advice in England and Wales* (1945) (the report of the "Rushcliff" Committee).

3. The expectation that the new legal advice centers would be created led, unfortunately, to the anticipatory closing of a number of the charitable advice centers inherited from the poor man's lawyers (Abel-Smith and Stevens, 1967:328). It should be noted that some provision for legal advice by private solicitors was implemented through the "pink form" scheme in 1959, discussed in Pollock (1975:80–81), and the "green form" scheme of 1972, discussed below.

4. For example, see the *Report of the Committee on Local Authority and Allied Personal Social Services* (1968) (The Seebohm Report). According to Marris and Rein,

> "[T]hey are searching, by much the same means, to resolve the same fundamental problems—the growing disparity between the demands upon the social services and their resources, which no increases in taxation or contributions seem likely in themselves to meet; the assimilation of newcomers; and the alienation of democratic control in a completely interdependent society" (1972:20) (see also Freeman, 1974:173).

5. Professor Michael Zander's energy and interest, it might be noted, have had a very strong influence on the growth of a "public sector" of legal aid in England. He also has published more articles and books on the subject than anyone else. Of

particular interest is his very recent study, *Legal Services for the Community* (1978).

6. The problem in defining a "neighbourhood law centre" should be mentioned, since solicitors may act in the same role without being salaried, receiving substantial public funds, or having waivers from the Law Society. For example, the Holloway Neighbourhood Law Centre was created in October of 1971, but, lacking waivers and substantial public or charitable funds, was not then considered a "law centre" by most commentators (Holloway Neighbourhood Law Centre, 1974). This problem of definition is raised in some detail in Lydiate (1975). Since my concern is with the emergence of a law center movement as a serious alternative to public legal aid under judicare, I shall recognize "official" law centers that have waivers from the Law Society or are part of the Law Centres Working Group. At present, there are only two law centers that have waivers but are not part of the Law Centres Working Group (see also Legal Action Group, 1976).

7. As of August 1975, according to the Zander and Russell survey, local authorities provided 49% of the funding for the then fifteen law centers (Zander and Russell, 1976:208). The funding varied considerably among the law centers. North Kensington, for example, received 48% of its funds from legal aid revenues, while eight of the centers received 5% or less of their funding from legal aid. Five of the centers depended almost entirely on local authorities.

8. According to a statement by the Law Centres Working Group on 7 March 1978, they are now assisting twenty groups to set up new law centers in their areas. Letter from Phil Leask, Convenor of the Development Subcommittee, to local authorities in regard to a Conference in Birmingham on 20 May 1978, on "how to set up a law centre."

9. Byles and Morris were researchers for the Nuffield Foundation's Legal Advice Research Unit. The plan for the Newham Centre was inspired in large part from their "legal needs" study (Morris, Cooper, and Byles, 1973).

10. Of the twelve CDPs, six employed lawyers, four (Benwell, Coventry, Liverpool, and Birmingham) had separate legal facilities, and two more had lawyers on their staff (Zander, 1978:82).

11. A Circular (100/35) issued on 18 June 1975, for example, stated that, under the Urban Program,

> "Projects may take the form of salaried law centres or the provision of lawyers to work with the existing advice centres or community projects. They may also take the form of legal assistance in the context of groups of existing projects. It is considered appropriate that legal services should be managed by voluntary agencies and the number of lawyers employed in such schemes shall not normally be less than two."

The Saltley Action Centre, for example, was funded by the Birmingham CDP, whose funding ended in August 1977. Two of the Birmingham CDP projects were to be continued after that date, one of which was the Saltley Action Center. Funding by the Home Office was made available (although local authority problems delayed the receipt of the grant) (Saltley Action Centre, 1977).

12. The Newham Rights Centre's membership is open to "representatives of any organization whose 'principal purposes ... include the improvement or protection of the working or living conditions of that organization,' as long as a substantial number of members live or work in the London Borough of Newham" (Newham Rights Centre, 1977:3).

13. Examples include the Balham Neighbourhood Law Centre (1977:3) (546 referrals); Brent Community Law Centre (1976:iii) (69 referrals—15% of the casework); Camden Community Law Centre (1977:7) (598 referrals); Hillingdon Community Law Centre (1976:10) (134 referrals); Paddington Neighbourhood Advice Bureau and Law Centre (1976:Table 9) (Referrals are by the CAB attached to the centre); Small Heath Community Law Centre (1977:App. I) (97 referrals out of 930 cases). The Newham Rights Centre's approach is to utilize local solicitors in "Neighbourhood Advice Sessions" to handle individual cases (Newham Rights Centre, 1977:14). (See generally Zander and Russell, 1976:214.)

14. The following examples can be listed: Balham Neighbourhood Law Centre (1977:3) (16% of "actions" criminal); Camden Community Law Centre (1977:7) (6% of cases taken); North Kensington Law Centre (1976:4) (49% of files criminal); Islington Community Law Centre (1975:2) (14.6% of ongoing cases criminal).

15. Rule 1 of the Solicitors' Practice Rules states:

> "A solicitor shall not obtain or attempt to obtain professional business by (a) directly or indirectly without reasonable justification inviting instructions for such business, or (b) doing anything which by its manner, frequency or otherwise advertises his practice as a solicitor, or (c) doing or permitting to be done anything which may reasonably be regarded as touting [soliciting]."

Rule 5 allows the Society to waive any of the rules. Some similar issues have come up with barristers, who until December 1974 were not even permitted to become salaried employees at such centers. The Bar Rules permitting barrister employment at law centers were revised in March, 1977. There are still some problems to be worked out, however (Law Centres Working Group, 1978:App. 2 at 1-5).

16. For example, the Small Heath Community Law Centre received a five year commitment from the Home Office. It is still necessary for 25% of the funding to be provided by the local authority, but once the commitment is made, the 25% need not be requested anew each year (Small Heath Community Law Centre (1977:20). The 25% requirement may, however, prevent a Home Office grant from being made in the first place.

17. There are two solicitors, a judge, a nonpracticing barrister, the former director of the Legal Action Group, a legal journalist, a sociologist, a trade unionist, the director of the Consumers' Association, an economist, a former headmistress, a university lecturer in social administration, and two accountants. One of the accountants, Sir Henry Benson, is Chairman (see Zander, 1979:393).

18. In 1976, the Labour Government also made clear its opposition to a Legal Services Commission (*Hansard*, House of Commons, written answers, 26 January 1976, col. 10).

19. Interestingly, the proposal borrows from the LAG suggestion made originally in 1974 (LAG, 1974), with the key difference that under the Law Society's proposal the committees would be responsible to the Law Society (see Legal Action Group, 1977:19).

20. According to Zander (1979:420), "The solution is clear. The legal services committees should be off-shoots of the Minister's Advisory Committee with its terms of reference expanded to include *all* legal services—private sector as well as public. Secondly, the members of such committees should be appointed by the Minister rather than by the profession."

Chapter 4

Canada

Canadian legal aid developments have been powerfully influenced by its two closest allies, the United States and the United Kingdom. The OEO program sparked idealistic lawyers and students who favored a movement for change, while the English judicare system, in effect in Ontario since 1967, continued to attract the organized profession's support. The two models competed in what has been termed a "Great Canadian Debate"; the result was a series of "Canadian Compromises" in the provinces (Penner, 1977).

The focus of the Canadian story is on the ten provinces, each of which holds "exclusive legislative authority in the administration of justice and in matters of property and civil rights" (British North America Act of 1867, §92, para. 13, 14). The federal government may share costs and make grants for particular projects, and this power has been extremely important to Canadian NLFs, but no national civil legal aid program exists.[1] The provinces have considerably more autonomy than individual states in the United States.

The provincial developments will not be described in as much detail as was utilized in the previous two chapters. Partly this limitation is imposed by the general absence of detailed studies of NLFs in the various provinces, and partly it is self-imposed in order to keep the length of this chapter from becoming excessive.

I. The Canadian Debate—Judicare vs. Decentralized Staff Legal Aid Systems

In the United States the OEO program and its model of advocacy developed before the local bar associations discovered the virtues of judicare and were able to push it into the legal aid picture, and in England NLF advocates chipped away at the well-established judicare system. Ontario's experience was much like England's, but for the rest of Canada the question actually was which system—staff or judicare—to *choose*.

U.S. developments created a climate in Canada in 1969–1971 in which "there was no question of the need for a vast expansion of legal aid and for government funds to support such expansion" (Penner, 1977:14). Should the various provinces "follow the English model of simply extending existing services to a greater number of individuals or were they to become activist on the 'social welfare' model pioneered by the OEO offices, and be a legal vanguard in the war on poverty?" (Penner, 1977:14). Reforms were indeed enacted to such an extent in the early and mid-1970s that legal aid expenditures in Canada outside of Ontario went from $1 million (civil and criminal) in 1971 to over $48 million in 1977/78 (see Zemans, 1978:664).

Idealistic students and members of law faculties were the first in Canada to experiment with new forms of legal aid—often clinical legal education programs—oriented toward the NLF model (Brooke, 1977:542; Penner, 1977:10; Taman, 1978:669). In 1969 and 1970, for example, important legal assistance clinics were set up in connection with Osgoode Hall Law School (Toronto, Ontario), the Dalhousie University Faculty of Law (Halifax, Nova Scotia), the Universities of Montreal and McGill (Montreal, Quebec), the Saskatchewan Law College (Saskatoon), and the University of British Columbia (Vancouver).

Conferences and writings—many by participants in the clinics—fueled the debate considerably (see Taman, 1976:371). In September of 1971, for example, Larry Taman, the first director (as a student) of the Osgoode Hall Law School "Legal Aid Services Programme," published *The Legal Services Controversy: An Examination of the Evidence*, a powerful statement of the case for NLFs (Taman, 1971). Borrowing extensively from the writings of the Cahns, Carlin and Howard, and other influential U.S. sources, he drew attention to "legal needs" unmet by the Ontario judicare system. He called for an OEO-like system of legal aid "embodying *creative* and *active* measures aimed directly at effective alteration of the circumstances of the poor..." (emphasis in original) (Taman, 1971:6).

The movement gained momentum in October 1971, when an important "Conference on Law and Poverty" took place in Ottawa. Most of the Canadian pro-NLF leaders were there, and Edgar and Jean Cahn gave a major address as guest speakers (see the proceedings edited by Cotler and Marx, 1977).

The most decisive contribution to the debate, however, came from the Canadian federal government, which early saw the virtues of NLFs. The principal concerns were probably similar to those behind the War on Poverty in the United States and the English Home Office's Urban Program. The result was that Canada's federal Department of Health and Welfare in 1970–71 made "demonstration" grants to four community law projects, all of which had begun through law student–law faculty initiatives. The four were Parkdale Community Service in Toronto, Ontario; Dalhousie Legal Aid Service in Halifax, Nova Scotia; Community Legal Services Inc. in Point St. Charles, Montreal, Quebec; and Saskatoon Community Legal Assistance Society in Saskatoon, Saskatchewan.[2] These federal grants, according to all commentators, provided the decisive catalyst for legal aid change (e.g., Brooke, 1977:536–37; Cowie, 1975, in Canadian Council on Social Development, 1975:315; Penner, 1977:148).

Each of these federally-funded projects promoted a social-change-oriented NLF model. The Dalhousie Legal Aid Service, for example, emphasized from the outset that it not only would provide basic legal services to individuals and groups, but also that it would engage in "preventive law, drafting and lobbying for reform, organizing and animating community groups, research and many other similar activities" (quoted in Penner, 1977:81).

Community Legal Services Inc. in Point St. Charles accentuated "work to change and modify the law where necessary"; the elaboration of a "truly community clinic, responsive to the needs and priorities of the people of the district"; and the tactic of community organization, as reflected in the plan to hire two experienced organizers ("*animateurs specialisés*") (Penner, 1977:121–22; on Parkway see id. at 31; and on Saskatoon see id. at 28 and Zemans, 1978:676–77).

While there were different emphases among the federally-funded programs, all fit well the broad NLF (as used in this essay) definition. That they were supposed to fit that definition is apparent from the choice in 1972 of Robert Cooper, the first staff attorney hired by the Point St. Charles Project, as evaluator of the demonstration projects. Cooper was very concerned with the social change activities of these projects as well as "the issue of community participation at several levels: governance group activities, formation of groups, and use of paralegals" (Penner, 1977:30). Clearly the federal grants sought to foster NLF innovation, and they succeeded to a remarkable extent, providing powerful models of and advocates for provincial change.

II. The Canadian Compromise—Provincial Reform and the NLF Model

From 1971 to 1975, every Canadian province made significant changes in its legal aid system. The great debate produced a number of diverse programs, but virtually all, including Ontario, were forced to include some kind of salaried staff component. While the various attitudes and postures of provincial law societies and provincial governments cannot here be traced in detail, it will suffice to describe the most important of the provincial skirmishes. They involve themes and create patterns similar to those discussed in more detail with respect to England and the United States.

A. *Nova Scotia*

The first provincial government to move toward a staff system of legal aid was Nova Scotia, and change was accomplished with comparatively little controversy. In 1970 the provincial Attorney General constituted a committee to recommend reforms of the clearly outmoded charitable legal aid system. The committee was evidently influenced strongly by an important study by David Lowry, the Executive Director of the federally-funded Dalhousie office; he submitted an impressive written brief emphasizing unmet legal needs and favoring "Neighborhood Legal Services" on the U.S. model (Lowry, 1970). In 1971 the committee reported in favor of the adoption of the system of legal aid by salaried lawyers (Report of the Committee for the Study of Legal Aid in Nova Scotia, 1971:42). Subsequently the Province of Nova Scotia and the Nova Scotia Barristers' Society agreed to follow that recommendation—at least on an experimental basis—and the Barristers' Society was given the statutory power to administer the new program (Legal Aid Planning Act, S.N.S. 1970–71, ch. 14; see generally Nova Scotia Legal Aid, 1977). Since that time Nova Scotia has had an almost exclusively staff system of legal aid for both civil and criminal cases.

A second important advisory group on legal aid was established by the Attorney General in 1975 to evaluate the experimental programs. Its report in May of 1976 further supported "lawyers employed on a full-time basis in community offices ... as the principal method for delivering legal aid in Nova Scotia" and it also made recommendations to bolster the NLF dimension of the program (Report of the Advisory Committee on Legal Aid in Nova Scotia, 1976:4). It proposed that legal aid offices undertake more innovative activities, and it suggested that Legal Aid Nova Scotia take over the funding, but not the direct administration, of the Dalhousie office. Finally, the Report suggested that the management of the provincial system be removed from the Barristers' Society and transferred to an independent Legal Aid Commission. Legislation passed in 1977 created the Commission of fifteen directors, only seven of whom are to be nominated by the Barrister's Society (Nova Scotia Legal Aid, 1977:3–4).

The new law does not state what activities the new Commission should encourage. The dilution of the Barristers' Society's influence, however, may pave the way for more widespread pursuit of the activities exemplified by the Dalhousie office. Under the Society, some thirty-three staff attorneys were employed, servicing nine "regional offices" and three "suboffices," but there is no evidence that they did much more than provide individualized services. The 1977 report even states that there is a "priority on handling the criminal and family problem cases" (Nova Scotia Legal Aid, 1977:7). The NLF idea is still alive in Nova Scotia with the Dalhousie office, but it remains to be seen whether the idea will infuse substantially the work of the other provincial legal aid offices.[3]

B. Manitoba

Manitoba was the second province to take steps towards institutionalizing a staff system. Manitoba's essentially charitable system of legal aid in civil cases had resulted in the 1960s in increasing burdens on the attorneys of the Manitoba Law Society, and they were pleased to take advantage of the reform energies unleashed in the late 1960s (Larsen, 1977:164–65). Sharing an interest in change, the Attorney General of the newly-elected government appointed a task force on legal aid in March, 1970. Its findings, reported one year later, became the basis of the unique and innovative "combined" Manitoba legal aid plan enacted into law in July 1971 (Legal Aid Service Society of Manitoba Act, S.M. 1971, ch. L705 as amended).

The new law had a strong judicare component, following the basic format of the Ontario judicare plan, but it attempted to overcome Ontario's weaknesses. First, the Law Society's domination was eliminated. The Board of Directors of the newly-created Legal Aid Services Society is now composed of eleven persons selected by the Lieutenant Governor, only four of whom are from nominations by the Law Society (and four of whom cannot be solicitors).[4] Second, the statute and subsequent regulations provide specifically for staff lawyers in neighborhood or community law offices established and operated by the Board in order to supplement the judicare system. According to the *First Annual Report* (1973:2–3),

The legal aid system in Manitoba was clearly intended to be more than a mere quantitative extension of the partial system previously operated under the direction of the Law Society. It was envisaged that largely through community or neighborhood legal aid offices a wide range of legal services including preventive legal services would be made accessible to the people of Manitoba.

The Law Society was evidently content with this novel combined model, including its NLF component. Indeed, the quoted passage was written by the former Secretary of the Law Society's legal aid scheme, Ron Meyers, who became the Executive Director in charge of administering the plan. (As of late 1977, he still held that position.)

The first Community Law Office opened in late 1972. Located in Winnipeg, it was staffed by three lawyers, two secretaries, and two students. At the same time, Legal Aid Manitoba issued regulations concerning the Community Law Offices and their work. The regulations provide that social workers may be hired, that legal education is to be promoted, and that "subject to the approval of the executive director, [the office may] advise, assist, and represent such groups and organizations as is deemed advisable by the executive director" (Regulation under the Legal Aid Services Society of Manitoba Act, *Manitoba Regulation* 106/72, as amended by M.R. 12/73, 146/73, 235/73, 58/74, 78/74, §53). The latter restriction may seem to be aimed at curbing group work, but part of its function is most likely to insure that groups can meet legal aid eligibility requirements. Further, the *First Annual Report*, published in early 1973 and referred to in subsequent reports, emphasized as a top priority, after "preventive law," "aiding and representing groups and organizations within its community in matters related to 'poverty law'" (Legal Aid Manitoba, 1973:3). The regulations also provide for an "advisory committee" for each community office, appointed by the Legal Aid Manitoba Board "from a list of nominees submitted by community organizations with the particular community" (Regulation Under the Legal Aid Services Society of Manitoba Act, §§56(1) and (2)).

While rhetoric about social change on behalf of the poor has been absent in the reports of Legal Aid Manitoba, the type of local office it envisions is very much like NLFs seen elsewhere. There is the typical emphasis on education, preventive law, group work, and accountability to the community.[5]

In practice there has been a steadily increasing role for the Community Law Centers, which as of 1977 numbered six. The amount of funding provided to Community Law Centers, compared to that of "Fees for Services," went from 25 percent in fiscal year 1973–74 to 48 percent in 1974–75, to 62 percent in 1975–76.[6] The available evidence, in addition, suggests that these offices have retained a commitment to innovative, nontraditional legal aid.[7] The "combined model" in Manitoba seems to have resulted in a program essentially freed from bar and governmental restrictions and able and willing to implement an increasingly significant NLF component.

90

C. Quebec

Legal aid developments in Quebec, Canada's second most populous province, are among the most interesting and highly praised in the world. Quebec went from a strictly charitable system of civil legal aid in 1971 (with a criminal "public defender" system) to another "combined model" emphasizing the staff system and enjoying the highest per capita expenditure—$4.20—in Canada.

Events began essentially with Community Legal Services Inc. in Point St. Charles, Montreal, the important federally-funded demonstration project described before. When the Quebec Ministry of Justice announced in 1971 that it would introduce a new system of civil and criminal legal aid, it turned to the NLF model being implemented in Point St. Charles. Robert Cooper, the first director of the Point St. Charles clinic, was appointed special advisor for legal aid to the Minister of Justice, and he undertook the principal drafting of the Ministry's proposed new plan.

The new plan was embodied in "Bill 10," introduced to the Quebec legislature in March 1972. This remarkable bill sought "to create a neighborhood legal services scheme in Quebec similar to the American model established under the Economic Opportunity Act, 1964" (Zemans, 1978:670 n.36). Building on the Point St. Charles experience, the bill proposed an even more community-oriented model than that developed in the United States. It proposed that legal services be provided by full-time staff attorneys serving local corporations with boards of directors composed of at least one-third local residents and one-third lawyers. The U.S. program, in contrast, required more than a majority of lawyers on governing boards.

Considerable opposition arose from the Quebec bar association, which favored the adoption of a judicare system similar to Ontario's (see Zemans, 1978:670–71). Some bar leaders were willing to compromise in favor of a combined system, and the Quebec government relented to some of the bar's primary objections. The Legal Aid Act, signed into law on 8 July 1972, reflects these compromises (S.Q. 1972, ch. 14).

The act retained the provision establishing a *Commission des services juridiques*, or Legal Services Commission, governed by twelve members chosen by the Lieutenant Governor in Council for their expertise in "the legal problems of the underprivileged" (Legal Aid Act of 1972, §13). It differed significantly from the proposed bill in allowing qualified legal aid clients, as in Manitoba, to choose a private lawyer rather than the staff legal aid attorney (§52). Further, the Legal Aid Act deemphasized the local control provisions patterned after Point St. Charles.

The Act still provides for the funding of "local corporations" with their own boards of directors, but the basic staff system is through other local legal aid offices administered by "regional corporations" (§§29–39). The latter local offices are tied to the community principally through "advisory committees" appointed or recognized by the regional corporation (§32(d)). The boards of directors of the regional corporations, appointed by the Commission, must be composed of at least one-third lawyers and one-third "persons residing in the region served" (§35). There are eleven regional corporations to serve Quebec's 6.2 million population.

The general statutory orientation, therefore, is not as locally oriented as it might have been, and it represents a "combined model" rather than the proposed pure NLF system, but clearly the act contemplates the creation of a large network of decentralized offices providing legal services along the lines of the NLF model developed in the United States. In the words of two leading Canadian commentators, "Quebec thus became the first province to operationalize with some vigour the view that more than legal expertise is needed to administer and develop a programme which, while law-oriented, is also a programme of social service, and social change" (Taman and Zemans, 1973:33–34). While precise data are unavailable, it is clear that community education, test cases, and action-oriented research have characterized the operation of the program, which now includes ninety-one full-time offices employing some 313 staff lawyers (Commission des services juridiques, 1978:37). The Board as of late 1977 included seven lawyers and four laymen, with one vacancy (Zander, 1979:404).

There are some questions, however, about the program's current orientation. First, the regulations adopted concerning group representation evince some hostility to such activities.[8] Second, although now the subject of some concern in the Quebec Commission, the "advisory committees" to the local offices have to date either not been created or have failed to play a significant policy-making role (Deschamps, in Commission des services juridiques, 1977:107). Third, the especially innovative NLF model represented by the Point St. Charles clinic (see Clinique juridique communautaire, 1977) and others has had a difficult time under the new law. As mentioned before, the 1972 law expressly recognized existing independent "local corporations" such as Point St. Charles, and it even allowed for the creation of new ones. The Commission may fund such corporations and must ensure that a local corporation's activities "are integrated into all the legal services offered in the region and see that it complies with this act and the regulations" (Legal Aid Act, 1972, §33).

92

The Commission, according to several sources, has failed to support these local corporations and their brand of work. There were four such local clinics in operation when the Act was passed; by 1974 there were five. In 1975 and 1976 the Commission revoked the status of corporations in two cases and denied it for the first time in another; and one more withdrew from the Quebec legal aid network (Commission des services juridiques, 1976:43; Commission des services juridiques, 1977:38; Commission des services juridiques, 1978:33). As of mid-1977, only Point St. Charles and another remained, and reportedly even their status was in doubt (Morris, 1979:291). According to Penner, "The heart of the problem seems to be the imposition of impossible caseload quotas on the individual lawyers such that there is simply no time left for group actions, community legal education and law reform work" (Penner, 1977:139). Zemans cites a Montreal newspaper article in mid-1977 saying that these clinics "didn't harmonize too well with legal aid bureau's bureaucrats. They were based on ideas of citizen participation, popular services, community needs, and local decision-making" (Zeman, 1978:672, n.52). These events may reveal an unfortunate overemphasis by the Commission on individual casework and uniform standards imposed from above.

The situation in Quebec is still evolving. It may well be that the Commission has downgraded certain reform activities.[9] Nevertheless, it is clear that the NLFs in Quebec are comparatively well-funded and have found a secure institutional form in the combined legal aid system. The idea of staff lawyers doing more than just providing individual service work has been promoted and implemented. Quebec's ninety-one staff offices, which compare to some 700 in the United States (with a population thirty-five times Quebec's) and twenty-seven in England and Wales, have a unique potential.

D. Saskatchewan

In Saskatchewan the "Great Canadian Debate" resulted in late 1974 in the unmitigated victory of the NLF approach and in an extremely innovative statutory scheme. Prior to 1969, civil legal aid in Saskatchewan was essentially voluntary; a judicare system had existed since 1967 for criminal cases. The movement for change, as noted before, was begun by students and law professors who then found a federal ally. In June 1971 a $30,000 federal demonstration grant was made to the Saskatoon Legal Assistance Clinic (Saskatchewan Community Legal Services Commission, 1975:5), which used the grant to develop into a model NLF with a strong social reform and community control orientation (see, e.g., Zemans, 1978:676–77).

93

The Saskatoon model's impact became apparent in 1972. The governing cabinet of the New Democratic Party (a Socialist or Labor Party) appointed "The Attorney General's Committee on Legal Aid" to recommend the adoption of a new legal aid system (Zemans, 1979:677). The seven-person committee, called the "Carter Committee" after its chairman, the Dean of the College of Law, contained only two Law Society representatives, as well as two lay persons and the Director of the Saskatoon Clinic, Linton Smith. The Clinic's representations to the Committee strongly advocated a staff system able to engage actively in "fighting poverty," and this approach was adopted in the Carter Committee Report published in March 1973 (see Cowie, in Canadian Council on Social Development, 1976:11).

The report completely embraced the NLF model, insisting that "A legal aid scheme should be capable of acting, on proper occasions, as a vehicle for social change."[10] It found judicare systems incapable of such activities. In addition, the report emphasized "community involvement," which it foresaw through "advisory committees," and it felt that such involvement would be very difficult in a nonsalaried system.

The law enacted in August 1974 followed the Carter Committee's recommendations and set up a strictly staff system except for criminal cases, in which the client may choose a private solicitor (Community Legal Services (Saskatchewan) Act of 1974, §21). The Saskatchewan Community Legal Services Commission administers the program (§4). It consists of nine persons: one must be a lawyer designated by the Law Society and another a lawyer designated by the Attorney General of Canada; three members are appointed by the Lieutenant Governor in Council; and three members by the chairman of the "area governing boards" (described below) from "amongst their number." The commission then selects a "provincial director." In theory this breaks down to at least three lawyers, three citizen taxpayers, and three persons representing the client community. This arrangement is a unique one.

The administration of the thirteen "community legal services areas," covering Saskatchewan's population of almost one million, is also quite innovative. The statute gives the thirteen "area boards" much more power than the "advisory boards" envisioned by the Carter Report. These community-elected boards, which administer the community legal services office or offices in their area (except for the rural area administered by the commission), have absolute power over the hiring and dismissal of all staff except for solicitors (§15(f) and (h)). For the latter the approval of the Commission or its repre-

94

sentatives is required. Significantly, there is no requirement that any lawyers serve on the governing boards.[11]

The program's orientation has evidently been in the spirit of the NLF model suggested by the statute and the Carter Report. The first Provincial Director selected was Linton Smith, who, as noted before, served on the Carter Committee and directed the Saskatchewan Clinic. The reports of the Legal Services Commission show that, while individual casework is undertaken, there is a definite emphasis on helping the poor as a class. The first report dwells on the themes of local control and group work. It notes, for example, that "groups can often exercise collective strength which individually they would not possess. A legal aid plan is in a key position to encourage the development of such groups" (Saskatchewan Community Legal Services Commission, 1975:15). And it emphasizes above all "the fact that each of the community law offices under the plan is governed and administered by an independent community elected board of directors" (1975:22). These area boards, in fact, have formed an "Association of Legal Assistance Boards," which "functions as an inside critic of the Saskatchewan Community Legal Services Plan" (1975:10).

It is further suggestive that, in contrast to the problems of the Point St. Charles Clinic in Montreal, the Saskatoon clinic has prospered; its budget more than doubled from 1975 to 1976, and it receives over twenty percent of the funds allocated to the legal services clinics (Saskatchewan Community Legal Services Commission, 1976:23).

The Saskatchewan legal aid scheme is now the third best-financed system per capita in Canada, spending $3.43 per capita in 1977–78 (Zemans, 1978:664, n.6). It represents the institutional triumph of a unique NLF scheme. This triumph is not easy to explain, given the power of judicare-oriented Law Societies seen elsewhere. It appears, however, that there was a very strong governmental commitment in Saskatchewan and the Law Society chose not to challenge it, content to preserve the judicare option for criminal legal aid.

E. British Columbia

British Columbia about the same time also had a New Democratic Party government intrigued with the ideas of local control and legal aid through NLFs (see Morris and Stern, 1976:75), but the existence of a stronger and more established Law Society program, coupled with a timely change in government, led to a much lesser role for NLFs than was the case in Saskatchewan.

From 1952 to 1970, the provincial Law Society operated a strictly

95

voluntary legal aid plan administered through legal aid clinics under the local bar associations. In 1970, with the understanding that the provincial Attorney General's Department would contribute funding to a new system of regional legal aid offices, the Law Society officially created the Legal Aid Society. New offices provided direct legal assistance and made referrals to private practitioners. Compensation was available to the latter only for criminal and family cases; other types of cases were handled by the staff of the regional offices. By 1974 there were six such legal aid offices and plans to open eight more (Justice Development Commission, 1974:2–3).

The NLF idea, meanwhile, took hold in British Columbia as it had in other provinces. Beginning in 1969, law students and faculty established a legal advice clinic at the University of British Columbia in Vancouver. Federal funding in 1971 again turned an important experiment into an influential model. An outgrowth of the University clinic, the Vancouver Community Legal Assistance Society (VCLAS) received its funds principally from the Department of Justice. The Vancouver Community Legal Assistance Society has promoted the range of typical NLF activities and appears to have concentrated on class actions and test cases (Morris and Stern, 1976: 18; Justice Development Commission, 1974:13–15; Legal Services Commission, 1976:22–23).

The British Columbia government in 1973 created a Justice Development Commission, which in turn created the Delivery of Legal Services Project, headed by Peter Leask. Leask was formally advised by two representatives of the Law Society. In addition to preparing policy recommendations, Leask sought to encourage local groups to apply for provincial funding to provide legal services. Several such groups did thereby begin to provide "quasi-legal services utilizing paraprofessionals" (Legal Services Commission, 1976:4). (VCLAS also began to receive provincial support around this time.)

The Leask Report, published in December 1974, strongly criticized the limitations of a strictly judicare system and praised the concept of NLFs. The main recommendation, however, was somewhat ambiguous. The report suggested,

> ...that this province adopt a legal service delivery mechanism which places emphasis on local communities to assess their own problems, devise their own solutions and implement them with assistance from a central administrative body which would control granting of funds, provision of information and whatever expert assistance might be required (Justice Development Commission, 1974:49).

While an appealing statement, it avoided the problems of what type

96

of system to have and what the role of the Law Society and its existing offices should be.

The Legal Services Commission Act of 1975 (1975 S.B.C. ch. 36), which came into force on 1 August 1975, similarly avoided deciding what type of system British Columbia should have. According to Morris and Stern, who evaluated the system in 1976, "the legislation ... was insufficiently well thought out, having been written with a view to political expediency and in such a way as to try to avoid offending the bar..." (1976:74). The Act, passed unanimously by the legislature, sets up a Legal Services Commission with a vague mandate to see that "legal services are effectively provided to, and readily obtainable by, the people of British Columbia, with special emphasis on those people to whom those services are not presently available for financial and other reasons" (§3). The Commission's function is to plan the system of legal aid and fund organizations wishing to deliver legal services. The British Columbia Commission has five members, two designated by the Law Society, two by the Lieutenant Governor in Council, and one by the provincial Attorney General.[12]

The Commission's initial task was to take over the funding of the operations that had previously been handled by the Attorney General's Department. These operations included particularly the funding of the Legal Aid Society, which then had fifteen offices, Vancouver Community Legal Assistance Society, and eleven Community Law Offices (CLOs) or Legal Information Centers (the difference is that those staffed by a full-time lawyer were called "Law Offices"). These eleven offices were those funded by the New Democratic Party government prior to the adoption of the new law, and they evidently were supposed to evolve into community-controlled NLFs.

The first report of the Commission highlighted the nontraditional role envisioned for the Community Law Offices. The CLOs were to be engaged in "battles with government bureaucracies" and, with the help of local paraprofessionals, could engage in "organizing sections of the community to both take group action and to engage in self-help projects" (Legal Services Commission, 1976:14).

The main problem was that the relationship between the Legal Aid Society offices and CLOs—some of which were even located very near to existing Legal Aid offices—remained unclear. There is no doubt that the Law Society and local bar association resented the unorthodox competition of the Community Law Offices. Moreover, they feared, with some justification, I think, that the future emphasis would be on CLOs. The Leask Report, for example, hinted at the future by saying that "the largest single recipient of funds, *at least in the short term*, would be the Legal Aid Society" (emphasis added) (Justice Development Commission, 1974:40). Any such plans for the long term, however, were thwarted when the chief sponsor of the CLOs, the New Democratic Party government, was voted out of office in December 1975. The Legal Services Commission, appointed when the New Democratic Party was still in office, has continued to support CLOs, but, as could be expected, the lack of guidance from the statute, coupled with the uncertain present situation, has hindered— perhaps even crippled—the development of the CLOs.[13]

A study completed in late 1976 of the Community Law Offices and the Legal Aid Society Offices found that, with the exception of the Vancouver Legal Assistance Society, the system was only engaged in traditional legal aid. Criticizing the Commission for its understandable but regrettable lack of leadership, the study concluded:

> [T]he stated philosophy underlying the setting-up of CLOs is either not understood by those running them and working in them or, where it is understood, the constraints thought to be imposed by the local community, by the Bar, by certain Board members, and to a lesser extent by budgetary concerns, result in this philosophy being ignored and being replaced by an inefficient, confused and generally very traditional model of service delivery (Morris and Stern, 1976:73).

Evidently there is still this confusion and ambiguity (e.g., Morris, 1979:294), but there are some hopeful signs. In particular, a new "law centre" was funded by the Commission in January 1977 (Gold, 1977:88). The center culminated an effort initiated by the University of Victoria law faculty in late 1975 and early 1976 to bring together the Legal Aid Society, a CLO, and a clinical teaching program. It succeeded, according to the law center's director, because "both the Legal Aid Society of British Columbia's local office in Victoria and the Community Law Office perceived an opportunity to meet the criticisms of the other" (Gold, 1977:89). The new center has combined some of the staff of the CLO and the Legal Aid Society Office to build a new type of British Columbia law center.

This law center puts a heavy emphasis on innovative NLF activities. According to its director, "It must adopt a philosophy consistent with redistribution of wealth, property and therefore power" (Gold, 1977:89; see also Gold, 1979). It remains to be seen how successful this new experiment will be, or whether it can serve as a model of cooperation that will end conflict between the types of legal aid offices. But it is clear that the effort to develop NLFs in British Columbia is continuing.

98

F. Ontario

Since Ontario's judicare system, set up in 1966, was modeled on the English one,[14] it is perhaps not surprising that the movement for NLFs in this province has many similarities and parallels to the English one. NLFs have had a hard time becoming institutionalized at the provincial level. A judicare program administered by a Law Society gives the legal profession a strong stake in the status quo and a powerful position from which to resist change. Nevertheless, the NLF idea now appears firmly rooted in Ontario, as it is in England.

The principal provincial model challenging the judicare system was the federally-funded Parkway Community Legal Services, set up in 1971. As with the other federally funded programs, it developed into an important community-based NLF (Penner, 1977:70). Other such local clinics also were created independently of the provincial legal aid scheme and "[e]ach of these took a continuing, professional interest in changing the system" (Taman, 1976:372). Ontario's Law Society argued vehemently, however, that no basic change was necessary.

In addition to the strong criticisms coming from Parkway and others, two other factors helped spur the government to act—the examples of other provinces adding salaried staff components to their systems and the accelerating costs of judicare in Ontario. The judicare costs went from $7 million in 1968-69 to $17 million in 1974-75 (Taman, 1976:372).

In December 1973 the government created a Task Force on Legal Aid to review in depth the Ontario judicare plan and make recommendations for legal aid reform. Justice John Osler of the Supreme Court of Ontario was named Chairman of the Task Force, and there were also two representatives of the Law Society of Upper Canada, a social worker, a journalist, a former chairman of the Ontario Human Rights Commission, and a law professor. The Committee completed its report in late 1974 (the Report was made public in March 1975) (*Report of the Task Force on Legal Aid, 1974*—the Osler Report).

The Osler Report is a remarkably thorough and well-reasoned document. Its analysis and conclusions clearly show the influence of the critics of judicare and the Task Force's susceptibility to arguments about "unmet need" similar to those made against judicare in England. The Report even quotes at length the remarks of the English Lord Chancellor's Advisory Committee about rights "going wholly by default" (1974:19), and notes that the legal profession, despite the judicare system, has not dealt with "a wide range of social welfare, landlord and tenant, and compensation legislation" (1974:21). The heart of the Committee's recommendations is the transfer of control over the plan from the Law Society to a statutory nonprofit corporation named Legal Aid Ontario (with a twenty-person board), and the development of "staffed neighborhood legal aid clinics" to "complement" the judicare system (1974:27, 54).

The Committee's appreciation of the NLF concept is especially apparent from its proposed division of labor between the private bar and the "neighborhood legal aid clinics."

> Generally speaking, ... clinic staff will be encouraged to give priority to requests for legal advice and assistance, community group advice and representation and the development of community education programmes....
>
> To reduce the case load upon each professional or paraprofessional in a neighborhood legal aid clinic, the clinic director should be instructed to encourage applicants to consult the private bar in traditional areas of services. We think particularly that divorce, matrimonial work and conventional criminal and civil litigation should continue wherever possible ... to be conducted by the private bar (1974:55).

This proposal, which resembles strikingly what subsequently developed in England according to the "waiver agreement" between the Law Society and the Law Centres Working Group, shows a desire to free the local clinics to concentrate on work benefiting groups of the poor (1974:98–101).

The Osler Report is not specific on how many such neighborhood legal aid clinics there should be; it avoids the question by suggesting that such decisions can be made by the Board of Directors of Legal Aid Ontario, advised by the forty-six "Area Committees" composed of eight persons, half of whom would be lawyers (1974:30). The Report can be criticized for avoiding the key question of "the appropriate mix" of NLFs and judicare (Taman, 1976:376), but its very strong support of NLFs is nevertheless of great importance in the ongoing Ontario debate.

The Ontario government has not yet moved to adopt the recommendations of the Committee, but the Osler Report has precipitated several other important developments. First, the Law Society added ten lay members and one law student to its Legal Aid Committee. Second, and more pertinent to this inquiry, the Ontario Legal Aid Plan began funding "some 18 autonomous street and neighborhood clinics," including Parkdale, whose federal grant had expired (Penner, 1977:7; Taman, 1976:378–79). For a variety of reasons, including the influence of the Osler Report, the Legal Aid Society's position has clearly been modified; the Chairman of the Legal Aid Committee now expressly affirms the importance of clinics such as Parkdale.[15]

Whether a new law will be introduced or, if not, how much emphasis will be given to NLFs, is unclear, but NLFs will no doubt remain a component of the legal aid system. Ontario has been virtually the last of the major provinces to proclaim the adoption of any NLF approach, but this was to be expected. As in England, formal acceptance by the Law Society came late, but the appeal of NLFs could not be completely resisted.

G. *Alberta*

I have very little material on legal aid in Alberta, the fourth most populous Canadian province, but it is useful to note that the influence of the NLF approach is now also being felt there. Since 1970 Alberta has had a strictly judicare system set up by agreement between the Law Society of Alberta and the Attorney General (Legal Profession Act, 1970 R.S.A. ch. 203). The Law Society administered the program itself initially, and it created the Legal Aid Society to do so in 1973. In late 1975 a Joint Committee of the Legal Aid Society of Alberta recommended that services be expanded through legal aid clinics and neighborhood law offices. That recommendation apparently had not been implemented as of late 1976 (see Saint-Cyr, 1977:14).

H. *Newfoundland*

Newfoundland established a judicare plan in 1968 under the Law Society's administration, but a new law in force since January 1976 created a Legal Aid Commission to take over legal aid matters (Legal Aid Act, S.N. 1975 ch. 42). The ten-person Commission is composed of five members appointed by the Lieutenant Governor in Council, the Deputy Minister of Justice serving *ex officio*, three persons nominated by the Law Society, and the Provincial Director. This Commission was given the power, inter alia, to set up neighborhood law centers (see Saint-Cyr, 1977:23).

III. Conclusion[16]

The variety of Canadian compromises cannot easily be summarized, but a few concluding observations can be made. First, it is clear that the NLF movement in the United States captured the imagination of Canadian law students in the late 1960s, and the federal government, particularly the Department of Health and Welfare, was willing to encourage several of the most important outgrowths. A major debate took place and in virtually every province the virtues of NLFs ultimately were recognized.

The resulting programs vary substantially, from Saskatchewan's virtual embracing of the federally-funded model through a wide variety of systems combining judicare and neighborhood offices. To a great extent one can account for these differences by comparing the relative stakes of the Law Societies in a judicare system and the relative commitments of the provincial governments to reform, but, of course, much depends on more subtle factors such as individual attitudes and personalities. The main point, however, is that the case of Canada well illustrates the power of the NLF idea. Activist lawyers and law students, welfare state governments, and sooner or later, professional lawyers' organizations all find it difficult to resist the attractions of the NLF.

Notes

1. The federal government has exclusive legislative authority in matters of criminal law, which has led to a greater federal involvement in criminal legal aid (British North America Act of 1867, §91, para. 27; see Saint-Cyr, 1977:4).

2. The Federal Department of Justice funded the Vancouver Legal Assistance Society in British Columbia in 1971 (Penner, 1977:7).

3. The lawyers provided advice in 2,000 cases, opened files in 8,000 cases, and referred a number to private attorneys. One problem with the program may be funding. The roughly $1 million provided in 1976–77 was only seventh per capita in Canada (the population of Nova Scotia is about 830,000) (Nova Scotia Legal Aid, 1977).

4. The original law provided for a nine-member board; 1975 amendments (S.M. 1975, c. 42, §32) enlarged the board to eleven and required that at least four members be lay persons. As of October 1976, there were six lawyers, one social worker, a women's rights representative, and a community representative (Department of Justice, 1974:21; Zander, 1979:404).

5. It also appears that the program is trying to make the individual cases correspond to the "legal needs of the poor" rather than just family and criminal cases. The 1974 Report, for example, complained about the number of matrimonial cases:

"The relatively high proportion of matrimonial cases in our caseload is a cause for concern insofar as it appears to indicate that we are as yet not sufficiently developed in detecting and dealing with unmet legal needs in the general field of what is popularly referred to as 'poverty law' (consumer protection, housing, welfare rights, worker compensation and unemployment insurance)" (Legal Aid Service Society of Manitoba, 1974:4).

6. For 1974 the relevant figures were $786,097 and $196,327 (see Legal Aid Services Society of Manitoba, 1974:12); for 1975 they were $859,820 and $415,444; and for 1976 $1,472,640 and $911,293 (see Legal Aid Services Society of Manitoba, 1976:29). The total expenditures in 1975-76 were $3,107,427 (the population of Manitoba was just over 1 million).

With respect to the number of legal aid certificates issued, in 1974–75 80% were handled by the private bar; in 1975–76 the figure was 75%, and for 1977–78 it was estimated to be 65%. Clients may generally choose between a private or public lawyer.

7. According to a letter from Mr. Ron J. Meyers, Executive Director, to Bryant Garth, 24 October 1977, "we try to have our lawyers spend about 50% of their time on traditional law work and another 50% on poverty law and community education, etc." Roland Penner, the Chairman of the Board of Directors, pointed out that for the staff lawyers "new case intake is, as a matter of policy, restricted to a maximum of 144 per staff per year" (Penner, 1977:129). This is very low compared to other places.

8. The Legal Aid Act of 1972, §1, provides that "person" within the meaning of the Act includes "a group of persons or a nonprofit corporation whose members are economically underprivileged physical persons," and legal aid is available to "any economically underprivileged person establishing the probable existence of a right." §63. The regulations, however, as amended in 1975, require that group applicants must:

"(a) describe the objectives of the group and the territory served or to be served;
 (b) give the number of members of the group and an explanation of the accounting system;
 (c) describe the group's present and estimated property and revenue, debts or commitments where applicable;
 (d) fully describe the facts which lead the group to believe it requires legal services;
 (e) give all relevant information."

Regulation Under the Legal Aid Act, §3.11. According to Zemans, the regulations require "the names, addresses, occupations, assets and debts of *each* member of the group." He says that the group eligibility criteria "seem to have been designed, in fact, to deter groups from seeking legal services" (Zemans, 1978:673, n.63).

9. Zemans (1978:675) is very pessimistic about the present situation:

"Despite the initiatives in poverty law research, community education and test case litigation, the Quebec scheme during its early years has not fought the poverty war battle that it had proclaimed but rather has emphasized a case-by-case approach to legal aid."

This appraisal is shared by other leading commentators (e.g., Morris, 1979:291).

10. "General Conclusions of the Final Report of Saskatchewan Legal Aid Committee," in Saskatchewan Community Legal Services Commission (1975:34). The Report also argues that in setting eligibility criteria, "'reasonable' is not to be judged by comparing the cash value of the services with the cash value of the result. The criterion must be the seriousness of the case or problem to the particular individual."

11. Also of interest is the statute's explicit mention of "legal services to ...

103

organizations in respect of civil and criminal matters where such ... organizations are financially unable to secure such services..." (Community Legal Services (Saskatchewan) Act of 1974, §3(1)). The Regulations are also liberal for group representation, requiring membership only of "predominantly eligible persons" (Regulations Made Under the Community Legal Services (Saskatchewan) Act, §2(5).

12. The Lieutenant Governor in Council designates the chairman from among these members. It is notable that the Leask Report proposed a nine-person commission, with three government and three public representatives to go with the two from the Law Society and one named by the Attorney General (Justice Development Commission, 1974:37). The bill as passed eliminated the three public members and one government-appointed member in favor of a relative strengthening of the Law Society's influence.

13. Budgetary restraints imposed by the new government have exacerbated the situation considerably. Accordingly to Jabour (the Chairman of the board) (1977:3),

"The main consideration adopted by the Commission was to preserve the offices and personnel in existence, because these are the backbone of legal services in British Columbia. These are the bases from which legal services will expand when more adequate funding is available."

14. The Legal Aid Act of 1966, R.S.O. 1970, Ch. 239, amended by S.O. 1973, ch. 50. The difference between England and Ontario is that the latter's scheme entrusts criminal as well as civil cases to the Law Society's administration.

15. In late 1976, John Bowlby, the Chairman of the Legal Aid Committee of the Law Society of Upper Canada, said that, "It has become apparent to us that in certain legal areas which for the lack of a better term, have been called those involving 'poverty law' the clinical approach best serves the public" (Bowlby, 1977).

16. I have left out the small provinces of Prince Edward Island and New Brunswick, neither of which, according to Saint-Cyr, provides legal aid in civil cases (Saint-Cyr, 1977:21, 31).

Chapter 5

Australia

In contrast to the Canadian government, the federal or commonwealth government in Australia sought to do more than finance pilot legal aid projects; it tried to implement a nationwide system of staff legal aid offices—the Australian Legal Aid Office (ALAO). For a number of reasons considered in this chapter, the program was not very successful. Its political problems were especially grave, above all because it strongly antagonized a private legal profession which had been content with state judicare systems. In the absence of support by the profession, the ALAO did not develop sufficient prestige and power to avoid being crippled when its major sponsor, the Labor government, was voted ·out of office in 1975. Legal aid reform is still underway in Australia and the NLF idea is very much alive, but the institutional successes seen elsewhere have not been replicated. In this sense, Australia is unique among the countries covered in this study.

I. Background to the Australian Legal Aid Office

Australia is a federal commonwealth. As in Canada, legal aid policies have been set at the state level, either because of tradition or because of potential constitutional limitations on such central government activities. Showing the influence of English developments, by 1970 each of the Australian states had adopted an essentially judicare system for civil legal aid, administered in each state by the Law Society.[1] Around that time, as in Canada and England, law students and concerned legal professionals were attracted to the social model of advocacy being developed in the United States. A number of largely voluntary law centers were formed, beginning in late 1972 with the Fitzroy Legal Service in Victoria (see Epstein, 1977a:35–37).

Fitzroy, still the most important of these independent and relatively low-budget centers (Epstein, 1977b), proclaimed a number of optimistic goals, typifying the approach articulated throughout the NLF movement elsewhere. It proposed:

1. that it be a legal service for people in neighbouring suburbs, easily reached and providing its services free;
2. that it function as a centre which would develop a local awareness of legal rights;
3. that it should forestall legal problems by practicing "preventive" law; and
4. that (as a corollary and extension of the second point) it should provide legal education and foster community development (see Sackville, 1975b:111).

As in Canada some federal government money helped Fitzroy develop as a "pilot scheme," but it appears to have been the only such scheme funded in Australia (Harkins, 1977: App. 3; Epstein, 1977a:36; Sackville, 1975b:165). The government did not focus its attention on demonstration projects. Instead the Labour government elected in December 1972—the first Labour government in twenty-three years —chose to create its own new and ambitious legal aid scheme.

In February 1973 the Attorney General of the new government, Senator Lionel K. Murphy, stated the intention of the government to reform legal aid (see Purcell, 1977). On 25 July, 1973, he announced —without even having consulted representatives of the legal profession—that an Australian Legal Aid Office (ALAO) would be created to provide free legal advice in federal and matrimonial matters and in areas where the Australian commonwealth government has a "special responsibility." These limits were imposed partly for constitutional reasons (Epstein, 1977a:11–13; Sackville, 1975:51). The new system was to supplement state programs through a wide network of legal advice centers, staffed by full-time salaried lawyers. In September the government unilaterally created the new ALAO system by a Directive of the Attorney General; the new offices, initially replacing the "Legal Service Bureaus" already providing assistance to servicemen, veterans, and their dependants, were to be empowered to undertake advice and some litigation in a relatively wide variety of areas.

The actual role envisioned for these new offices was never very clear, but some hints can be taken from a speech by the Attorney General to the Senate in December (reprinted in Harkins, 1977). Attorney General Murphy stated that, in the view of the government, "legal assistance to socially disadvantaged persons can most effectively be provided through a salaried legal service." Noting his favorable impression with "overseas developments," the Attorney General went on to praise "storefront offices" as opposed to "the traditional conservative approach to legal aid": "I see the role of the Australian Legal Aid Office as taking the law to the people who most need it." He thus provided a "legal need" justification for decentralized offices. This view of NLFs is a limited one, lacking in any recognition of the role of law reform, group work, and other NLF activities, but the suggested proactive role comports with at least one powerful component of the NLF ideology seen in other countries. There was the hope "that the young lawyer with a social conscience will be attracted to join the office."

II. The ALAO is Established

With the Attorney General's Directive, the very limited existing federal Legal Service Bureaus became the first components of the ALAO. They were primarily one-lawyer offices except for the one in Sydney, which had five lawyers and eight "lay advocates." Thirteen persons on the initial Australian Legal Aid Office staff of thirty-one were lawyers (Harkins, 1977:10–11).

The ALAO began its expansion by advertising for lawyers in late 1973 and early 1974. In March the Director, J.P. Harkins (from the Office of the Attorney General), was appointed, and in April and May six new offices were opened—one in each state. The government then enlarged the program as rapidly as possible. By September 1975 the ALAO had established thirty-three new offices located in shopping centers and similarly accessible locations. Although "economic and budgetary problems" of the government limited expansion somewhat—the plan was for sixty-two regional offices—federal expenditures on the ALAO reached almost $12 million in the fiscal year 1975–76 (see Harkins, 1977:Att.H). Suddenly the federal government was a major provider of a new form of legal aid.

The ALAO regional offices succeeded in attracting large numbers of individual poor clients, about one-third of whom sought help in family matters (Disney et al., 1977:400). They demonstrated the existence of the proverbial unmet need. But they made no commitment to substantial law reform efforts (except for some environmental cases), nor provided any significant amount of assistance to groups (Disney et al., 1977:406–411). According to a critical study of the ALAO in New South Wales (the most populous state),

> The ALA lawyers completely eschew the idea that their role in providing legal aid is in any way different from the role of the lawyer in private practice. Like the traditional lawyer, the ALA lawyer remains in his office to await his clients and deals with the problem of each client as an individual matter. He does not see his role as one of promoting law reform or disclosing injustice on a wide scale (Ross and Mossman, 1975:12–13; see also Sackville, 1975a:40–41).

The ALAO, in fact, has increasingly become a referral agency to private practitioners. As in the English judicare system, the latter are compensated at 90 percent of normal fees for their services. It is suggestive that of 99,251 personal *interviews* in the year ending 30 June 1975, 20,326 cases were referred to private practitioners at a cost of over $6 million. The following year the interview number was 151, 948, the referrals 45,706, and the cost almost $12 million (Harkins, 1977:Att.G). The ALAO thus resulted in an essentially traditional legal aid service—even if through staff lawyers—and through referrals it increasingly bolstered the income of private lawyers who before had only the Law Society schemes to turn to. Nevertheless, the organized bar forcefully opposed the new federal system.

III. The ALAO and the Legal Profession

The Attorney General repeatedly assured the private legal profession that he wanted only to supplement "the talents of the private legal profession" (Purcell, 1977:18), and the operation of the ALAO bore him out, but other statements by the Attorney General made the state Law Societies uneasy. For example, Senator Murphy stated his conviction that the staff system of legal aid was superior to judicare; he spoke in mid-1974 of plans for "legal aid centres" which would provide "one spot shopping" for legal aid, and he accused the profession of being overly "conservative" (Purcell, 1977:20–21).[2] Such statements, as well as the failure to consult with leaders of the profession, seemed to threaten the predominance of the Law Societies in the legal aid field and the very existence of the judicare schemes which they administered and benefitted from—both financially and in improved public relations.

Law Society leaders reacted strongly (see Purcell, 1977:18–27). Statements by leaders of the profession emphasized the necessity of chanelling federal funds "through or under the guidance of the ... [state] Legal Aid Committee," and the importance of consulting the profession and taking it "into the confidence of government." The President of the Law Society of New South Wales insisted that public staff offices should not be established unless "after proper consultation, study and investigation [the private profession] is shown unable to provide at least as good a service and as economical a service..." Another professional leader added the explicit concern about "unfair competition," suggesting that the referrals to the private bar made by ALAO offices might not "compensate for work taken from the profession on uneven terms." The ALAO program even faced problems in *court* hostility to the new scheme, epitomized by a ruling in March 1975 of the Supreme Court of the Australian

Capital Territory that, since staff lawyers of the ALAO were retained by the government, they could not be sufficiently independent to be recognized as solicitors serving their legal aid clientele (*Re Bannister; ex parte Harstein*, (1975) 5 A.C.T.R. 100; see O'Connor, 1975).

Overt manifestations of Law Society hostility added to the ALAO's problems. Publicity given to ALAO lawyers in South Australia, for example, brought Law Society threats of disciplinary action on the grounds of advertising (Harkins, 1977:25–26). Most dramatically, the Law Institute of Victoria (the name of the Victorian Law Society) was directed by its members to file a lawsuit in 1975 challenging the constitutionality of the ALAO (Harkins, 1977:26–27; Purcell, 1977:27–29). The suit was brought (as a relator action) in August 1975 (although subsequent events, including the change in government, made further action unnecessary). The ALAO may not have undertaken any politically controversial NLF activities, but it clearly caused a remarkable wave of protest from the profession.

It appears that bar hostility gradually diminished, partly because the controversial Labour Attorney General, Lionel Murphy, was appointed to the High Court of Australia and a more conciliatory appointee succeeded him. State Law Societies and the ALAO also reached agreements coordinating responsibility and setting boundaries for ALAO "competition" with private attorneys (Purcell, 1977:22–23; Epstein, 1977a:33). The federal government and the organized profession did thus manage to develop a working relationship, but the profession as a whole remained rather unenthusiastic about the ALAO. Private lawyers were too suspicious about what a federally-imposed staff system might do to the state judicare systems essentially controlled by the profession.

IV. Efforts to Provide a Wider Range of NLF Services and a Statutory Basis for the Staff System

The ALAO's failure to implement an NLF approach beyond meeting individual legal needs is unusual. The program did not develop toward activism on behalf of the poor as a class. The Fitzroy Legal Service formula for an innovative program, for example, seems to have had little impact. The ALAO's "maturing" as an NLF program was further hindered by its lack of a statutory base. Efforts to solve these problems will be considered here.

A. The Legal Aid Review Committee

The Legal Aid Review Committee might have spurred the ALAO to some further innovation. The Attorney General created this Committee at the same time he announced plans for the ALAO. Its relatively broad mandate was to assess "areas of need," the role of "salaried legal services," and the means for financing such services (Purcell, 1977:30). Unfortunately, this Committee did not develop into a very influential or innovative body. It issued two reports, one in September 1974 and one in March 1975, and they provided some further justification for a staff legal services system, but in general the reports did little to guide the ALAO or further reform efforts. Rather, as one leading Australian commentator noted, the Committee became "preoccupied with detail and [did] not attempt to seek a wide response to the broader issues" (Purcell, 1977:34).

B. The Commission of Inquiry into Poverty

Stronger arguments and pressures for activist NLFs in Australia developed from the "Law and Poverty" section of the Commission of Inquiry into Poverty. The Commission was established one year prior to the victory of the Labour party. As in the United States, England, and Canada, poverty was rediscovered in Australia in the 1960s. After the Labour victory, the Labour Prime Minister widened the Commission's scope; the most important of the new terms of reference concerned law and poverty. The task of the new research program was to evaluate (1) "the effect of the law and the legal system upon the poor and other disadvantaged groups," (2) the substantive laws of "special significance to the poor," and (3) the "delivery of legal services to the poor ... and their effectiveness in meeting the perceived and unperceived needs of the poor" (Sackville, 1975a:ix).

Unlike the ALAO and the Legal Aid Review Committee, both of which emanated only from the Attorney General's office, the Law and Poverty section was rooted in an antipoverty program; it accordingly embraced NLFs as a tool for combating poverty. In a survey critical of Australian state judicare schemes, published in final form in 1975, for example, Professor Sackville recognized that,

> [O]ne of the basic choices to be made in establishing or reorganising a system of legal aid is to determine whether the services provided should be confined solely to meeting the needs of individual clients or should extend to the use of the legal process to attempt to change the political, economic and social status of the poor (Sackville, 1975b:3).

110

He opted for the latter approach, referring especially to the U.S. experience with OEO legal services and the Legal Services Corporation Act of 1974.

Fortified by a "legal needs" study published in 1975 (Cass and Sackville, 1975) and the critical assessment of how the Law Society judicare schemes met these needs, the Law and Poverty section forcefully advocated the establishment of an independent Legal Services Commission whose "primary task ... should be to establish and administer a network of local legal centres, building on the offices already established by the ALAO" (Sackville, 1975a:53). It grounded its policy recommendations on the following argument:

> A network of community-based legal centres, staffed principally by salaried lawyers, offers the greatest potential for reaching people in need of legal assistance, exploring new avenues for redressing imbalances in the legal system, which historically has worked to the disadvantage of the poor, and for involving local residents actively in the administration. The establishment of the ALAO is a major step in the right direction, but does not of itself ensure that the goals will be attained (Sackville, 1975a:41).

These proposals favored a "combined system" with referrals in some cases to compensated private practitioners, but the overall aim was to turn the ALAO into a broad system of NLFs under an independent Legal Services Commission.

The strong statements in the Law and Poverty reports, however, have had little influence on policy developments. One reason for this relative lack of influence to date is that legal aid policies had already been established and continued to be set in the Attorney General's office. That office was outside of antipoverty policies. Also, in addition to its already evident unwillingness or incapacity to encourage the ALAO to undertake nontraditional NLF activities, the Attorney General's office was put on the defensive by the profession's hostility to the ALAO. It was necessary to placate the legal profession in order to obtain support for a bill that would give statutory support and some permanence to the ALAO.

C. The Legal Aid Bill of 1975

The bill introduced in the Australian Parliament by the Labour government in June 1975 proposed that the ALAO be managed by a board of three persons appointed by the Governor General (see Sackville, 1975a:20–21, 38–39). One was to be director; a second, taken from the ranks of judges or "private practitioners of high standing," would serve part-time as chairman; and the third appointee was required to be a barrister or solicitor. The board's powers were to be somewhat limited, ensuring that the Attorney General's office would still have a very strong influence.[3] The bill provided further that an independent Legal Aid Commission would be established to advise on matters of legal aid policy, but only when requested. The Commission was to be composed of not less than seven nor more than twelve part-time commissioners.[4]

The government bill envisioned no broader NLF role for the ALAO. The ALAO's work would continue to be concentrated on individual advice and, according to the Attorney General, the bill assumed "that a large proportion of the work of the ... office will be referred to the private profession" (Purcell, 1977:41).

Not surprisingly, in view of the lack of commitment to NLF activities and the weak measures for lay participation in the administration of the ALAO, NLF proponents such as Sackville tended to be at best lukewarm in their attitude toward the bill (e.g., Sackville, 1975a:18–53). The bill also did not succeed in winning the support of the legal profession, principally because the ALAO Management Board was not considered "independent," meaning free from the control of the government (but not the profession) (Purcell, 1977:45–48). The profession's spokesmen had modified their positions somewhat; they now all recognized that "salaried government services ... have an important role." But they were still concerned that "[a]id schemes should be administered substantially by the profession...." In other words, they were now willing to concede that publicly-salaried legal aid lawyers were a necessary supplement to judicare, but they did not want to relinquish control over the work of those salaried lawyers.

In the formal debates on the bill, the parliamentary opposition expressed the concerns of the profession as well as a desire to reduce the federal role in this area. Opposition leaders proposed that any staff system be set up within the states, with the legal profession playing "a leading role" (Purcell, 1977:44). The opposition had a majority in the Senate, and without the support of the legal profession, the bill failed to gain approval in that branch.[5] The bold effort of the Labour government to create a permanent system of widespread staff legal aid offices was unable to obtain the momentum seen outside of Australia.

112

V. The ALAO and State Legal Aid after the Fall of the Labour Government

A. The Fate of the ALAO

The Labour government collapsed (for other reasons) just after the failure to pass the Legal Aid Bill. The Liberal–National Coalition came to power in December 1975, and the leader of the opposition to the Legal Aid Bill became Attorney General. The new government has continued to express interest in legal aid, and the federal budget continued to rise, but the government has created a number of difficulties for the ALAO. On 8 March 1976, new and very severe eligibility guidelines took effect, and as of early 1978 they had not been altered: "The effects of inflation ensure that fewer and fewer persons are eligible for assistance; even so, whole areas of law can no longer be covered" ("Legal Aid—A Meaner Means Test," 1977). Whether or not the ALAO is being "dismantled," as some commentators have charged (e.g., Purcell, 1977:54), its future is highly uncertain. The new government has sought to transfer legal aid administration to the states; in that setting the ALAOs may be taken over or eliminated, depending on the outcome of state deliberations.

B. Reform at the State Level

The Liberal–National government in late 1976 developed a plan for legal aid reform at the state level, and these proposals were supported in great part by the organized legal profession (see Disney et al., 1977:430; Harkins, 1977:36). The plan was for each state to establish an independent Legal Aid Commission, with "substantial representation" of the legal profession. The Commissions are then to set financial priorities and administer all legal aid services, including the ALAO, in a state (or territory). Finally, they are to "provide legal aid by making available the services of salaried lawyers or by referral of cases to private lawyers in accordance with policies determined by the respective Commission" (see Harkins, 1977:36).

A model statute drafted by the commonwealth government suggested seven-member, part-time Commissions composed of three nominees of the private profession; two of state government (one of which would be Chairman); one of federal government; and one nominee of the Council of Social Services. The model statute also proposed that local advisory committees, called "Consultative Committees," be created. (Such committees had also been envisioned by the Labour bill.)

As of early 1978 several states had enacted new laws and others were still discussing how to implement the federal plan and gain commonwealth funding for their revised legal aid schemes. In addition, the commonwealth created an eight-person Legal Aid Commission to support the state programs (Commonwealth Legal Aid Act 1977).

The first state to act was West Australia, which in late 1976 passed a new law, effective 1 July 1977 (West Australia Legal Aid Commission Act 1976; see.also Khan and Hacket, 1977). The West Australian Legal Aid Commission it established has seven members, at least four of whom are drawn from among practicing lawyers. The new law recognized a role for the ALAO, which the Commission has taken over, but it was a very limited one. The law established Legal Aid Committees, consisting of three private practitioners appointed on the nomination of the Law Society, and the Committees were to decide themselves whether to refer eligible persons to a private practitioner or to a staff attorney. The West Australia Law Society clearly had a very strong influence on the new scheme, and the potential for a salaried component appeared to be very limited indeed. Recent amendments, however, have evidently made the system less dominated by private practitioners (Hermandad, 1978:76). Much now depends on how the new Commission implements the law.

A second state to act was South Australia, where the South Australian Legal Services Commission Act of 1977 became law on 12 May 1977 (see Sexton, 1977). The law provides for a ten-person commission, including three nominees of the Law Society, three of the State Attorney General, and one person to represent the client community. The new Commission has not yet been created, however, since it is awaiting the outcome of negotiations with the Commonwealth Government over funding and the ALAO, and it is also unclear here what role the ALAO or any other staff component will have. Finally, the Australian Capital Territory passed a Legal Aid Ordinance in 1977, and it too leaves the difficult decisions to a Commission with substantial representation by the legal profession (see "Legal Aid in the A.C.T.," 1978).

Thus far, therefore, the states have created new commissions with the power to take over the ALAO in the state or set up their own offices, but the mixture of staff and judicare is left open. Each of the commissions has substantial representation of the legal profession, but the idea that control should not be solely with the profession seems to have taken hold. The NLF idea as used here—as opposed to simply the staff system—has not yet been very influential at the state level. The staff model tends to be the ALAO rather than a more innovative type of program. NLFs, however, may be given more recognition in the two largest states—Victoria and New South Wales—since some important local law centers continue to exist and provide models for a more activist legal aid system.

In Victoria, Fitzroy Legal Services still provides an influential model of an NLF (see Baynes, 1977). It has taken a very active role in the ongoing legal aid debate in Victoria, urging that there be strong consumer representation on the proposed Commission and that staff lawyers in a combined system be encouraged to undertake test cases and law reform actions (Fitzroy Legal Service, 1977). And in New South Wales, since 1975 the Law Society has itself operated a "Community Law Centre" located at Mount Druitt (see Kershaw, in Purcell, 1977:65), and, the Redfern Legal Centre, an independent law center funded mainly by the Sydney Municipal Council, opened in early 1977 near Sydney ("Redfern Legal Centre," 1977). There is not much evidence on how active or influential these law centers are, but they may exemplify NLF advocacy beyond that of the ALAO.

In sum, there is now general agreement in Australia that staff lawyers will contribute to the new state schemes, but the nature of that contribution remains unclear. The Law Societies recognize the need for staff lawyers, but not for NLFs, and there is not any powerful federal or other pressure favoring NLFs. The prognosis is thus for more or less "mixed" systems, but the mixture appears to be judicare with the ALAO, rather than with an active NLF component as advocated by Fitzroy and by the "Law and Poverty" reports made under Professor Sackville's direction.

VI. Conclusion

The NLF idea still has a large number of proponents in Australia, but it has found no institutional embodiment. As in other countries, the federal government took the lead in Australia with the ALAO, the Legal Aid Review Committee, and the Law and Poverty section of the Commission of Inquiry into Poverty. The federal government, however, faced well-established state judicare programs controlled by and in the interests of the legal profession. Rather than concentrating on "pilot projects," as was done in Canada, or on cooperation with existing programs, the Attorney General overambitiously proclaimed a new national program. The profession predictably resisted and ultimately killed the ALAO by failing to support the bill giving statutory recognition. Aside from this political overestimation, the Labour government failed in my opinion by *limiting* its sights too much.

115

The ALAO was the creation of the Attorney General's office and did not partake of the "community action" or antipoverty orientation of federally-sponsored NLFs in Canada, England, and the United States. It never developed into an innovative alternative to traditional legal aid. Significantly, the Sackville studies arose outside of the Attorney General's office. The conclusion of Terence Purcell, a leading Australian commentator, supports this analysis,

> The government could have made use of the Australian Assistance Plan (AAP.) which was modelled on the Canadian Assistance Plan and which was not dissimilar from OEO's Community Action Programs. By using this procedure it would have been capable of sponsoring a series of truly community-based legal service programs in a total community service environment (Purcell, 1977:53).[6]

The ALAO alienated the profession by challenging the control of their Law Society programs and raising the spectre of lost judicare business, but the ALAO never really developed and implemented an affirmative NLF program. As a result, Australia—unlike the United States, England, and Canada—is still waiting for the strong governmental initiatives necessary for an NLF system to be implemented.

Notes

1. The statutory schemes are as follows: New South Wales—Legal Practitioners (Legal Aid) Act of 1970; Queensland—Legal Assistance Act of 1965-1974; South Australia—Legal Practitioners Amendment Act of 1969; Tasmania—Legal Assistance Act of 1962 and Legal Assistance Scheme of 1974; Victoria—Legal Aid Act of 1969; West Australia—Legal Contribution Trust Act of 1967 and Legal Assistance Rules of 1971. The latter scheme was replaced on 1 July 1977 by the Legal Aid Commission Act of 1976 (West Australia).

These schemes are described in great detail by Sackville (1975b). The major source of funding for these schemes was the interest on solicitors' trust accounts. The major exceptions to the judicare systems were Public Defender programs in New South Wales and Queensland and Public Solicitor offices in Victoria and New South Wales. Only the latter, however, offered legal aid in a substantial number of civil cases.

2. According to Harkins, the Attorney General's office at one point even leased land for a pilot "legal aid centre" in Adelaide, South Australia, but the project was shelved when agreement could not be reached between the Attorney General and the Law Society of South Australia (Harkins, 1977:23).

3. The board was to be required to inform the Attorney General of any policy proposals regarding the ALAO. The Governor General would then resolve any disagreement between the Board and the Attorney General (see Sackville, 1975a:21).

4. The Labour Attorney General indicated that he planned to appoint, aside from

116

the lawyer-chairperson, one representative of his department; two private practitioners; one person each from a state law society, the ALAO, and a state government legal aid scheme; one person from the Australian Council of Social Service; one person expert in "law reform"; and three persons from among groups and persons interested in legal aid (see Disney et al., 1977:429).

5. According to Purcell, whose account of these developments is excellent,

"[T]he Bill's failure was probably due to its being an attempt to enshrine in the Australian social fabric a legal aid policy which did not by and large find favour with the Australian legal establishment" (1977:47).

6. Purcell adds that to choose the AAP approach "would have meant ministerial cooperation, as the AAP was the brainchild of the Social Security Minister, Mr. Hayden. Unfortunately, cooperation at that level was not one of the prominent features of the Labour period in office; in fact, the opposite was frequently the case."

Chapter 6

The Netherlands, Belgium, and Norway

Aside from the Canadian province of Quebec, the discussion has thus far been only of "common law" jurisdictions. It may be that lawyers in "civil law" countries are less likely candidates for enlistment in wars on poverty. After all, judges tend to assume more of the fact-finding responsibilities in civil law jurisdictions, and less attention is given to a single, lawyer-dominated trial (see, e.g., Rueschmeyer, 1973). The absence, or at least attenuation, of the doctrine of case law precedents makes test cases less useful and cuts down the opportunity for making new law by creative legal arguments. Nevertheless, much of a lawyer's work anywhere is outside of a litigation setting, and in any event, lawyers are still considered essential to decipher codes and other legal rules. The experience of the Netherlands, Belgium, and Norway suggests that the forces that have created the NLF movement elsewhere are sufficiently strong to blur civil law–common law distinctions, given the overriding similarities among Western, "welfare state" countries.[1]

This chapter will primarily treat developments in the Netherlands, since they are to date more pronounced and important than those in the other two countries. The "law shops" in the Netherlands, furthermore, inspired the Belgium "*boutiques de droit*," and the principal Norwegian example, the "*juss buss*," is still relatively isolated and has not had much impact in promoting legislative legal aid reform.

I. The Netherlands[2]

Since 1957 the Netherlands has had a comprehensive judicare system modeled on the English scheme (Royal Decree of 24 December, 1957, most recently amended 9 December 1975). Interestingly, the 1957 reform was the result of an initiative launched by a Minister of Justice, Mr. Donker, who strongly favored a staff system of legal aid. His plan was to implement a salaried staff system that would build on a legal aid system begun before the First World War. Legal services

118

had been provided by salaried lawyers in private municipality-subsidized offices. That essentially charitable system declined in the 1920s and after due to economic crises and the Second World War (see Griffiths, 1977:261).

Mr. Donkers died before he was able to enact his plan, which of course did not contemplate NLFs in the sense of the 1960s and 1970s, and in his absence the pressure from the organized bar was sufficient to persuade the government to adopt a judicare rather than a salaried system. The 1957 law set up quite an advanced legal aid system for that time, and it has been quite successful according to a number of criteria. The number of legally-aided cases tripled between 1958 and 1972, and in 1972 such cases represented almost half of the Dutch civil caseload (Schuyt et al., 1977:99). As in England and elsewhere, however, the standards for evaluating a legal aid system began to shift, and very strong attacks on the judicare system began in the late 1960s.

A. The "Law Shop" Movement and the Challenge to Judicare

In late 1969 some students in the faculty of law in Tilburg created the first "law shop" in the Netherlands (see de Jong, 1977). They did not then follow any model or gain inspiration from any foreign experiences. In the wake of the student movement and the awakening of social conscience which took place around this time, they wanted simply to offer some legal advice to the needy, and make their legal skills socially useful. They obtained an office in which to provide such advice at certain hours. The idea of a law shop (*rechtswinkel*) struck a very responsive chord among law students; it spread to other law faculties, gained inspiration from developments elsewhere, and encouraged law students to question explicitly the adequacy of the judicare system. A special issue of the Dutch student law journal in June 1970, for example, was dedicated to "unmet needs" and the alleged failings of private lawyers in meeting those needs (see Schuyt et al., 1977:99).

Activist students set up law shops in all the major universities. By 1972 there were thirteen law shops, which became twenty-eight in 1973, fifty-four in 1974, sixty in 1975, and peaked at around ninety in 1976. At present there are roughly eighty law shops (Griffiths, 1977:262).

These law shops vary considerably in size, organization, and methods of work.[3] They are all, however, staffed almost exclusively by student volunteers who are aided by socially-oriented lawyers and law professors (see Bruinsma, 1976). "Law shoppers" may give

119

advice, but they do not undertake litigation except at times in the Canton Courts (lower courts where representation by lawyers is not required). As in England, they may refer cases to lawyers who can obtain legal aid money for litigating cases. The very limited funding provided to the law shops comes mainly from the universities and municipalities with some also from central government.[4]

The law shops, especially the eight large ones (Amsterdam, Groningen, The Hague, Leyden, Nijmegen, Rotterdam, Tilburg, Utrecht), have sought to provide precisely the services typical of NLFs in England and the United States. According to Professor Kees Schuyt, the work of OEO lawyers and law shops has a great deal in common: "In their ideology both projects are almost identical (stress on legal impact cases, highly decentralized, active in poverty areas, etc.)" (Schuyt et al., 1977:100). They have sought to concentrate their individual cases—which take up most of their time—in "poverty law" areas such as housing and social security, and the indications are that they have succeeded in this regard. Roughly one-quarter of the matters handled in Leyden and Amsterdam in 1974, for example, were housing matters, and about another quarter were labor and social insurance matters (see Chapter 8). Law shops have also been involved in education programs such as radio shows; and many—an increasing number—have sought "to transcend individual assistance to concentrate more on structural work" (Bruinsma, 1976:6). By "structural" is meant "assistance with an end of social change, in addition to or instead of protection of individual interests" (Griffiths, 1977:261). As in England, this may mean a particular emphasis on group organization and support, rather than simply litigation.

The emergence of this law shop movement sparked the criticism of the 1957 judicare scheme and then helped make it plausible. As elsewhere, the evidence of "unmet need" revealed by the popularity of the law shops was compelling: "The enormous popularity of the law shops underscore[d] ... the grave inadequacies of the free legal aid system" (Houtappel, 1978:591). As in England, it was clear that the judicare system was not leading to legal aid work in consumer, social welfare, or similar matters involving new rights on behalf of the disadvantaged. The judicare scheme in Holland dealt almost exclusively with litigation in traditional legal matters, about sixty-five percent of which concerned matrimonial issues (Griffiths, 1977:262; Council of Europe, 1977:187). The organized legal profession, naturally sensitive to its prestige and that of its legal aid system, had to respond to the situation.

120

B. The Organized Bar's Response and a New Challenge

The organized legal profession responded to criticism with a proposal for change, described as follows by one Dutch commentator.

> The bar association initially rejected the law shops' critiques. Instead it argued that private attorneys could ably assist those going to the law shops, if the government would only increase remunerations. Such bar association assertions were influential in the government's 1972 decision to increase compensation for free legal aid (Houtappel, 1978:592).

The first reaction was thus to insist that better incentives for private lawyers would enable them to meet the need revealed by law shops. The government complied, and legal aid compensation was raised some 50 percent. Still, however, this did not lessen the demand for the law shops' services.

The large law shops themselves began to organize in 1974 and put pressure on the bar and the government to adopt a new system of legal aid through publicly supported NLFs (de Jong, 1977; Bruinsma, 1976:5). They recognized that their own offices were not the answer to the problem, since they had to rely on students and could not easily bring court action. The bar association responded to further criticisms of the judicare program, and a 1975 report made several new recommendations (see Houtappel, 1978:592). While rejecting the law shops' proposals on grounds very similar to those seen in England, i.e., that public offices would be a step backward by creating two classes of clients, the report admitted the need for local offices able to provide legal advice and assistance *other than court representation*. This proposal, reminiscent of the English Law Society's emphasis on advice centers and CABs, was again heavily criticized by the law shops as inadequate. They wanted well-funded, full-service NLFs (see Bruinsma, 1976:5; Houtappel, 1978:592–93).

The Ministry of Justice—the key Dutch governmental office in this area—again supported the bar's proposals, this time providing funding for a new network of offices called *bureaus voor rechtshulp*. According to the State Secretary for Justice, the new offices were designed to take over the work of the law shops, which had served the function of revealing "most clearly" the "defects" in the judicare scheme ("Address by Mr. H. J. Zeevalking," in Council of Europe, 1976:9). He stated that the new offices would provide a "countrywide network of Legal Advice Centres equivalent perhaps to the English Citizens Advice Bureaus. The organisation would be run by a central authority, comparable to the English Law Society."[5] The first of these new offices opened in Amsterdam in 1974. Since late 1977

121

there has been one in each of the nineteen districts in the Netherlands. Government support amounted to 2.3 million guilders in 1976 (Council of Europe, 1977:181).

Most of these advice centers are very small, with a staff of about three, and much of their work is merely approving legal aid applications for referrals to private practice. The Amsterdam *bureau*, however, is the prototype for a more ambitious scheme. It has a very large staff of fourteen, at least nine of whom are law graduates (who would be lawyers if they had gone through the required three-year apprenticeship period). The staff is accountable to a board appointed by the Ministry of Justice and composed one-half of members of the bar, plus a court clerk, a notary, a representative of the Ministry of Justice, and a member of one of the Amsterdam law shops. The chairman is a judge.

As a replacement for the law shops and an answer to the problem of unmet need, the new advice centers are something of a success. The demand for advice from the new centers has been substantial, and the number of law shops began to decline. It is not clear, however, as discussed below, whether the limitation to legal advice—the principal reason for the bar's endorsement of this alternative to NLFs— will survive further developments in the Dutch NLF movement. Further, the advice centers may themselves generate pressures for an expanded role and even for "structural work." Significantly, the Amsterdam office was staffed by former members of the Amsterdam law shop, and it was clear from a visit there that they are already endeavoring to expand services somewhat beyond simple legal advice. Finally, the *bureau*'s ideological proximity to law shops generates new support and a clientele for another important component of the present NLF movement in the Netherlands—the law collectives.

The Dutch law collective (*advokaten kollektief*) is a unique outgrowth of the NLF movement. The bar's efforts to make legal aid lucrative for private practitioners, as evidenced by the 1972 raise in legal fees for legal aid (and another such raise in 1975), made it possible for these "NLF judicare offices" to be established.

The Amsterdam law collective opened in October 1974 with nine lawyers, one of whom had been the founder of the Amsterdam law shop (cf. Boer, 1978). While the Ministry of Justice, showing its changing attitude, provides a "minimum guaranteed fee" (465,000 guilders in 1976), the law collective is funded essentially by revenues from the judicare system. The collective, however, handles no divorce actions, which generate most of the judicare revenue to private practitioners. The lawyers, in fact, turn away some forty percent of

122

the clients who come to them, preferring to concentrate on politically important cases and cases they feel the private bar cannot handle. Many matters are referred to them by their politically sympathetic friends at the law shops and the Amsterdam *bureau voor rechtshulp*. Although over 30 percent of the cases taken are criminal cases (criminal cases are better compensated for than the others taken by the collective), the law collective's work is very much oriented toward group work and social reform. It has also become a national leader in organizing NLF proponents and urging reform of legal aid toward salaried NLFs.

The members of a law collective receive only modest salaries, and the bar still has some controls over law collectives, particularly since law collectives may need "patrons" to sponsor young lawyers through their three-year apprenticeship.[6] But this limitation has not prevented at least eight law collectives from organizing in cities such as Utrecht and Nijmegen.

The law shop movement, in short, has taken the bar-sponsored reforms aimed at diffusing the movement and transformed them into new components of the movement. Law shops have started to decline in number, but the legal advice centers and the law collectives have strengthened the call for the adoption of a permanent salaried NLF system. The Ministry of Justice is once again considering statutory reform, which may move further toward institutionalizing NLFs in the Netherlands. Already the Ministry is involved in subsidizing law shops, to the extent of 120,000 guilders in 1976, and in helping ensure the existence of at least the Amsterdam law collective.

C. The Current Situation and Future Prospects

The Ministry of Justice is currently working on a new legal aid law. Partly this is because the advice centers do not yet have a statutory basis, but it is also because the Dutch NLF movement and its aftermath have created strong pressures for further reform. Besides those mentioned in this chapter, there is now the well-publicized and important study of legal needs financed by the Ministry of Justice and undertaken by Schuyt, Groenendyk, and Sloot (see Schuyt et al., 1977). The completed study, published in 1976, favored a "pluriformity" of legal advice and assistance agencies, but it explicitly recognized and legitimated the need for legal services such as those provided by the law shops. Professor Schuyt is now a consultant on legal aid for the Ministry of Justice. Adding particularly to reform pressure was the formation, in late 1977, by law shops, law collectives, and other interested activists, of a "Legal Aid Association" (an outgrowth of the earlier law shop organization). It has already become a strong advocate of reform. The Ministry of Justice—now accepting the desirability of NLF advocacy—recognizes this group and consults with it in the same way as with the bar association. The new respectability means that the bar can no longer work out policies by itself with the Ministry.

Opposed to the Legal Aid Association is the Bar Association, still firmly against salaried lawyers other than the law graduates in the legal advice centers. The bar even issued a rule recently against lawyers receiving salaries from organizations, and the leader of the bar wrote an article saying there was no need for publicly-salaried lawyers except for legal advice. The bar's position seems to be motivated primarily by economic concerns. Legal aid revenues—primarily from divorce cases—are now a quantitatively important part of the average lawyer's practice. For many lawyers in the cities and for even more in rural areas, 50 percent of their income is from the judicare scheme. On the other hand, the large commercial firms located in Rotterdam and Amsterdam, according to Professor Schuyt, are willing to support a staff system. This division is remarkably similar to that seen in the U.S. NLF movement except that, unlike the American Bar Association, it appears that the Dutch bar association has a relatively broad base; its position is therefore closer to the more representative private practitioners.

The outcome of this debate is still in doubt, but it appears that if a compromise can be worked out with the bar—perhaps something like the English waiver agreement—the way would be paved to grant lawyer status to the law graduates in the advice centers. This type of reform obviously would cause the number of law shops to further dwindle, but this would not be a problem. The law shops can be seen more as catalysts for change than permanent NLFs. Student volunteers cannot take cases to court, and their inevitably conflicting commitments make continuity difficult to maintain. Even assuming the nineteen legal advice bureaus are given the status of law firms, however, questions remain about how they will be governed and funded, and whether they can further decentralize to reach more of the population. The situation is still open, but the rise to power and respectability of the movement has already caused lasting change. The rise of judicare-funded law collectives is a particularly remarkable Dutch accomplishment.

II. Belgium

The legal aid situation is also uncertain in Belgium. The organized bar is seeking to reform the charitable legal aid system in favor of a judicare one, while *boutiques de droit* favor the adoption of a strong NLF component. Without going into detail, it is useful to describe here briefly the origins, extent, and orientation of the movement in Belgium.

It is necessary to begin with the charitable system that has long been in operation in Belgium (Code of Civil Procedure, art, 455; see generally Pelgrims, 1977; Pelgrims, 1978; Godding, 1975). Under this system there is an office in each of the twenty-six judicial *arrondissements*, located usually at the courthouse. The offices, called *bureaux de consultation et de defense*, are administered by the legal profession, the *Ordres d'avocats*, and contain a President (an established lawyer) and several *stagiaires* (legal apprentices). They are open generally only a few hours a week, and there are relatively fixed income limits to qualify—15,000 Belgian francs for full legal aid in 1978 and 25,000 for partial legal aid. As could be expected, the types of matters brought to these *bureaux* have generally been criminal defense (50 percent) and family (30 percent) (Pelgrims, 1978:352; see also Pelgrims, 1977:21).

This system underwent the same kind of criticism found elsewhere in the late 1960s and early 1970s, particularly with the establishment of Belgian "law shops," *wetswinkels* or *boutiques de droit*, the name depending on whether they are located in the Flemish- or French-speaking part of the country. The first law shops in 1972 followed the Dutch example, well-known to Flemish speakers, in the Flemish part of the country—Ghent and Louvain (see Pelgrims, 1977; Pelgrims, 1978; Godding, 1975).

In 1973, six of these *boutiques* opened in Brussels, and by late 1977 twenty-five of them existed in various parts of the country—although most were concentrated in the north. They are staffed primarily by students, with help from young lawyers. Like the Dutch law shops, the Belgian *boutiques de droit* vary widely in methods and strategies, but again the aims are united in a general sense. One general aim is to provide assistance in matters not generally brought to lawyers or handled by the *bureaux de consultation et de defense*: *"La fonction première des boutiques est de déceler et de cerner les aires énormes négligées par le droit"* (Panier, 1977:153). For example, according to Pelgrims' data, the Belgian law shops handled forty-one percent housing matters, compared to nine percent housing in the Brussels *bureau* (Pelgrims, 1977:21; see Pelgrims, 1978:362–63). A second aim is to use their position to promote actions that favor groups of people: *"de rechercher les causes sociales du problème, de replacer celui-ci dans sons contexte et de depasser la solution juridique par la recherche d'une transformation sociale"* (Godding, 1975:56; see also Pelgrims, 1977:104–11; Pelgrims, 1978:364–66; Panier, 1977:154). Like the law shops in Holland, these student-run institutions suffer somewhat from a lack of funding, a lack of continuity, and the inability to go beyond legal advice without regular staff lawyers, but they too have provoked a debate about the future of legal aid.

Again, the terms of the debate gradually shifted, beginning with local bar efforts to hinder the law shop movement in Louvain and Brussels by refusing to allow lawyers to collaborate (see Pelgrims, 1977). The need for law shops forced the bar to acquiesce in that collaboration, but they sought to defuse the movement by upgrading their own legal aid service through the *bureaux*. The means test was relaxed, requiring less documentary proof, and several *bureaux* began to remain open for longer hours and to provide office hours in certain times at more locations. Similarly, consistent with the bar's argument that compensation for private attorneys would help close the gap in unmet need by upgrading the quality and extent of their system (see Van de Heuvel, 1976), the organized bar persuaded the Ministry of Justice to enact a further reform in late 1978. The reform, as described by Pelgrims (1978:357), eases the burden on young lawyers by allowing those designated by the *bureau* to recover personal expenses necessitated by taking a case.

Beyond this upgrading of the charitable system, a second response by the public authorities and legal profession to the challenge of the Belgian law shops has been the development of public social assistance centers (*centres publics d'aide sociale* (see generally Pelgrims, 1978:368–73)). These centers, which evidently grew out of private initiatives providing specialized legal advice, were created by a law of 8 July 1976. They are open to all persons and provide only legal advice. The staff is composed of lawyers who are compensated for their time. Some forty lawyers participate in the six offices in Brussels. Significantly, the law creating these offices partakes of the language of NLFs and unmet need. The goals are that it *"assure non seulement une aide palliative ou curative, mais encore une aide préventive"* (art. 57). Similarly, it is stated that *"Le centre fournit tous les renseignements utiles et effectue les démarches de nature à procurer aux intéressés tous les droits et avantages aux quels ils peuvent prétendre dans le cadre de la legislation belge où étrangère"* (art. 60). In other words, the emphasis is supposed to be on enforcing rights and on preventive law, not simply providing advice to whoever seeks it.

126

It is too early to know how these public centers have affected the legal aid debate in Belgium, but no doubt as in Holland there will be questions about whether these new offices go far enough. Certainly they do not provide the "social change" orientation of the law shops, and they limit the staff to legal advice. Again, however, the point is that the legal profession and the government have been placed on the defensive by the law shop challenge. They have sought to diffuse the movement by finding means short of NLFs to meet the legal needs revealed by the law shops, but the issues are still very much open.

III. Norway[7]

The *juss buss*, or "law bus," in Oslo, Norway, was organized in 1969 and implemented in 1971 as an experiment in alternatives to the existing judicare system. Like the law shops, it is staffed principally by students (twenty-five to thirty) but they are paid for their time in Norway (at a rate of about U.S. $7 per hour for twelve to fifteen hours of work per week). It is called the *juss buss* because it began by using a traveling mobile trailer to give legal advice in various parts of the city of Oslo.

The founders of the *juss buss* were a small group of persons, including the present director, who were interested in doing some practical work for the poor and some research into the poor's legal problems. They were to some extent inspired by developments in the United States, but they were not trying specifically to copy them. They sought funding to pay students to work with them and found it from the University of Oslo Institute of Sociology of Law, with whom they affiliated, as well as from the city of Oslo and the Department of Justice. For the latter the *juss buss* was considered an experiment in legal aid.

For a long time the *buss* concentrated on providing legal advice in individual cases, but recently the *buss* decided to change its emphasis. Advice (except for two three-week periods during the year) is now offered only to persons brought by groups involved with foreigners, gypsies, tenants, the handicapped, and prisoners. The members of the *buss* are also seeking to redress the problems of the underprivileged by broader NLF strategies, particularly by doing research into and publicizing injustices.

The *juss buss* is an important NLF phenomenon in Norway, even if it has evidently had little or no impact on legal aid policy makers. There is a similar legal advice organization in Bergen, the only other Norwegian city with a law faculty, and there are now two hundred "graduates" of the *buss* in practice in Norway. The NLF idea has

127

reached Norway, but whether it will have any impact there on further legal aid reform remains to be seen.

Notes

1. Another non-common law jurisdiction with somewhat similar developments is Sweden, where a well-funded "combined model" of legal aid was created in 1972. For a variety of reasons, however, I would not say that the public legal aid offices in Sweden can be characterized as NLFs as the term is used in this study. The public legal aid offices are not intended to be staffed by salaried lawyers, but rather are supposed to compete with private attorneys for judicare funding, and the activities of these offices cannot be characterized as those of NLFs as I have defined them (see generally Cappelletti et al., 1975:525–84; Muther, 1975; Hellners, 1976). As an indication of the work of these offices, Hellners reports that "81 percent of the cases in which counsel came from a public law office were matters of family law. The corresponding figure for private practicing lawyers was 65 percent" (Hellners, 1976:93). As will be seen, this is not the kind of caseload characteristic of NLFs.

2. The information reported here came to a great extent from my visit to the Netherlands in June 1977, and from the seminars led by Professor Kees Schuyt of Nijmegen at the European University Institute on 14 and 21 March 1978. I prepared a summary of my visit to the Netherlands entitled, "Legal Aid at the Local Level in the Netherlands and Norway: Report to the Florence Access-to-Justice Project" (4 July 1977).

3. The Amsterdam law shop, for example, is divided into five essentially independent section—labor and social insurance, family, consumer, landlord–tenant, and "diverse," which includes problems of foreign workers and immigrants. Law shop policies are set up by a board composed of one member of each section. Twice a week the students hold advice sessions, seeing about eighty persons per session. Every Monday the sections meet with volunteer attorney advisers to go over advice that was given and to decide on difficult cases where advice was postponed (see Boer, 1978).

The Tilburg Law Shop only handles housing, labor, and social benefit matters, and its emphasis is clearly more on social change as opposed to simply meeting individual legal needs. It seeks to put the law shop's activities "at the disposal of the organizations, already existing, or still to be founded, of labourers ... [,] people who are entitled to social benefits and ... tenants" (de Jong, 1977).

4. The average subsidy from the *central government* was between 2,000 and 7,500 guilders per lawship, totaling 120,000 guilders in 1976 (Council of Europe, 1977:181).

5. The new offices were formed to replace the "legal aid boards" which had been set up in each of nineteen districts to grant or refuse legal aid applications (Council of Europe, 1977:154–55).

6. Special permission is required from the bar if the sponsoring patron does not work in the same office. For the Amsterdam collective, such permission was obtained

to allow one patron in the office and six outside patrons to sponsor the eight law graduates.

7. All the following information is based on conversations with the members of the *juss buss*, including the director, Mr. Gunner da Capua, in June 1977, in the Netherlands. The *juss buss* law students and director toured the law shops at the same time as I did.

Chapter 7

The Emergence and Development of the Neighborhood Law Firm as an Institution: A Comparative Conclusion

A tentative answer can be given to Stuart Scheingold's suggestive question posed at the outset of this study. "The winds of change," he wrote, had been detected before; "Would it be different this time?" The answer is that neighborhood law firms, with their idealistic goals, have survived. Seeking to bring the poor into the legal system, where they can vindicate their rights, and pushing to overcome the fundamental problems of "class justice," NLFs were not just a phenomenon of the late 1960s. The movement has spread to many countries, gained strength, and increasingly put judicare systems and their proponents in the organized profession on the defensive. In a growing number of countries, despite a growing scarcity of public funds, NLF reformers have been able to secure stable public funding, a large degree of independence from government and from professional organizations, and some type of permanent institutional form.

This chapter, which concludes Part Two of this study, will pause to reflect on the continuing institutional evolution, examining comparatively some of the principal themes that have emerged from the previous chapters. It will seek to demonstrate the differences, but especially the similarities in how lawyers, bar associations, and welfare state governments in various countries have reacted to the NLF idea.

Before proceeding with this comparative discussion, however, a few qualifying remarks are necessary; they will help explain why I wish to give only a "tentative" answer at this point to Scheingold's challenge. First, the definition of NLFs used thus far encompasses a bundle of activities, including individual casework, especially in areas of "unmet need"; law reform, either through the courts or the legislatures; "group work"; and community education. This definition is justifiable because the NLF ideology encompasses all these activities and, moreover, unites them with the general aim of improving the position of the poor not just as individuals, but also as a class. Still, it avoids the important differences among NLFs in regard to how they implement these strategies, and it neglects the question of which combination of tactics is most effective toward the "social change" end. "Institutionalization" might even shift the mix of tactics in such a way that the social change goal would in practice be ignored. To return to Scheingold's terms, the "difference" this time could be illusory. Second, in showing the growth of the NLF movement, I have had to rely often on statements of participants as to their ideology and goals and on their own assessments of the significance of their NLF activities. Seeking social change and making social change may not, however, be the same. Both these qualifications will be treated in subsequent parts of this essay, but for the moment they will serve to caution us not to overestimate the significance of the NLF movement and its evident successes in becoming institutionalized.

Nevertheless, institutional victories are vital to the continuation of a movement, and ideological pronouncements are important in showing what NLF lawyers and staff personnel will be permitted or encouraged to do. It is, therefore, useful to analyze and compare the forces that have promoted and hindered NLFs in the various countries studied and that have led to the current status as pictured in the preceding five chapters.

I. The Prime Movers

The NLF movement is a movement for a welfare state reform of the legal profession in order to help the poor, but it had its intellectual origins neither with welfare state governments, the organized bar, nor the demands of the poor. It began with the rediscovery of poverty and the revival of social consciousness in the mid-1960s, when law students, law professors, and lawyers not yet settled into traditional careers increasingly questioned the neutrality of lawyers and the law. Sensitive students of the law became concerned that they were being trained mainly to serve as "hired guns" for wealthy persons and institutions. They learned that poor persons have a wide range of relatively new welfare state rights that—so it seemed—required legal assistance to be enforced, and that the traditional legal aid mechanisms, whether charitable or judicare, did not provide that assistance. The equal justice proclaimed by the legal ideology was clearly not the reality. Law students looked for new ways to make the legal system more accessible to the poor, and NLFs were a logical answer. The new model of legal aid, in fact, served a double purpose for these students: (1) it gave law students and lawyers the chance to help the poor; and (2) it held the promise of jobs in which one could avoid "selling out" to work in traditional legal practices. There has been great pressure, especially in the late 1960s and early 1970s, to find non-"establishment" careers.

At the same time many academic lawyers and a growing new breed of "legal sociologists" took an interest in the legal problems of poverty. They began to do empirical research to find and test "solutions." Their studies, as has been noted, fueled the movement and helped greatly to direct student energies. Further, once the movement began in the United States and elsewhere, the existing NLF model proved contagious as it provided a concrete example and rallying point for legal aid reform.

The experiences described in this Part varied considerably in detail, but the importance of these law students, academic lawyers and the growing new breed of policy-oriented legal sociologists is uniformly evident. In the United States the influential article by Edgar and Jean Cahn was written while Edgar Cahn was a law student, and the Cahns then went to work in Washington, D.C., at the outset of the War on Poverty. At the same time, lawyers and legal sociologists were revealing the "unmet legal need" and finding the solution of NLFs well adapted for that need. The first issue of the *Law and Society Review* published an important legal need study in 1966, and the co-author of that and an earlier study, Jerome Carlin, became the first director of one of the more important legal services programs, the San Francisco Neighborhood Legal Assistance Foundation.

In England the *Society of Labour Lawyers*, prompted especially by an academic lawyer, Michael Zander, was initially most prominent, and Zander also worked on the first large study of legal needs in England. And in Canada, Australia, Holland and Belgium, law students were the first to promote the NLF idea and actively take initiative to implement certain aspects of it.

By that time, of course, the students also could build their arguments on the success of NLFs elsewhere, beginning with those set up in 1965 in the United States. Indeed, the influence of this "foreign" NLF model, derived initially from peculiarly American roots, is one of the striking aspects of this study. England, Canada, Australia, and Norway all felt the very strong influence of the U.S. model (at least initially), as it was translated to them through descriptions published in the late 1960s. While it is more difficult to trace influences on the Dutch program, it is fairly clear that it received momentum from a relatively early acquaintance with U.S. and English developments. It is clear, in addition, that Dutch law shops inspired the Belgian law shops and the *boutiques de droit* in French-speaking Belgium, and we could also trace the influence further to the more recent French *boutiques de droit* (Boutiques de droit, 1978), which have the potential to grow into a major force there as well. The NLF movement is thus a leading recent example in the practical uses of comparative law.

132

II. The Policy Makers

Law students and academic lawyers were, as noted, the first group to agitate for NLFs, and they often also helped set up university-affiliated law centers. But students and professors obviously cannot sustain a movement unless it strikes a responsive chord with more important pressure groups and policy makers.

By "policy makers" I mean both governments and influential private foundations concerned with "social engineering." Such foundations are most notably found in the United States and to a lesser extent in England. They are closely linked to governmental policy makers, and their programs fit perfectly with the governmental approach found throughout the history of NLFs. Poverty in the 1960s seemed to many of these policy makers to be the result of a "technical" failure of the welfare state. Governments had created many social programs and enacted many laws to ameliorate the conditions of the poor, yet the poor—victims of the "cycle of poverty"—were unable to take advantage of new opportunities to uplift themselves. There was an unmet need. The "unmet legal need," once uncovered by law students and legal academics, was taken very seriously by policy makers in the welfare states. In the United States, the Ford Foundation and the federal government began to emphasize and support legal services experiments beyond their earlier community action programs. Interestingly, the influential Abel-Smith, Zander, and Brooke "legal needs" study (1973) in England was also funded by the Ford Foundation. The Nuffield Foundation in England sponsored an investigation of unmet need (Morris, Cooper, and Byles, 1973) and the Newham Rights Centre— an experimental NLF to meet that need. The government itself funded legal need studies in at least the Netherlands (Schuyt et al., 1976) and Australia (Cass and Sackville, 1975).

NLFs have generally been sold to policy makers as a means to overcome the problem of the "underutilization" of lawyers to enforce legal rights—the problem revealed by the need studies. This approach sought to add a legal component to wars and battles against poverty. The Cahns and their allies in the United States, for example, were able to convince the director of the antipoverty agency, Sargent Shriver, to implement NLFs; and antipoverty programs in England, such as the Urban Program and the Community Development Project, and in Canada gave vital boosts to the NLF movements there. The failure of the Australian Legal Aid Office to develop into an innovative NLF system can in part be attributed to its lack of contact and coordination with Australia's antipoverty program,

133

which sought a more activist NLF component. NLFs provide an attractive program to combat poverty in the welfare state. Even the European Economic Community's Antipoverty Program funds at least one law center, the South Wales Antipoverty Action Centre.

Technical solutions to poverty, however, are incomplete. They are bound to make political opponents if they become serious attempts to better the position of the poor. To upgrade the position of the "have-nots" requires some stepping on the toes of the "haves." To the extent data are available, the history of NLFs verifies this point. Considerable controversy has surrounded activist NLFs. Lawsuits against governments, campaigns to rouse citizens to assert their rights, and efforts to change the law can encounter and at times have encountered powerful and sustained opposition. The U.S. experience particularly illustrates the kind of controversy that can be generated. The program was singled out for attack by Congressmen, Governors, and even the Vice President, and it was nearly destroyed. The English problems with local governments are also instructive. Funding was cut off in a couple of instances, and one prominent local council-man called a law center a "Centre for the dissemination of vicious propaganda."

This controversy, however, should not be exaggerated. Indeed, what is surprising is how little controversy there has been, considering the "brave paradox of government backing for programmes which challenge government" (Marris and Rein, 1972:230). Problems in the United States, for example, were especially severe at the local or state level and in the federal House of Representatives, a body particularly susceptible to local pressures. The rhetoric surrounding the OEO Legal Services Program, in addition, probably alarmed as many people as program actions. The data available to date suggest that political hostility against NLFs results primarily from particular actions generating an almost "irrational" local anger among those being sued or subjected to other strong legal pressures. Upon reflec-tion, most local governments favor NLFs; and from a more detached national perspective their activities, including relatively controversial ones, appear desirable. Local governments, for example, have some-times been very hostile to neighborhood law centers in England, but they have tended on balance to support them, while the Home Office and the Labour Lord Chancellor and his Advisory Committee have increasingly been willing to finance the law centers and their type of advocacy. The movement elsewhere also shows a steadily growing legitimacy, especially among national policy makers.

The activities of lawyers may create enemies, but lawyers have two basic characteristics that make their activities less annoying to

134

"conservatives" than, for example, might be a "community action agency" aiming only to give the poor more local power. First, lawyers can hide behind the mask of professional independence, as was done especially well in the United States. If the lawyer acts as an advocate for an unpopular cause, he or she can often disclaim political responsibility. After all, lawyers zealously serving large corporate interests are not generally held accountable for the actions of their clients.

Second, lawyers bring people within the rule of law. The availability of lawyers to the disadvantaged inevitably encourages people to try to use legal channels for change. President Nixon, for example, stated in 1971 that "legal service has reaffirmed faith in our government of laws" and given the poor "a new reason to believe they are part of the system" (Presidential Message to Congress, 5 May 1971). Similarly, the English Lord Chancellor in 1978 discussed urban problems as follows:

> One of the elements in this situation is a disturbing alienation of people from the legal order and the hitherto accepted legal and administrative machinery. It is in just these communities that there are special needs for legal services. And it is just these services which, I believe, can restore people's confidence in the ability of the law, the courts and the legal system to redress their grievances, to protect their lawful rights and to provide a framework for an ordered community (Speech to Law Centres Working Group Conference, September 22, 1978, at 3).

The stabilizing function of NLFs will be discussed in more detail in connection with the examination of what they in fact do, but the importance of that function in gaining and holding political support must be recognized. NLFs, like the welfare state itself, imply both social change and social control (see Janovitz, 1976).

III. The Organized Bar and NLFs

The implementation of NLFs, unlike many other welfare state policies, confronts a very powerful interest group—the organized bar—which exists in some form in all the countries studied. The organized bar's actions are crucial to the success or failure of an NLF program. The American Bar Association, for example, supported the OEO Legal Services Program and enabled it to survive a very hostile and conservative administration. It was the only controversial OEO program to survive. The Australian law societies, in contrast, ensured that the Australian Legal Aid Office program would collapse with the demise of the Labour government, while the English Law Society has increasingly accepted the need for neighborhood law centers as presently organized and functioning. Canadian law societies at times inhibited NLF developments, as in Ontario and British Columbia, while in other cases fostered them, most notably in Saskatchewan. And new Dutch developments depend to a great extent on how the organized bar finally reacts to staff attorneys. It appears that the bar there is evolving in a fashion similar to the English Law Society.

While different bar associations can certainly adopt divergent positions, closer analysis reveals some strong unifying themes, which will now be discussed. First will be the role of narrow financial interest in shaping the bar's attitude. A second theme is the effort of the organized profession to "control" new NLF developments. Third is the relationship of the bar to the more controversial, nontraditional NLF activities, and, finally, there is the importance of image—the legitimacy of the profession—which emerges strongly from the NLF histories.

A. The Financial Interests of the Profession and Judicare

The power of the pocketbook is evident throughout the NLF story. This power is most evident where the bar's legal aid system already receives a certain amount of government funding, as in Australia, England, Holland, and Ontario, but even small-time lawyers in the United States feared a loss of income if free access is given to potential clients among the poor. If lawyers receive a certain part of their income from public funds, however, they are especially loathe to lose their legal aid clients to publicly-funded offices. Clearly the loss of even a small percentage of a lawyer's income can mean the difference between a good economic year and a bad one. It is thus not surprising that no existing judicare system has yet been *replaced* by a staff one; the result has been at most a combined model calculated to protect the private practitioner's legal aid practice.

If a judicare system has not been created, strong segments of the organized bar will continue to press for one. The prospect of judicare income is not as vital as income already received, but it is very attractive to most private practitioners. In Canada, for example, the "great debate" nearly always resulted in the adoption of at least some judicare component in the reformed system. The only real exception was Nova Scotia, where the Barristers' Society was content to administer the experimental staff program. The lure of judicare dollars is also quite apparent in the United States, particularly among state and local bar associations. Only the power of the national bar, the ABA, prevented a proliferation of judicare plans very early in the life of the program, and the Legal Services Corporation Act may have added new impetus to judicare experiments. A number of such experiments are now taking place.

There are other reasons, besides the narrow financial interests of lawyers, to favor judicare over or at least along with staff lawyers, but the single-mindedness of most segments of the organized legal profession on the judicare issue is due principally to financial concerns. Lawyers are a very strong interest group, and recent history shows that the preservation of judicare income is an issue capable of mobilizing the full power of the profession.

B. The Bar and the Control of NLFs

A second theme underlying the developments reported here is the legal profession's evident desire to "control" NLFs. The organized bar often emphasizes the need for legal aid programs to be "independent," but the independence sought is from the government, not the bar. Again and again one sees the organized bar trying to gain a position from which it can shape legal aid developments to its own interests. The American Bar Association's initial—and successful—effort to gain a dominating influence with the Legal Services Program in the United States is one example. Others include the Law Society's effort to assume the administration of law centers in England and decide through waiver agreements where and in what fields law centers can operate. In Australia the law societies also emphasized their desire to control any experiments with staff offices such as those under the Australian Legal Aid Office. In the heat of conflict, it may appear that the question is one of ideology, but closer inspection shows what really matters to the legal profession in these countries. Control is not an end in itself; the more important issue is *why* the organized professional groups wish to control legal aid developments.

The profession quite naturally fears the unknown, and it wants to ensure that its primary interests threatened by legal aid reforms—its interest in lawyers' financial prosperity and in preventing "socialized law" (analogous to "socialized medicine," with the implication of less income)—will not be threatened. "Control" is a way to protect the profession's interests, and, depending on the profession's fears and apprehensions, may take a variety of forms. In the United States, the profession's position under OEO was supposed to be protected by assurances from the OEO leadership, the activities of the National Advisory Council, the condition that local bars approve the programs, and the requirement that at least a majority of the governing boards of NLFs be lawyers. Under the 1974 Legal Services Corporation Act, local governing boards must be composed 60 percent of lawyers. These mechanisms of influence and control have more than satisfied the American Bar Association. Significantly, in Australia, where the Labour government created the ALAO without even any consultation with the organized legal profession, the law societies opposed the program from the start. They saw a threat, and there was no way to see that their interests would not be endangered. In the Netherlands, the requirements that the boards of the new *bureaus voor rechtshulp*—which are supposed to replace the law shops— be composed one-half of members of the bar is another effort to protect the bar's interests. In contrast to these various professionally-oriented formulas for control by lawyers, the English position is at first glance remarkable. The Law Society now supports management committees that are normally supposed to consist of a majority of *lay* persons. The reason, however, as explained earlier, is most likely that the Society feared control from the funding sources of the neighborhood law centers more than the centers' management committees. Management committees could provide some insulation (and of course law society representatives generally had some representation on the committees).

The example of England underlines the significance of the control issue as a defensive one. The concern is to ensure that the bar's interests will not be compromised, and it can be expressed in a variety of ad hoc ways. It is not that the bar insists on control for its own sake. When programs operate for a while, moreover, and it is seen that the bar's vital interests are not likely to be jeopardized—indeed may be promoted—the bar is much less concerned with formal mechanisms of control. There was evidently little controversy, for example, when in 1975 Manitoba expanded its system's governing board from nine to eleven, with the number of Law Society representatives kept at four. And the Board of Governors of the U.S. Legal Services Corporation was just changed to allow up to three client representatives on the Board. For the legal profession to support or at least not attempt to undermine or destroy a legal aid program, it is necessary not that it have formal control, but only that it feel its essential interests are not threatened. One reason for the trend toward lay involvement in the legal profession (see Zander, 1979) is simply a recognition that it need not be inconsistent with perceived vital professional interests.

C. *The Bar and NLF Activities*

The discussion of the preceding two themes points to the third one. If the profession actually does control the program, the program is less likely to develop in an innovative fashion. The influence of local bars in the United States, for example, was to diminish law reform and other nontraditional activities. The English Law Society's proposed "Section 16" legal centers, designed to preempt the independent law centers, were originally to be given a very narrow role. In Nova Scotia and British Columbia in Canada, where the bar administered a staff system, NLF activities never really developed within the bar program.

Nevertheless, comparative data suggest that the organized profession does not have a strong interest in curbing such NLF activities; it simply does what it has always done rather than take the initiative to innovate. In places where more innovative and controversial activities have taken place, however, they have not necessarily been opposed by the bar. Again, once the profession sees that these activities bring no real harm to their individual interests—indeed may through referrals create business—or the interests of the profession, the attitude has been at least tolerance, if not outright support. Again, it is significant that one of the least innovative programs discussed here, the Australian Legal Aid Office, was that which excited the most opposition within the profession, while in England the Law Society is not now critical of the "group work" emphasis of the law centers. The profession's concerns are above all with its economic interests and its overall image. These concerns can tolerate—even promote—a wide range of NLF activities.

D. *The Importance of the Profession's Image*

Before discussing how the concern with image affects the profession's actions, it is useful to discuss briefly the divisions within the profession as they affected the actions discussed in this study. Those most concerned with economic interest tend naturally enough to be those who need judicare money or see potential gain from it. These are the more or less average lawyers who represent individuals in divorces, handle some criminal matters, etc. Those who serve mainly corporate interests do not need legal aid funds, and they can afford to care more for the profession's image. It may also be that those who serve the large corporate interests have a certain stake, both psychological and professional, in equal justice. Their one-sided advocacy of the interests of the "haves" is more justifiable to themselves and to others if the "have-nots" also have their advocates and have their legal needs met. If all groups have their advocates, the adversary system can ensure that justice will be fair. It is thus instructive that the American Bar Association, the one professional organization that most clearly represents the bar's corporate elite, has been the most zealous legal professional defender of NLFs against judicare. Similarly, the large commercial lawyers in Holland are more willing to support NLFs than is the mainstream of the profession.

Even if concern with judicare income is crucial to a professional organization as presently constituted, however, the organization *must* respond to the challenge of the NLF movement and its "welfare state" supporters in the government. The English, Dutch and Ontario materials in particular show how the bar's position may shift in response to the perceived failures of judicare and the growing pressures for reform. First came the suggestion that increased judicare compensation would take care of the unmet need. Second came the recognition that some staff component would be necessary, preferably limited to legal advice. And finally, at least in England, the Law Society recognized the need to continue and provide stable funding to the existing NLFs. Of course, the bar seeks to protect its judicare incomes every step of the way, for example, by the "waiver" agreement which the Law Society and the law centers reached, but it is notable that the bar feels compelled to propose and lobby for a series of reforms designed to make the legal aid system capable of meeting the poor's legal needs.

A question that cannot yet be answered is how far this concern with image will go outside of the United States. In the United States the American Bar Association, as already noted, strongly defended a very controversial program. The success and survival of the program became identified with the interests of the ABA in making the legal system work better for the poor. It remains to be seen how much affirmative support the Law Society in England, for example, would give to neighborhood law centers under similar conditions. The Law Society now recognizes the need for the law centers, but it is doubtful that it believes that their survival is vital to the Law Society's interests. It is clear, however, that the bar's interests are not just financial, and the interest in improving the public image of the legal system and lawyers' activities has played an important role in the organized professions' reactions to NLFs.

IV. The Continuing NLF Movement

In fifteen years the NLF movement has come very far, and further developments can certainly be expected. Already the *boutiques de droit* in Paris suggest that the French will follow a similar pattern. Without attempting to predict the future extension of the NLF movement, it might be helpful to summarize what factors appear to have made it such a contagious idea in these countries in recent years.

140

First, all these countries can be considered welfare states, with the government committed to ameliorating the situation of those who cannot succeed on their own in the market economic system. Second, the relevant actors and activists in the NLF history believe in change through law, implying both that such change is possible within the existing legal and constitutional arrangements and that sufficient change can be effected within these existing arrangements. Third, there is a well-developed legal profession, typically growing very quickly and composed therefore of many who are relatively young. Fourth, the welfare state in these countries contemplates state intervention to mobilize the target groups of governmental policy to ensure that they obtain the benefits of the policy. This allows the development of concepts such as that of "legal need," which can be invoked to justify state action. Fifth, the reformist and proactive orientations promote sociological research that is policy oriented but tries to avoid being partisan. It fosters relatively uncontroversial, pragmatic reform. Sixth, despite the general prosperity of these countries since the Second World War, there are important segments of the society, particulary racial and ethnic minorities, who have not been integrated into the economic system. Such groups can be and have been disruptive, particularly in urban areas, and a function of reform is to prevent such disruption. Seventh, these countries are experiencing some scarcity of public funds for social programs. NLFs are a very visible reform that does not really cost very much when compared to other social programs.

Perhaps other characteristics shared by these countries and relevant to NLFs could be enumerated. The list does not seek to explain the details of national developments which, it can be seen, have owed much to the particular power and characteristics of the legal profession and liberal or labor governments. Nevertheless, it is clear that the NLF idea has taken hold in welfare states fitting the above description, and as this chapter shows, the idea has great staying power for an often controversial antipoverty program.

The blending of the zeal of young legal activists, the plans of welfare state governments, and the interests of professional associations has therefore produced a variety of legal aid schemes with NLF components. The United States and Saskatchewan presently have the least involvement of the private profession (through judicare) in the legal aid programs studied; while the result in Australia was (at least temporarily) an almost complete defeat for the publicly-salaried NLF movement. In between are a variety of "combined models," some resulting in formal political independence and with statutory form and others, most notably those of England, Belgium,

Holland, and Ontario, still awaiting a new legal aid law. While public funds may become scarcer and the conservative reaction to social programs develop further, we still can expect the NLF idea to continue to spread and gain legitimacy.

Part Three

The Strategies and Methods of Neighborhood Law Firms

Introduction

Partisans of neighborhood law firms, armed with persuasive sociological studies, insisted that NLFs could undertake a number of essential activities for the poor. First, they could be set up in poverty areas and made attractive to residents of poor neighborhoods. This would enable them to reach the poor, bring them into the legal system, and provide the legal representation essential to make the poor's new welfare state rights effective. By enforcing those rights—above all consumer rights, rights to decent housing, and social welfare rights— NLFs could contribute toward putting the welfare state's ideals into practice.

Second, NLFs could play a leading role in reforming the law on behalf of the poor. Poor people's lawyers would be uniquely situated to learn the legal problems of the poor and to propose new remedies. The advocacy powers of lawyers would counterbalance the powerful advocates of corporate and governmental interests. These powers would be utilized principally in test cases, where legal reasoning is most important, but legislative reforms would be promoted as well. In these ways lawyers would be able to better the position of poor people as a class. Combined with efforts to make laws favorable to the poor effective, this strategy could turn the NLF institution into a powerful weapon in the fight against poverty.

A third strategy, the bolstering, or even organizing of neighborhood interest groups, does not follow quite so neatly from legal need studies, but it has always been part of the NLF arsenal. If lawyers take seriously their assignments in the war on poverty, they will often turn to strategies which will develop local groups. Such organized groups can monitor the impact of laws in the community, refer their members to lawyers when necessary, and push for legislative or administrative reforms at the local level. Sometimes this strategy is stated boldly in pragmatic, nonlegal terms: to help the poor, you must organize them to give them political power.

143

"Community education," a fourth category of NLF activity, complements the preceding ones. NLF lawyers are to be "proactive," meaning that they affirmatively alert the poor of their rights and their possibilities to improve themselves through legal action. Community education is the effort to reach out, and it can encompass numerous types of activities. It is convenient, therefore, to treat this general topic after the previous three in order to first suggest the basic ends for which community education can be designed—meeting individual needs, bringing test cases, or bolstering groups.

A fifth strategy or method of NLFs is to involve the poor in the program's operation. This aim is often ambiguous and in one sense is less relevant to what NLFs affirmatively do for the poor. But this participation theme is an increasingly strong one in the NLF movement, and it has taken on the characteristics of an affirmative strategy to help the poor. Moreover, an examination of the activities of NLFs just described raises serious policy dilemmas. The choice of strategies can be very difficult and controversial. The question then becomes who ought to decide these policy issues—the government, the funding agencies, professional bar associations, NLF lawyers, or the client community. A growing concern is for the poor to have the most responsibility in determining how their legal needs should be met.

The balance of the operating methods selected has a fundamental impact on a NLF's orientation and effectiveness. It affects decisions about the location of NLF offices, such as how decentralized and accessible they should be. It may determine issues of staffing, including the number of lawyers versus paraprofessionals or community workers. And, of course, it sets the priorities for the work of the NLF staff. The following three chapters will examine these basic strategies, suggest what they mean in practice, and subject them to some critical scrutiny. After that is done, a concluding chapter to this Part will discuss how these strategies have been combined and some implications of these combinations. This will prepare the way for the more general conclusion in Part Four which, among other things, will address the question of whether the NLF movement, given the limitations of its various strategies, is developing into a lasting force for change on behalf of the underprivileged, or whether, despite strong pronouncements and protestations to the contrary, it is having little meaningful impact.

Chapter 8

Individual Services: Meeting the Legal Needs
of the Poor

I. The Importance of Individual Casework

Traditional legal aid programs, whether charitable or judicare, have been heavily criticized, partly because they failed to satisfy the poor's "unmet legal needs." Those needs, as noted in Part One, arise above all in new areas of the law designed to benefit the poor in their capacities as tenants, consumers, unemployed persons, or simply as poor people needing social welfare benefits. The social laws were not being enforced, and only new methods of legal aid could remedy the situation. NLFs were designed to be geographically and culturally accessible, able to reach these needy poor persons and help them vindicate their rights and obtain their welfare state entitlements.

While policy makers have supported other NLF activities, there is no doubt that much of the program's current legitimacy depends on satisfying or appearing to satisfy this unmet need. It is also clear that, with a few notable exceptions, most programs spend the largest part of their time on individual cases.

In the United States, for example, while there is some controversy about how much time is spent on individual services versus law reform in a project, the debate is a relatively narrow one. The most conservative estimate is that 70–80 percent of a program's time is spent on individual cases (Hollingsworth, 1977:307; Handler et al., 1978:52–63),[1] and the average attorney still handles some five hundred cases per year (Legal Services Corporation, 1978:18).[2] Moreover, the importance to policymakers of these individual cases—especially those concerning the unmet legal need mentioned above—is evident from the approach taken by the Legal Services Corporation over the past several years. The Corporation has been emphasizing the goal of reaching as many as possible of the poor's estimated seven million annual *individual* legal problems, "involving housing law, consumer law, family law, and administrative benefits" (Legal Services Corporation, 1978:7–8). This goal necessarily implies a commitment to utilizing the program's resources to servicing *those* problems in increasing numbers.

145

In England the situation is similar, even if law centers are increasingly seeking to avoid individual work. Individual work has to date been essential to the centers' popular success. The Law Society, for example, respects the law centers primarily for their "expertise in certain specialized fields such as housing and welfare law" (Law Society, 1977:204). The Law Centres Working Group has further pointed out:

> The popular image of Centres is as principally casework agencies; these are the models which funding agencies most readily accept and tend to opt for in new areas. Central government, too, inclines towards this model by insisting that individual Centres make up an ever-increasing amount of their budgets through use of the legal aid system on individual cases (Law Centres Working Group, 1977:29).

Canadian examples also support the importance of a substantial individual casework component of NLFs. For Saskatchewan "the meeting of the immediate legal needs of the poor remains the first priority" (Saskatchewan Community Legal Services Commission, 1976:14), and in Quebec it may be recalled that the problems of some local NLFs stem from the imposition by the central *Commission des services juridiques* of difficult minimum caseload standards.

In Australia individual casework was practically the only activity of the federal Australian Legal Aid Office, and in Holland individual advice takes up most of a typical law shop's time. Without belaboring the point, it is obvious that meeting the immediate needs of the poor is generally considered vital for NLFs—by themselves and by the relevant policy makers. The interesting but difficult question, which will be discussed in the following chapter, is how much the legitimacy of NLFs is tied to this individual casework.

II. Eligibility Requirements and the Needs of the Poor

Before seeing what kinds of legal needs law centers meet in practice, it is useful to look briefly at what needs they are permitted to address. This involves examining the eligibility requirements and policies of NLFs, which are summarized in Table 1. Most of the meaningful prohibitions, such as that on fee-generating cases where contingent fees are available, are designed to avoid competition with the private bar. The long list in England is to protect the judicare income of private solicitors, who depend on their subsidized fees from divorces and criminal cases. Table 1 also shows the peculiar "federal law" limitation in Australia, which may have been required by the Constitution, and it indicates the politically unpopular cases that the U.S. Congress sought to prevent legal services lawyers from taking.

146

The most important contrast in Table 1 is that between the English approach to eligibility and those of the other NLF legal aid and advice programs. The English law centers set no formal poverty line but instead use only a geographic one. Persons living outside the boundaries of the law center's target area are generally turned away, even if poorer than the clients who are served. The English approach seems odd if one is seeking primarily to meet individual legal needs of the poor. Resources should presumably be allocated to the "neediest," and that allocation should not depend on where they live (see Zander, 1978.94–100). The English centers, however, seek to help certain geographically-defined *communities* rather than poor individuals. This is a basic characteristic of the English law centers, and it will be seen throughout the discussion of NLF strategies in this part. It is one way to ease the problem caused by the inevitable choice between serving all the needy and trying to develop into effective proponents of community change for the poor.

III. How the Need is Met in Practice: NLFs vs. Judicare (or Charitable) Legal Aid Systems

The assertion is often made that judicare or charitable legal aid systems cannot match NLFs in reaching poor persons with legal problems in nontraditional areas, i.e., the areas of unmet need. We can examine the validity of this point roughly by comparing reported caseloads. The question we must consider is, given that NLFs spend much of their time on individual casework, is this the type of casework that would not normally be brought to a lawyer in private practice (even if the lawyer would be willing to take the case if subsidized by the state)? Obviously, the answer is important for NLFs and their "legal need" justification.

Tables 2 to 8 summarize the available data from the United States (Table 2), England and Wales (Table 3), Quebec (Table 4), Saskatchewan (Table 5), Australia (Table 6), the Netherlands (Table 7), and France (Table 8). To these tables may be added three further items: (1) In Manitoba, where 90 percent of the civil legal aid cases for the scheme in general are matrimonial, the comparable percentage for the community law offices was 65 percent (with 17.5 percent of the remainder involving representation before tribunals (Legal Aid Service Society of Manitoba, 1975:4–5); (2) the judicare system in the Federal Republic of Germany handles almost exclusively family matters (Council of Europe, 1977:150); and (3) Swedish data indicate that staff legal aid lawyers handle *more* divorce cases (81 percent) than compensated private lawyers (65 percent) (Hellners,

Table 1. *Eligibility Requirements and Policies of NLFs*

	Statutory or official prohibitions of individual cases	Eligibility requirements for individuals
U.S.	Fee-generating cases; criminal cases; action for the desegregation of schools cases; litigation for a "nontherapeutic" abortion; military deserters or draft evaders[a]	Roughly income 125 percent of official poverty line (e.g., 1976, $6,874 per family of four; 1977, $7,250)[b]; may also be a geographic limit
England	With some general exceptions, divorce cases; conveyancing; commercial matters; probate matters, except personal applications involving small estates; criminal matters where defendant is over 21 years old[c]	No formal means test but generally limit clients to "catchment area"; most will not act for landlords[d]
Canada		
Manitoba	Certain fee-generating cases; actions for breach of marriage promise; actions for alienation of affections, etc.; actions for criminal conversation[e]	Family of four (1976) $8,175 (Canadian dollars)[f]
Quebec	Action for defamation, libel; action for breach of marriage promise; action for alienation of affections; certain fee-generating cases; cases concerning parking violations[g]	Family of four (1976) $8,060 (Canadian dollars)[h]

148

Table 1 (*continued*)

	Statutory of official prohibitions of individual cases	Eligibility requirements for individuals
Saskatchewan	Fee-generating cases[i]	When person received social assistance or would be eligible if required to pay costs of an attorney[j]
Australia (ALAO)	Allowed only for federal law matters, and assistance generally to pensioners, military personnel and dependents, aborigines, migrants, and others to whom the federal government owes a special duty[k]	Family of four, $4,420 "disposable income" (Australian dollars)[l]
Holland	Law shops, none;	Informal; most will not represent landlords
	Bureau voor rechtschulp (advice only)	Apparently no limitations[m]

[a] Legal Services Corporation Act of 1974, §1007(b), as amended by Legal Services Corporation Act Amendments of 1977, Public Law No. 95-222. The amendments eliminated a general ban on representing juveniles, also modified slightly the prohibition on representing persons charged with evasion of the draft, and allowed legal advice in school desegregation cases.

[b] 45 CFR §1611 (effective 23 December 1976); Legal Services Corporation, *Annual Report 1977*, at 8, 16 (Washington, D.C., 1978).

[c] See "Waivers of the Solicitors Practice Rules 1936–72 for Law Centres and Similar Organizations," 75 *Law Society's Gazette* 698 (1977). The centers may nevertheless handle such cases in situations of emergency or where private practitioners are unavailable. The waivers represent an agreement under the auspices of the Lord Chancellor's Office but have no statutory force.

(*Continued on following page*)

1976:93). The summaries must be taken with some caution, given differences in reporting and the absence of information about relative time and resource commitments. Nevertheless, the figures are rather dramatic; they suggest strongly that, in contrast to judicare legal aid systems, NLFs—although, as the Swedish example shows, not necessarily all public legal aid offices—are reaching significant numbers of people with problems in nontraditional areas of the law. Judicare systems, whether or not supplemented by NLFs, succeed mainly in attracting family and criminal matters.

The contrast in England and in the Netherlands, given that NLFs and judicare exist side by side, is particularly notable. In England, despite differences between individual law centers, it is clear that law centers undertake mostly individual work concerning the rights of tenants, followed by varying degrees of involvement in consumer and social welfare problems (see also Zander and Russell, 1975:726). These are the areas of the so-called unmet need. The English civil legal aid and advice schemes, in sharp contrast, are overwhelmingly dominated by family matters. The figures for the Netherlands are equally persuasive.

To give meaning to this comparison, it is necessary to know why NLFs succeed better than judicare systems in reaching this "unmet

---

(*Continued from previous page*)

[d] See Zander and Russell, "Law Centres' Survey," 73 *Law Society's Gazette* 726 (1975) (answers to questions 30, 33, 34).

[e] Regulations Under the Legal Aid Services Society of Manitoba Act, *Manitoba Regulations* 106/72, as amended by *M.R.* 12/73, 146/73, 235/73, 58/74, and 78/74, §§29, 21(1).

[f] See Legal Aid Service Society of Manitoba, *Annual Report 1976*, at 14 (Winnipeg, 1976). Those somewhat over the limit may receive services by making a contribution.

[g] Regulations under the Legal Aid Act (Quebec), §3.19.

[h] Regulations under the Legal Aid Act (Quebec), §3.14.

[i] Community Legal Services (Saskatchewan) Act of 1974, §3.

[j] The latter category may have to make a contribution. Regulations Made Under the Community Legal Services (Saskatchewan) Act, §2.

[k] Directive of the Attorney General, Lionel Murphy, Establishing the Australian Legal Aid Office, 6 September 1973, §5(a).

[l] Australian Legal Aid Office, "Means and Needs Test and Contributions Change in Guidelines," in J. Disney, J. Basten, P. Redmond, and S. Ross, *Lawyers* 409–10 (Sydney, The Law Book Company, Ltd., 1977).

[m] See B. Garth, Legal Aid at the Local Level in the Netherlands and Norway: A Report to the Florence Access-to-Justice Project (4 July 1977).

Table 2. Caseloads for Legal Aid in the United States

Caseload	1967[a] Traditional programs	1967[b] OEO	1967[d] OEO	1971[e] OEO	1972[g] OEO	1977[h] OEO
Family	35.0	29.7	30.4	36.6	21.7	29.2
Consumer and debt	17.5	14.1	24.1	15.9	21.6	13.7
Landlord–tenant	7.5	10.5	18.2	14.4	23.3	17.8
Welfare and other problems with government	9.2	14.4	6.2	11.2	12.2	17.6
Others	30.8	31.3	21.1	21.9	21.2	21.7
Total number	–	350,000[c]	–	1.2 million[f]	–	1.2 million

[a] K. Fisher and C. Ivie, *Franchising Justice: The Office of Economic Opportunity Legal Services Program and Traditional Legal Aid* 10 (Chicago, American Bar Foundation, 1971).

[b] Id.

[c] Note, "Legal Services—Past and Present," 59 *Cornell Law Review* 967 (1968).

[d] J. Handler, E. Hollingsworth, and H. Erlanger, *Lawyers and the Pursuit of Rights* 52 (Madison, Wis., Institute for Research on Poverty, 1978).

[e] National Legal Aid and Defender Association, *1971 Statistics of Legal Assistance Work* iv (Chicago, 1971).

[f] Note, note c above

[g] J. Handler et al, note d above.

[h] Legal Services Corporation, *Annual Report 1977*, at 16 (Washington, D.C., 1978).

151

Table 3. Caseloads for Legal Aid in England and Wales

Caseload	Civil legal aid scheme 1975/76[a]	Civil legal advice scheme 1975/76[b]	Civil legal aid scheme 1976/77[c]	Civil legal advice scheme 1976/77[d]	Adamsdown Law Centre (18 mos. ending 12/31/76)[e]	Balham Neighbourhood Law Centre (Year ending 3/77)	
						Advice	Action[f]
Divorce and family	86%	56.8%	85%	56.4%	–	16.4%	16.2%
Landlord–tenant	N.A.	4.7%	N.A.	4.6%	28 %	34.4%	36.3%
Social welfare	N.A.	N.A.	N.A.	N.A.	32 %	7.0%	8.0%
Consumer	N.A.	3.4%	N.A.	3.3%	8 %	10.5%	4.4%
Employment	N.A.	N.A.	N.A.	0.9%	3 %	7.3%	6.6%
Other	14%	20.8%		20.0%	26 %	7.9%	12.3%
Criminal	handled under Home Office	14.3%	15%	14.8%	3 %	16.5%	16.2%
Number of cases	207,977	–		291,961	974	5,680	1,284

a Lord Chancellor's Office, *26th Legal Aid Annual Reports* [1975–76] 16 (London, H.M.S.O., 1976).
b Id. at 18.
c Lord Chancellor's Office, *27th Legal Aid Annual Reports* [1976–77] 25 (London, H.M.S.O., 1978).
d Id. at 21.
e Adamsdown Community Trust, *Community Need and Law Centre Practice: An Empirical Assessment* 78 (Adamsdown, Cardiff, 1978) (simple advice not included).
f Balham Neighbourhood Law Centre, *Into the Community: Annual Report April 1976–March 1977*, at 3 (London, 1977).

Table 3 (*continued*)

Caseload	Brent Community Law Centre (year ending 3/77)[g]	Camden Community Law Centre (year ending 3/77)[h]	Hackney Law Centre (5/76 to 3/77)[i]	Hillingdon Community Law Centre (10/20/65–12/31/76)[j]	Islington Community Law Centre (year ending 8/74)[k]
Divorce and family	7.2%	13%	5.2%	17.9%	3.8%
Landlord–tenant	34.9%	40%	49.6%	14.4%	53.4%
Social welfare	N.A.	6%	4.6%	7.3%	4.5%
Consumer	28.1%	N.A.	3.9%	7.8%	8.7%
Employment	17.2%	13%	16.6%	14.6%	6.5%
Other	2.3%	22%	14.3%	31.5%	8.5%
Criminal	10.3%	6%	5.8%	6.5%	14.6%
Number of cases	608	1,067	931	1,604	1,423

g Brent Community Law Centre, *Report January 1978*, Appendix at xiii (London, 1978) (simple advice not included, consumer includes tort).

h Camden Community Law Centre, *Annual Report 1976–77 7* (London 1977) (includes only cases taken).

i *Annual Report of Hackney Advice Bureau and Law Centre* 13 (London, 1977).

j Hillingdon Community Law Centre, *Annual Report 1975–76*, at 10 (London, 1976) (figure includes 909 cases dealt with in one interview).

k Islington Community Law Centre, *Report '74*, at 2 (London, 1975) (includes only ongoing cases).

153

Table 3 (*continued*)

Caseload	Newham Rights Centre (year ending 3/77)[l]	N. Kensington Neighborhood Law Centre (1975)[m]	Paddington Law Centre (year to 3/76)[n]	Small Heath Community Law Centre (1/77 to 6/77)[o]	Vauxhall Community Law Centre (year ending 6/76)[p]
Divorce and family	5.1%	2.1%	3%	3.3%	1%
Landlord–tenant	32.3%	20.3%	48%	37.8%	34%
Social welfare	22.9%	0.6%	2%	28.4%	4%
Consumer	4.5%	6.7%	7%	6.1%	16%
Employment	7.6%	6.4%	7%	5.9%	7%
Other	23.0%	14.3%	12%	14.4%	25%
Criminal	4.6%	49.6%	21%	4.1%	13%
Number of cases	846	796	816	917	439

[l] Newham Rights Centre, *Two Years Work 1975–1977: Lousy Houses and Dole Queues* (London, 1977).

[m] North Kensington Neighbourhood Law Centre, *Annual Report 1975*, at 5 (London, 1976) (number of files opened).

[n] Paddington Neighbourhood Advice Bureau and Law Centre, *Annual Report 1976*, at 35 (London, 1976).

[o] Small Heath Community Law Centre, *First Annual Report 1976–77*, at 41 (Birmingham, 1977) (appears to include simple advice).

[p] *Third Annual Report of the Vauxhall Community Law Centre, June 1975–June 1976*, at 13 (Liverpool, 1976) (includes only cases retained).

Table 4. *The Caseload of Quebec's Combined Model*

Caseload	Salaried advocates (year ending 31 March, 1977)[a]	Advocates in private practice (same year)[b]
Family	22.3%	38.5%
Other civil	42.7%	21.2%
Criminal	35.0%	40.3%
Number of cases	113,325	35,826

Commission des services juridiques, *5th Annual Report 31 March 1977*, at 35 (Quebec, 1977)

[b] Id. at 36.

Table 5. *The Caseload of the Saskatchewan Area Offices (Year Ending 31 March 1976)*

Family	20.6%
Consumer	4.8%
Social welfare	8.4%
Landlord–tenant	3%
Labor	1%
Other	24.1%
Criminal	38.1%
Number of cases	15,546

Source: The Saskatchewan Community Legal Services Commission, *Second Annual Report 1975–1976*, at 10–13 (Saskatoon, 1976).

Table 6. *Australian Caseloads*

Caseload	ALAO[a]	Victoria Judicare[b]
Family	36%	52%
Landlord–tenant	6%	N.A.
Consumer	6%	N.A.
Social welfare	2%	N.A.
Other	39%	21%
Criminal	11%	27%

[a] Based on a sample for June 1975. The number of matrimonial matters has since increased. J. Disney, J. Basten, P. Redmond, and S. Ross, *Lawyers* 400 (Sydney, The Law Book Company, Ltd., 1977).

[b] Id.

Table 7. *The Netherlands—Civil Legal Aid and Advice Caseloads*

Caseload	Judicare scheme[a]	Law shops[b]	Amsterdam law shop 1974[c]	Amsterdam advice bureau (Jan.–June 1975)[d]
Family	60–70%	Under 20%	15.1%	56.0%
Landlord–tenant	N.A.	N.A.	27.2%	25.9%
Consumer	N.A.	20%	N.A.	N.A.
Social and economic law	10–15%	40%	11.0%	N.A.
Labor	N.A.	N.A.	14.0%	3.5%
Other	N.A.	20%	32.7%	14.6%
Number of cases	80,000 (1974)		60,000	5,730

[a] From the Schuyt, Groenendijk, and Sloot study, cited in Griffiths, "The Distribution of Legal Services in the Netherlands," 4 *British Journal of Law and Society* 260, 262 (1977).

[b] Id. (the reference is only to advice).

[c] Council of Europe, Committee of Experts on Economic and Other Obstacles to Civil Proceedings Inter Alia Abroad, *Replies Made by Governments to the Questionnaire on Legal Aid and Advice* 184 (Strasbourg, 1977) (again only legal advice was given).

[d] Id. The Amsterdam Advice Bureau, the *Bureau voor rechtschulp*, also handles legal aid certificates under judicare. Thus, of the 5,730 cases, 2,691 resulted in the designation of a lawyer or bailiff. Only 1,814 persons, in fact, were advised by the staff personnel. Id. at 185.

Table 8. *French Judicare (1973)*

Family	70%
Landlord–tenant	10%
Social welfare	N.A.
Contract	5%
Civil responsibility	13%
Other	2%

Source: M. Valetas, *Aide judiciaire et accès á la justice* 23 (Paris, CREDOC, 1976).

156

legal need." What characteristics of NLFs enable them to reach this need, and could other institutions duplicate those characteristics? A few general reasons for NLF success have already been suggested, particularly in Chapter 1. First, persons tend not to go to lawyers except for problems that have traditionally been considered "legal" or where lawyers by law are required to obtain a given remedy. Examples are divorces, criminal defense, and certain property matters. Judicare does not correct for this natural tendency. To this may be added a typical bias of judicare systems against legal actions in the new areas of the law.

This bias originates in the method of determining judicare eligibility. Judicare systems must have some test of reasonableness in deciding whether to allow legal aid in an individual case (see e.g., Cappelletti et al., 1975:93–95). It is evident that the cost of judicare (and perhaps staff systems as well) would be prohibitive if qualified individuals could sue at public expense anytime they chose to do so. Some criteria must be set, and judicare systems, by definition seeking to give a poor *individual* the same services as a person able to afford legal services, tend to take a particular approach to criteria setting.

The English test, for example, is whether a "hypothetical paying client" would bring the legal action. An obvious problem is that many of the legal needs in new areas of law involve small amounts in controversy that would not be litigated by a reasonable middle-class person. Consumer problems, social welfare problems, and the like tend to involve relatively small amounts of money. A reasonable person will not retain a lawyer for them because the legal fees (or risk of paying such fees) would be higher than the expected recovery. An excellent empirical study of judicare in Birmingham thus concluded that the English test created a serious bias against many legal problems of the poor:

> First, use of this model means that middle-class standards as to what is reasonable are imposed on cases involving persons who are by definition among the poorer members of the community. In other words, legal aid committees are required to make a difficult and at times inappropriate comparison across class lines.... Second, to the extent that the hypothetical paying client is identified with *homo economicus*, the question of fruitless litigation tends to be decided without account being taken of the less tangible, nonfinancial interests that any applicant may have in taking legal proceedings. A third and closely related effect ... is that regard is had only to the interests of the individual applicant to the exclusion of the wider community interest that might be involved in the case (Bridges et al., 1975:159).

NLF programs, with their ideological mandate to help the poor *as a class*, can modify standards in individual cases. The criteria of reasonableness need not be middle-class ones. The reform commission in Saskatchewan, for example, expressly mentioned the type of "reasonableness" test which they felt NLFs should use: "'[R]easonable' is not to be judged by comparing the cash value of the services with the cash value of the result. The criterion must be the seriousness of the case or problem to the particular individual" (see Saskatchewan Community Legal Services Commission, 1975:34). The aim is to help the poor even if a middle-class person with the same problem might not seek legal assistance.

Given that NLFs will generally serve problems that might not be eligible for judicare services, there is still the question of what it is about NLFs in practice that breaks down barriers to access and attracts persons with nontraditional legal problems. Clearly the geographic accessibility of NLFs located in poor communities is one factor. Community education programs, discussed below, also contribute. According to a recent empirical study of the Adamsdown Law Centre in Wales, however, the most important factor is the "image" of the center (Adamsdown Community Trust, 1978:40–49). The image is what the members of the local community come to think about the law center and its availability to help them with certain types of problems.[3]

According to the Adamsdown study, people will generally take legal problems to helping agencies like law centers if such an agency is *known to them* and *perceived as useful* to the particular type of problem. The basic barrier to access is in identifying the relevant agency. According to the study, "once an agency has been identified, all of them are about as likely to be reached as one another" (1978:49). Given that finding, the success of the law center in attracting people stems from its ability: (1) to break down the narrow image people hold of lawyers and the law; and (2) to convince potential clients that the law center can help them with a wide range of problems not normally thought to be legal. The law center does this primarily through its affirmative involvement with the community and through word-of-mouth communication as the center's contacts increase.[4] The center can, through its expansive use of legal skills, reach the community and convince its members of the law center's utility.

Private lawyers could conceivably change their image too. Indeed, it is plausible to expect that financial incentives would lead private practitioners to a new type of practice and a corresponding new image. To date, however, this has not happened despite efforts to create such incentives. The 1972 £25 advice scheme in England has thus far failed to attract many nontraditional problems to private solicitors (see Table 3). The Adamsdown report is accordingly very skeptical about the prospect for change:

158

> Minor amendments of the financial, geographical or work pattern barriers to the use of private practice will not … create the new image that is necessary if people are to receive help on a proper basis. Such a strategy would represent an attempt to manipulate one minor part of the image of private practitioners. Our own assessment of the necessary strategies is that Law Centres can provide a distinctly different image and that they are the agencies most likely to have the capacity and outlook to project that new image (Adamsdown Community Trust, 1978:45–46).

While the statement is no doubt presented from the perspective of the law center, it is consistent with the comparative data here presented. The claim of legal sociologists that NLFs would be superior to private attorneys in reaching potential clients with nontraditional legal problems appears to have been substantiated. This is no doubt a vital reason for the institutional successes of NLFs and a leading rationale for their continued existence.

IV. Approaches to Utilizing NLFs for Individual Cases

NLFs have important advantages over judicare in reaching and helping persons with unenforced welfare state rights. There are several ways, however, that these advantages can be utilized to meet this latent demand for individual services, and the differences merit some attention. Three organizational methods will be considered here: (1) the strictly NLF model (at least for civil cases) in the United States and Saskatchewan; (2) the combined models exemplified by Quebec and, at a less formal level, England; and (3) a third approach which aims to reduce the need for lawyers to vindicate the new rights at the individual level.

A. The NLF Model by Itself

An exclusive reliance on NLFs to service individuals poses at least one serious problem. Legal services, whether provided by NLFs or private practitioners, attract family matters, especially divorces and related actions, more easily than other civil problems. Both the U.S. and Saskatchewan NLF programs as a result have had to handle a relatively high percentage of family matters, usually divorces. For Saskatchewan (Table 5) about 33 percent of civil cases involve family problems, while for the United States (Table 2) the most conservative figure is 21.7 percent, with more realistic figures around 30 percent. In addition, one reason for the relative decline in family matter cases in the United States was a conscious policy implemented locally to limit the number of such cases. The program had been criticized as a

159

"divorce mill" for the poor, and there was an effort to shift the caseload toward other problems (see Handler et al., 1978:52–54). Under the pure NLF system, however, it is not easy nor even necessarily desirable to turn to other problems.

Reducing the burden of divorces and the like tends to require NLFs to restrict the intake of such problems. Otherwise family matters will inevitably take a considerable amount of the NLF's time and resources, and the NLF may reach relatively few persons with nontraditional problems. The difficulty with cutting the family caseload, however, is that family problems can still be urgent and important, even if they seem to have relatively little to do with the new welfare state rights which are more associated with NLF services. To turn away divorces is to neglect an individual problem of vital personal importance. NLFs must therefore face a real dilemma if they wish to concentrate their energies on vindicating new rights (or, for that matter, on any of the other NLF activities beyond individual casework). This dilemma can be solved to an extent by the "combined models" discussed below.

B. Combining NLFs and Judicare

Combined judicare-NLF models are often praised because they can provide clients with a choice of a staff lawyer or private practitioner, and because the involvement of the private bar may make it possible to give legal aid as a right. These characteristics of a combined model are extremely important, as Professor Cappelletti and others have noted (Cappelletti, 1974). From the perspective of this study, however, another characteristic of the combined model merits attention. NFL lawyers in a combined system can leave a large number of family matters to private practitioners and concentrate on the new areas of law to which NFLs evidently are uniquely suited. The same is true, it should be noted, for criminal cases, which can also be handled by the private bar. Criminal cases made up a very large percentage of the Saskatchewan caseload (see Table 5), although they are not handled by NLFs in the United States. If it is true that family (and criminal) cases are the first to be brought to lawyers, including NLFs, and that those matters then take up a substantial portion of NLF resources, then the implementation of the proactive "image building" necessary to reach nontraditional problems may require that an alternative means be developed to handle the more traditional cases. Judicare is the logical alternative, since judicare systems clearly can attract traditional cases (see Tables 3, 6, 7, 8).

One way to combine judicare and NLFs is found in Quebec, where

160

clients can choose a private lawyer if they want. The data (Table 4) suggest that this creates a natural division of labor between private lawyers and NLFs. Private lawyers are chosen relatively more frequently than staff lawyers for family and criminal matters. As could be expected, the private practitioners evidently attract clients mainly in traditional areas of the law. This acts to reduce the caseload in these areas for the NLF attorneys. Nevertheless, staff NLF lawyers must handle family or criminal matters in 57.3 percent of the cases they take. This burden is a very substantial one, and it may be that a reduction in those traditional areas would be helpful to enable the NLF to reach people whose problems are more difficult to reach. From the point of view of "unmet needs," one can thus ask whether the element of choice in the combined system is overburdening the NLFs with matters that private attorneys could handle.

A different type of combined NLF-judicare model is that which has been created for the time being by the "waiver agreement" in England and which has been proposed for Ontario by the Osler Committee. This involves a more explicit division of labor. The Osler Report, for example, advocated the creation of a combined legal aid model, but it gave less of an emphasis to free choice than was seen for Quebec:

> [A]ny neighbourhood legal aid clinic may be given special priorities in its community.... Such priorities might require restrictions on the kind of work for which the clinic will be available, emphasis on particular clientele or specialized projects... (1974:54).

It generally recommended that "divorce, matrimonial work and conventional criminal and civil litigation should continue wherever possible and where the applicant so desires to be conducted by the private Bar" (1974:55). This proposal corresponds roughly to that sanctioned by the waiver agreement in England (see Table 1). Traditional legal matters will be left with the private profession, while NLFs seek to reach another set of problems.

This more formal division of labor offers definite advantages to both the private bar and the NLFs. It eliminates the main possibility for competition between the two programs, thus cutting down on private lawyer hostility to NLFs. Most importantly, from the legal need point of view, it maximizes the likelihood that lawyers will concentrate on individual cases in nontraditional areas of the law (and on other innovative activities). There are, of course, also some disadvantages to this model. For example, there is the problem of whether eliminating or severely restricting choice is desirable. This problem, however, could be minimized by a flexible arrangement whereby most cases would be channeled to the appropriate type of service, but clients could overcome this initial assignment. In England, in fact, the boundaries are not strict either way, and someone unhappy with a law center can always turn to a private lawyer. Also, a healthy competition between the public and private bar, rather than a division of the labor, might help raise the standards of both parts of the profession. Nevertheless, the values of choice and competition must be carefully weighed against the possibility that NLFs will be prevented from doing the work which they are best suited to undertake.

C. Beyond Combining NLFs and Judicare—Meeting Legal Needs Without Lawyers

A recurring theme for lawyers, legal sociologists, and policy makers has been that NLFs are necessary because of the "underutilization" of lawyers in matters concerning new welfare state rights. The comparison with judicare adds plausibility to that contention. The effort to make the new rights effective, however, can be taken beyond the call for a new type of legal aid. The problem may not be due so much to the underutilization of lawyers as to the overformality of the judicial system. A variety of less-formal, nonlawyer methods may be used to meet the same individual legal needs (see generally Cappelletti and Garth, 1978:1–123). These various methods going beyond legal aid need not be examined at length here, but the relevance of these reforms to the NLF movement must be considered.

The "unmet needs" of the poor, as has been noted, tend to involve areas of the law such as social welfare, consumer, creditor–debtor, and landlord–tenant areas. Violations of rights in these matters usually involve relatively small amounts of money. Claims to remedy these violations in the countries here studied are made increasingly in special administrative tribunals, small claims courts, and the like. The reasons for this trend include the following: lawyers cannot as a practical matter handle the vast number of problems in these fields; it is expensive to devote the services of relatively high-priced lawyers to these numerous small claims; and there is no reason to depend on lawyers if ways can be found to make rights effective without lawyers. A few examples of recent activity will illustrate this kind of reform.

The Rentalsman in British Columbia, introduced in 1974, has jurisdiction over virtually all landlord–tenant problems in that province (see Cappelletti and Garth, 1978:100–02). The officers of the Rentalsman investigate the problems and seek to bring the parties to an amicable solution. The solution, however, is supposed to be one consistent with the intent of new legislation that is much more favorable to tenants than previous law. An enforceable decision can also be made but is rarely necessary. According to Canadian observers, the Rentalsman system is working to make tenants' new rights effective; it has "effectively reoriented the landlord–tenant relationship" in British Columbia (see Cooper and Kastner, 1978:293–95). Considering that lawyers are reportedly involved in less than one percent of the matters handled by the Rentalsman office, this is a very important conclusion. Other specialized housing courts may be able to duplicate this evident success in landlord–tenant matters.

Another important example of reform involves certain small claims courts, such as the one established in 1972 in the Harlem district of New York City, a very poor minority community (see Johnson et al., 1978:946–50). The court is open on certain evenings as well as during the day, is very informal, and persons who wish to make or defend a claim are given considerable assistance by "community advocates." These advocates, in addition, act to make the court and its methods known in the Harlem community. This affirmatively builds an "image" reminiscent of that sought by the Adamsdown Law Centre. Courts, Rentalsman, and the like can also reach out to the community if properly designed and responsive to community needs.

Beyond the creation of new dispute-processing machinery, it is possible to make rights effective by simplifying eligibility standards, e.g., for welfare rights. Simplifications can make it so that lawyers will not normally be necessary. The need for lawyers is often due to the maze of technicalities and complex rules which determine a person's eligibility for benefits. No-fault divorce, while not a reform to make new social rights effective, is an important method of at least making lawyers less necessary.[5] It, too, can take the burden off lawyers' workloads.

Leaders of NLF programs are themselves beginning to see the virtues of reforms which may cut down the demand for their services. They are even assuming a positive role in urging that ways be found to make rights effective without lawyers.[6] The *Commission des services juridiques* in Quebec, for example, has proposed that the jurisdiction of the innovative Quebec small claims court be raised, no-fault automobile insurance be mandated, and that a "New Rental Code" be adopted with a "Unified Tribunal" to oversee it (Commission des services juridiques, 1977:60). The President of the U.S. Legal Services Corporation has also gone on record as favoring the development of alternatives to adjudication that will depend less on the service of lawyers (Ehrlich, 1977:67) (for England see, e.g., Morris, 1979:296–98).

A new model is thus emerging, even if it is still in the very early stages of its development. Alongside the judicare and NLF approaches to meeting legal needs, there is increasingly a "nonlawyer model." Obviously this new model has profound implications for the future of NLFs and the type of work they ought to do. Some of the more important considerations are the following.

First, new, less formal institutions and simpler standards will obviously take some pressure off NLFs. There are already some examples of this diversion. One of the leaders of the Manitoba legal aid system, for example, made the following remark about the Manitoba Rentalsman (which is similar to British Columbia's):

> [We] believed we would have to develop expertise in the landlord and tenant area ... because of the widespread interest in the new Landlord and Tenant Act of Manitoba. As it turned out, the provincial government's rentalsman office has handled most landlord–tenant problems, with only the rare case coming to Legal Aid (Larsen, in Canadian Council on Social Development, 1975:31).

Similarly, an English law center noted the positive effect of the nearby experimental Westminster Small Claims Court: "The Centre's work ... [in consumer protection] has continued on a relatively small scale due to the undoubted success of the Westminster Small Claims Court..." (Paddington Neighbourhood Advice Bureau and Law Centre, 1975:14). As these examples suggest, the most popular and persuasive (to policy makers) justification for NLFs may be in the process of being undermined; the classic "unmet need" is increasingly being met through more or less proactive institutions which do not require that lawyers be considered or retained.

NLFs may have a role to play in advising individuals how to find and use these new techniques and institutions, but this is a different role from the traditional one. NLFs must turn increasingly to a "self-help" strategy according to which individuals are prepared—even trained—to handle the matter effectively without formal legal assistance. Self-help is not new to the NLF movement. Often it served as a rationale to reduce caseload by referring people to small claims courts and the like.[7] This was generally undertaken, however, as a "second best" solution to get lawyers out from under a crushing caseload, and the small claims courts or other alternatives were generally little help to the poor (cf. Yngvesson and Hennessey, 1975). "Self-help" was similarly used to reduce caseload in divorce cases, where advantage could be taken of no-fault laws that made lawyers' services less necessary (e.g., Brickman, 1971:1215–17).

The self-help strategy has recently been given a slightly different aim and a more positive justification by some English law centers. According to the Camden Community Law Centre:

> In principle ... the client takes most of the action in the case with continuing advice and assistance from the Centre, sometimes over a period of months. We feel this is an important development because it means that clients have to take a more active part in understanding the nature of the legal processes in which they are involved. Although it may save time in administration in the Centre, it means more time is actually spent with the client and this helps to break down the barrier between "professionals" and "consumers" (Camden Community Law Centre, 1977:1).[8]

The purpose of this self-help strategy goes even beyond that of making rights effective. It aims to develop an individual's legal competence to handle similar matters with little or no legal assistance. It may thus complement efforts to "de-legalize" and "de-lawyerize." In conjunction with simplified procedures and standards, a self-help strategy such as this may free individuals from a dependence on lawyers without leaving them helpless to pursue their rights effectively.

Along with the self-help approach, which has considerable potential, there is another strategy that NLFs could utilize to continue the quest to enforce individuals' new rights. NLFs may have an essential role to play in monitoring the effects of new institutions and legal reforms. Small claims courts in particular have a long history of failing to help individuals against their typical institutional opponents—corporations, banks, and governments—and it is difficult to design and implement an institutional reform that will succeed in the task (see Cappelletti and Garth, 1978:9–19). As noted by one law center in England about administrative tribunals created there for enforcing new legislation, "Replacing the courts with administrative tribunals so that they can apply socialist legislation is no guarantee that a socialist view of justice will prevail" (Holloway Neighbourhood Law Centre, 1977:14). NLFs can be important in monitoring such agencies ostensibly designed to help the poor. There are a variety of ways this can be done, including follow-up of "self-help" cases and even active participation in new institutions. One lawyer from the Paddington law center, for example, has served as an adjudicator at the Westminster Small Claims Court (Paddington Neighbourhood Advice Bureau and Law Centre, 1976:18).

These tasks, however, are moving beyond efforts to help *individuals* toward actions on behalf of *classes* of people. The "legal need" justification for individual service work in "poverty law" areas has become a reason to do nonindividual work. Indeed, except for the "self-help" role, which itself may be supplanted by "community advocates" and advisers such as those connected to the Harlem Small Claims Court, the justification for the service work of NLFs may be losing its force. While NLFs clearly are active now in vindicating

165

nontraditional rights, the remarks of a leading Canadian commentator are perhaps increasingly true. According to Roland Penner:

> [T]he conditions of poverty (housing, welfare, employment, etc.) do not generate cases so much as they do the need for community and group action, in which the legal and the political intertwine. One of the reasons for this is the very significant and welcome development in the many areas of mediation-type services (rentalsmen, consumer protection bureaus) and more informal mechanisms (small claims courts, welfare appeal boards), all of which are both more suited to conflict resolution in poverty law areas than the traditional formal court mechanisms, and have the effect of leaving the individual "case" load in community clinics still showing a high proportion of "traditional" cases (Penner, 1977:91–92).

In other words, an indication of how successfully the unmet need is being handled may be the *absence* of legal aid in enforcing the nontraditional rights of persons. The need for legal aid may correspond to the failure to develop more advanced nonlawyer methods for enforcing rights at the individual level.

The logic of this third model for serving legal needs, assuming the model is becoming more widespread, points, as Penner suggested, to other strategies of NLFs if they are not simply going to serve "traditional" cases which could probably just as easily be handled by judicare lawyers. NLFs must increase their involvement in "community and group action."

V. Going Beyond Individual Needs

The conclusion of the preceding section already supported a reduced emphasis on individual casework, but the argument there depended for its force on the availability of effective nonlawyer alternatives to meet legal needs. There are also other compelling reasons, however, for going beyond *merely* individual problems, and they have been recognized throughout the NLF movement—indeed, have been a defining characteristic of that movement.

The theoretical reasons generally adduced for this type of social advocacy can be summarized as follows: the problems of the poor are the problems of groups or classes of people, and they cannot be solved by merely individual legal remedies that accept the existing law as given. Change is required in the law and in the practices of institutions that affect the lives of the poor. Moreover, tactics which can secure such changes are more cost-effective than a multitude of individual actions; one change in institutional practices, for example, may obviate the need to seek further individual remedies.

A further limitation of the strictly individual approach can be added on the basis of NLF experience. The "unmet need" is simply too great for a concerned network of NLFs to handle it. As Earl Johnson wrote in regard to the United States, "Within a few months after a legal assistance organization hired the lawyers and opened the offices made possible by OEO funds, those offices and attorneys were swamped by more needy clients than they could properly represent" (Johnson, 1974:127). It may be, as Wexler asserted in an important 1970 article, that "if all the lawyers in the country worked full-time, they could not deal with even the articulated legal problems of the poor. And even if somehow lawyers could deal with those articulated problems, they would not change very much the tangle of un-articulated legal troubles in which poor people live" (Wexler, 1970:1053; see also Legal Services Corporation, 1978:7–13).

Reports about the experience of NLFs elsewhere also suggest the same huge demand for their services. As a result, for example, the Brent Community Law Centre in London, in a very influential policy statement, announced its shift away from individual casework as follows:

> [T]he problem of unmet needs for legal services and of enforcement of laws designed to protect and benefit the less powerful sections of society is massive. So great is it and so feeble the response by government that it is questionable whether it is useful to go on making such laws if, as at present, they are then to go unenforced or largely unenforced. In these circumstances we are led to doubt that these laws are intended to be anything more than elaborate exercises in public relations. The problem is not simply that successive governments have failed to provide more than token resources to legal services. Rather it is a near total failure to plan for or provide the means to enforce much of the legislation which is at the moment, merely declaratory of rights and obligations (Brent Community Law Centre, 1975:30–31; see also Newham Rights Centre, 1975:31).

Lawyers cannot make these laws for the underprivileged effective by serving only individuals. In Brent's terms, "The service which is needed is one which can mobilize others rather than simply do every-thing itself" (1975:31).[9] NLFs that try to enforce the new rights of the poor only through individual actions may succeed in helping some individuals, but they will accomplish no change on behalf of the poor as a class. The social change implied in welfare state promises would remain a symbolic program, not a reality.

Moreover, such an outcome is worse than a failure of NLFs to have an important positive impact. It can result in a *disservice* to the poor. First, since NLFs would still have substantial caseloads in poverty law areas, in many people's eyes they would legitimize the present state of affairs. It would appear that the situation had noticeably improved;

those who needed help were getting help, even if closer analysis would reveal that there was no change in the situation of the vast majority of poor people. Reformers often have short attention spans. Publicity moves from one problem to another, and an apparent success in meeting legal needs may be enough to shift the focus away from welfare state rights in default.

Second, if strength comes from organization rather than isolation, the chances of poor people gaining political power may be reduced by too great a focus on individual legal problems. Lawyers concerned with individual legal rights tend to see the problems of the poor in only individual legal terms. To the extent this lawyers' view permeates the community, individuals will themselves look only to individual legal remedies to solve their problems. They may be blinded to the possibilities of affirmative political action at the group level.

The tendency of lawyers generally, including those in NLFs, to encourage a dependency on their skills can further aggravate the situation.[10] In short, there are a host of problems which may be created by well-intentioned efforts to solve individual problems. In one of the classic analyses of these dangers, Stephen Wexler made the following statement:

> Traditional practice hurts poor people by isolating them from each other, and fails to meet their need by completely misunderstanding that need. Poor people have few individual legal problems in the traditional sense; their problems are the product of poverty and are common to all poor people. The lawyer for poor individuals is likely, whether he wins cases or not, to leave his clients precisely where he found them, except that they will have developed a dependency on his skills to smooth out the roughest spots in their lives (Wexler, 1970:1053).

For a wide variety of reasons, therefore, NLFs look to other strategies besides meeting individual legal needs. There are, however, basic issues of how much to go beyond individual services, and for several reasons it may not be easy to implement other strategies. Despite the drawbacks of an individualized approach, it does help individuals survive, and it is often personally rewarding to provide that help. It is very difficult to turn away individual clients with problems in the name of a more abstract goal. This burden weighs especially heavy when there is no place else for the individuals to go. An important virtue of combined legal aid models and nonlawyer models is that they ease that burden—indeed may eliminate it for a category of cases. It is suggestive that the arguments reported about caseload burdens in Quebec concern a requirement of 200–300 active files per year, per lawyer (Penner, 1977:139), and in Manitoba the reported intake limit is 144 cases per year (Penner, 1977:129). Comparisons of caseloads are, of course, only approximate, but it is useful to compare these rough caseloads in combined systems to the 500 matters handled by the average U.S. legal services attorney. Even in the absence of effective alternatives, however, most NLFs have developed some commitment to actions designed to help the poor as a class. The principal strategies for this aim—law reform, group action, and community education—will be the focus of the next chapter.

Notes

1. An analysis of perhaps the most highly praised U.S. legal services program, California Rural Legal Assistance (CRLA), is instructive. A report in 1971 found that 95–98 percent of the caseload represented "routine matters," and that 80 percent of the time was allocated to "service cases" (Falk and Pollak, 1972:1289).

2. About 15 percent of these matters resulted in litigation. The 500 per year figure is consistent with earlier years under OEO (Auerbach Corporation, 1971:2–22).

3. For other sociological information on how an image is translated into practice, see Lochner (1975) and Mayhew (1975). Both these studies are consistent with the Adamsdown one.

4. It may take considerable time, however, to establish this new image throughout a community. The Adamsdown Centre, it must be admitted, services a population of only about ten thousand—the smallest of the English law centers. In North Kensington, where the area includes some eighty thousand people, the image was not so well-established. Interviews of 100 next-door neighbors of clients of the center showed that 57 had experienced problems similar to those of law center clients yet had not consulted the center (nor taken any alternative action) (see Byles and Morris, 1977:44–48). Nevertheless, this finding does not undermine the conclusion that law centers diffuse an image that reaches many who would otherwise not be mobilized to take legal action.

5. One of the sources of the Divorce Reform Act, 1969, in England was in fact the cost of divorces handled through legal aid at public expense (see Bridges et al., 1975:152).

6. Two pioneers of the NLF movement, Edgar and Jean Cahn, made the call for reforms such as those advocated in the text as far back as 1966 (Cahn and Cahn, 1966).

7. Carol Silver, for example, cited one U.S. legal services program which, overburdened with cases, referred clients "to any self-help facilities available (such as small claims court) or to the bar referral program, but with little expectation that such referral would yield any real assistance" (Silver, 1969:233).

8. The discussion of "self-help" by the Adamsdown Law Centre is also instructive:

> "Handing out leaflets should not be confused with working *with* the client in a way that can increase the client's awareness and abilities. The promotion of self-

169

help requires at least as much 'professional' input as a conveyance or a court appearance. The professional skills needed are rather different, but they should not be disparaged or under-resourced merely for that" (Adamsdown Community Trust, 1978:57).

9. The latest report of the U.S. Legal Services Corporation expresses the same sentiment:

"More and more, the attorneys and staff must concentrate on issues that can help large numbers of the poor, and continue to meet individual needs. Their major concern is identifying common problems and finding common solutions" (Legal Services Corporation, 1978:10).

10. According to Penner (1977:151):

"[I]t seems to me almost axiomatic that to the extent social services and legal aid delivery systems either create new dependencies or entrench old ones, they cannot but bolster the very system of power and value allocation which keeps literally millions of human beings in our society both poor and powerless.

In the words of the Saskatchewan Community Legal Services Commission (1975:13), "A plan which merely solved immediate problems would rapidly become just another social service upon which clients would become dependent."

Chapter 9

Strategies for Helping the Poor as a Class— Meeting the Collective Needs of the Poor

Lawyers can help poor individuals by making them aware of their rights and bringing legal actions to enforce them, but the cumulative effect of these individual actions will not do much to help the poor as a class: it will neither make welfare state rights effective for most poor individuals nor help unleash energies that will result in increased political power or economic strength to the poor. Rather, as was suggested in the previous chapter, the result might be quite the opposite—a reinforcement of the status quo.

The strategies designed explicitly to change the status quo in favor of the poor—a goal understood differently by different persons active in NLFs—are generally given as law reform, group action, and community education. Each of these general categories will be discussed in this chapter. The discussion will, in addition, highlight the differences between the approach in the United States, where "law reform" is emphasized, with that developing elsewhere, especially in England, with a focus more on "group work."

A question to consider in this chapter is how far NLFs can go without losing their legitimacy? Thus far it has been established that most NLFs that have been given a more or less permanent institutional form are in some manner deemed to be agents of "social change" on behalf of the poor. Yet it is also clear from the preceding chapter that individual service work has played a key role in the popularity and acceptability of NLFs. Needless to say, at this point, no definite answer can be provided to the question of how far NLFs can go beyond meeting individual needs towards what can be seen as more political ends. Nevertheless, it should be noted that, as will be seen in this chapter, the more innovative activities of NLFs may also serve relatively uncontroversial social goals, even from an essentially conservative viewpoint. NLFs are not only making change on behalf of the poor. The following defense of "law reform," made by an American Bar Association leader before the U.S. Congress, can be seen to apply to group work and community education as well:

A legal services program without law reform will never get to the place where it is intended. It will never bring equal rights for people, it will never stand out, it will never bring dissidents into our system with a feeling they have some stake here, and that problems can be solved within the system... (quoted in Johnson, 1974:169).

The statement nicely captures the ambiguity of social change through law as examined in this chapter. Reform is also a means of bringing dissidents within the existing system.

I. Law Reform

A. The Place of Law Reform in the NLF Movement

Law reform means simply changing the law on behalf of the poor. It may include legislative advocacy or "test case" litigation, in which the purpose of a case or series of cases is to challenge a law or practice as invalid on constitutional or other grounds. The purpose is to substitute a new law or practice by judicial order. Law reform in the United States also connotes "class actions," which usually seek both compensatory relief for members of a class who have been victimized by the challenged practice and a change in that practice. Most often, particularly in the United States where NLF activity began, the latter two litigation strategies have dominated law reform activity and discussion.

The origins of the NLF movement in the United States, it may be recalled, owed much to the popularity and evident success of test case litigation on behalf of Blacks by the NAACP Defense Fund. The Supreme Court under Chief Justice Earl Warren was highly receptive to these cases, and by 1965 test cases were recognized as a uniquely effective method of social change through law. Moreover, the methods of test case litigation—involving intricate legal arguments and work in the prestigious federal courts—were appealing to bright young attorneys. It allowed them to use the skills gained in law schools, and to earn the respect of their classmates who utilized similar sophisticated legal techniques on behalf of corporations.

It was natural for OEO to emphasize law reform through litigation as the chief method of promoting changes on behalf of the poor as a class. Earl Johnson, Jr., then Director of the Program, announced it officially on 17 March, 1967:

[T]he primary goal of the Legal Services Program should be law reform, to bring about changes in the structure of the world in which the poor people live. ... I believe law reform is vital because it is the means by which we can provide more for the poor than in any other way with less expenditure of time and

172

money. Law reform can provide the most bang for the buck, to use an OEO phrase (quoted in Johnson, 1974:133).

Law reform is still a basic goal, according to the current Executive Vice President, Clinton Bamberger (who was also the first Director in 1965). In late 1976, he stated that legal aid in the United States "has three characteristics which I consider immutable. ... Those characteristics are substantial public funding, reform of the law for the benefit of the poor, and full-time salaried lawyers..." (Bamberger, 1977:207). Legal aid priorities may now be set locally to a greater extent than before, but law reform is still the principal "social change" activity associated with the program.

Law reform through test cases is obviously less attractive outside of the United States. The United States is somewhat unique with its two-century history of a written constitution and judicial review. Nevertheless, the spread of NLF ideas outside the United States has generated substantial adherence to this law reform strategy. Little empirical data are available to measure the amount of time devoted to this strategy, but its importance is at least well recognized. In England, for example, the Law Centres Working Group recently emphasized that "test cases" are an "aspect of Law Centre casework which Centres not only already perform but believe it is their role to continue to perform" (Law Centres Working Group, 1978:35; see also, e.g., Partington, 1974; Tiplady, 1979). The Newham Rights Centre, in particular, stated that 9.7 percent of its caseload consisted of "potential test cases" (Newham Rights Centre, 1977:21). Law reform is also given a prominent role in the Canadian provincial programs (e.g., Penner, 1977:56–57, 106; Commission des services juridiques, 1977:28; Saskatchewan Community Legal Services Commission, 1976:14), and there was even some effort in the Australian Legal Aid Office to encourage test cases, at least in the environmental field (Harkins, 1977:18). Law reform is clearly part and parcel of the NLF movement. What "law reform" means in practice and what its potential benefits and limits are, however, can best be understood by a closer look at this strategy as implemented in the United States.

B. Law Reform in the United States

Most of the evaluative literature about the legal services program in the United States concerns the dichotomy of service work vs. law reform. It was generally assumed that law reform through test cases[1] meant that a program was making social change, while service work was considered traditional and less effective. Harry Stumpf thus

173

wrote from a critical perspective that, "from the majority of programs we can learn nothing about the impact of law reform activities because these programs practice almost exclusively traditional case-by-case, band-aid law" (Stumpf, 1975:274). He attributed this lack of activity to "local bar control" and the tendency of lawyers to stick to individual legal problems with which "most lawyers are familiar." On the other hand, there are data indicating that the average attorney in 1973 spent 31 percent of his or her time in law reform work (Handler et al., 1978:55). In any event, it is clear that at least 15 percent of the legal services budget goes exclusively to units specializing in law reform (see Johnson, 1977:316–17), and that law reform at the local level gained in importance as local bar influence attenuated and it became a national goal and criterion for program evaluation (e.g., Handler et al., 1978:54–55; Hannon, 1970). At present, as noted before, projects active before the Legal Services Corporation was created are probably continuing as before to emphasize law reform. Law reform is still the basic NLF strategy for change in the United States.

1. The Methods of Law Reform

Test case litigation, usually via the class action device, requires a very large commitment of lawyers who are expert in certain areas of substantive law. Three basic organizational methods evolved in the United States to encourage these actions and to assure that they could be handled efficiently. The first, and most important method, was the creation of back-up centers (now called support centers) to supplement litigation brought by local NLFs. There are now thirteen such centers and each of them specializes in an area of the law of particular concern to the poor, including consumer, housing, employment, and welfare law.[2] There are also "regional advocacy centers" and "statewide centers" specializing in law reform with a broad impact.

Second, approximately one-fourth of local legal services organizations have "appellate units" in which lawyers devote themselves to appellate litigation and other "high-impact work" (Johnson, 1977:317). This frees lawyers from a normal caseload and allows them to specialize. These units may vary in size from one to eight attorneys. For large projects, they usually are located in the central office, with local offices dispersed around a city.

Finally, information about developments in the law, current test cases being brought, and possibilities for new test cases, was and still is circulated through publications such as the *Clearinghouse Review*, funded directly by the legal services program (e.g., Huber, 1976:769–70). These publications have made specialized poverty law

174

available to lawyers in the field offices, particularly those specializing in appellate advocacy. As these three examples show, there was a major effort to organize the U.S. legal services program to foster law reform. The law reform units attracted the best lawyers, earned the most publicity, and appeared to do the most good. Given this emphasis, there obviously has been no comparable effort in the United States to orient resources in favor of other "impact" strategies.

2. *The Results of the Law Reform Strategy*

Much can be said in praise of law reform as practiced by legal services attorneys in the United States. The lawyers compiled a remarkable success ratio considering that their aim was to change the law to favor the weak. From 1967 to 1972, for example, 219 cases involving the rights of the poor were brought to the U.S. Supreme Court—most by legal services attorneys. One hundred thirty-six of these cases were decided on the merits, seventy-three in favor of extending the rights of the poor (Johnson, 1974:189). Test cases significantly expanded the rights of consumers, tenants, minority groups, and welfare recipients.[3] Test case victories have provided debtors with a right to a hearing before being deprived of their property by a creditor (*Fuentes* v. *Shevin* 407 U.S. 67 (1972), brought by Greater Miami Legal Services), strengthened tenants' rights to minimum standards of housing (see e.g., Ventantonio, 1976), and closed loopholes that prevented needy persons from obtaining welfare benefits (see, e.g., *King* v. *Smith*, 392 U.S. 309 (1968), holding void a state regulation denying welfare benefits to a mother cohabiting with a man); and *Shapiro* v. *Thompson*, 394 U.S. 618 (1969), holding state residency tests for welfare benefits void). It has been estimated that welfare test cases added some 5.5 million persons to the welfare rolls (Ventantonio, 1976:240). Test cases have no doubt contributed considerably to expanding the rights of the poor.

Test cases also created considerable controversy. Lawsuits aroused a vocal opposition, at least on the part of defendants, and the national controversy about the program centered on test case litigation. On the floor of Congress, it will be recalled, an amendment to the Legal Services Corporation Act was passed with the intent of destroying the back-up centers specializing in law reform. Nevertheless, test cases and back-up centers were not opposed by many conservatives such as President Nixon, who showed no such hostility in his bills for a Legal Services Corporation. He turned against the back-up centers only at the last minute when he sought to gain anti-impeachment votes. We must again recognize the dual nature of NLF activities; test cases and class actions also serve socially integrative functions. In San

175

Francisco, for example, a study found that there were numerous public officials who, "though publicly criticizing the [San Francisco Neighborhood Legal Assistance] Foundation, privately praised it. They thought that class action suits provided militants with a legitimate outlet for their dissatisfactions and frustrations" (Brill, 1970:51). Test cases, in any event, did survive the controversy and are still very much part of the program's continuing legitimate strategies.

There have, however, been serious criticisms of the law reform strategy by commentators both inside and outside of the program. It has been argued, to begin with, that class action litigation simply requires the commitment of too many scarce resources: "A single case may occupy a few lawyers for an entire year" (Brill, 1970:42). Second, the division between the prestigious "appellate units" and the other neighborhood lawyers may create friction, undermining project morale.[4] Another problem with law reform, particularly with its tendency to be confined to special "high impact units," is that it tends to increase the distance between the reform-oriented lawyers and the client community. Test cases are highly technical actions, and often they are initiated by lawyers who search out passive plaintiffs or class representatives to fit cases designed in advance (e.g., Rothstein, 1974:514; Bellow, 1977:58). The accountability problem referred to in other contexts looms larger as lawyers move farther from any real client contact.

Increasingly, moreover, the results of test cases are being criticized. A successful test case may result in a ruling favorable to the poor, but effective enforcement may be difficult or impossible. In the first place, official or corporate behavior may only be changed for a short time before it lapses back into the old challenged pattern. NLFs can (indeed must) monitor the results of some cases, but they do not have the resources to monitor and continually pressure a large number of institutions. According to Stuart Scheingold, whose powerful critique of NLFs identifies them mainly with test cases,

> Rights are declared as absolutes, but they ripple out into the world in an exceedingly conditional fashion. The declaration of rights is ordinarily the prelude to a political struggle, and according to the evidence that struggle is primarily coercive. When it comes to getting large numbers of people to conform to norms they oppose, power is indispensable... (Scheingold, 1974:123).

Large institutions, as Marc Galanter has amply demonstrated in his now famous article on "why the haves come out ahead," have a multitude of ways to avoid decisions that are unfavorable to them (Galanter, 1974; see also Handler, 1978).[5]

Second, enforcement may not do much good for the poor anyway.

176

One of the most celebrated welfare law test cases, for example, invalidated California's state residency requirements for welfare eligibility. The result, however, was that:

> Eligibility requirements were more vigorously enforced and tightened to exclude many poor people who had formerly been eligible; the new restrictions were so severe that, despite an increase in unemployment, the total number collecting welfare in California actually dropped (Brill, 1970:43).

In other words, the victory was a hollow one; no more resources were committed to the poor.

The weaknesses of litigation as a strategy for social change are increasingly apparent (see generally Horowitz, 1977). Given these limits, the next question must be the cost of failure in terms of alternative strategies. Clearly an unenforced reform proclaimed by the courts as a victory for the underprivileged "may become a substitute for redistribution of advantages" (Galanter, 1974). In Joel Handler's words, test case victories may turn out to be merely symbolic: "Symbols are used by the entrenched interests to assuage dissident groups, to give them the feeling that they have accomplished their objectives when in fact tangible results are withheld" (Handler, 1976:110).

C. Law Reform in a Broader Perspective

The critique of the test case strategy is a profound one, even if we recognize that there have been real accomplishments through this strategy in the United States. In some ways, however, the critique is too easy to make, especially now that the U.S. Supreme Court under Chief Justice Burger is not very receptive to the arguments of the poor and minorities. Moreover, the critique of test cases tends to imply that *legislative* rule change will overcome the deficiencies of law reform through the courts. Test case victories do have certain disadvantages when compared to legislation. They may lack the legitimacy of legislative rule change; it may be difficult to obtain public funds for affirmative activities ordered by courts; and a legislature may be in a better position to create enforcement machinery. Yet test cases have succeeded in areas where legislatures had refused to act, particularly in the United States.[6] One should not expect too much from U.S. legislatures, given the absence of a strong party system and the constitutional constraints on innovative legislative action (see Thompson, 1969). Minorities in other countries may also find the courts to be indispensable to the achievement of their substantive ends. Nevertheless, it is probably true that test case activity has been undertaken even when lobbying in legislatures would have been more effective (see, e.g., Brill, 1970:45; Hazard, 1970).

More fundamentally, law reform—legislative or judicial—is simply too limited a strategy for social change. In the words of Gary Bellow, one of the founders of California Rural Legal Assistance, it is a "dead end" (Yale Law Journal, 1970:1077). It must not be considered as an end in itself, as it has been throughout the U.S. legal services program, but rather as a *beginning* in an effort to bring new rights and entitlements to the poor. We are back to the problem of the previous chapter—that of making rights effective. It has already been seen that individual actions brought by NLF lawyers cannot by themselves accomplish the task, and it has been suggested that reform of the judicial system can be vital in enforcing rights in "poverty law" areas. NLFs, it was noted, can help monitor such reforms to see that they remain true to their purposes. The discussion of this function must now be developed further.

Monitoring raises two clear problems for NLFs. First, NLFs lack the resources to monitor the conduct of the great number of governmental agencies and private institutions whose activities impinge on the lives of the poor; and, second, their power to bring lawsuits may be insufficient to force necessary changes in institutional practices. As stated by the Brent Community Law Centre in the influential *First Report* cited before,

> The extralegal sanctions, economic and political, which a class of people can bring to bear cannot be separated from the legal sanctions in any negotiation— e.g., an attempt at enforcement of the obligations of the Local Authority or the standards of a manufacturer. These sanctions are, inevitably, in the background in representations made by the lawyers for a class. It is the clients not the lawyer who carry the political and economic punch" (Brent Community Law Centre, 1975:15).

Brent's conclusion regarding the "massive" failure to enforce laws on behalf of the poor is thus the following:

> What is needed is not simply to increase the resources available to the legal aid scheme or the public enforcement agencies, although this is certainly necessary; rather it is legal services which will help the poor and powerless to organize themselves so that they are capable of negotiating and enforcing rights and obligations and of having an effective voice in the decision making processes which effect them. The service which is needed is one which can mobilize others rather than simply do everything itself (1975:30–31).

This strategy of helping the poor organize, which is the strategy most favored by the English law center movement, will now be examined.

178

II. Organizing and Aiding Community Groups

"Group work" is not inconsistent with law reform activities, but it goes much beyond the focus on advocacy by lawyers of reforms on behalf of the poor. As expressed by the Newham Rights Centre in London, "organized groups can exert pressure in any number of ways on a whole range of public and private institutions, and in doing so, the use of the law is one tool amongst many, rather than the only and last resort of the unorganized (assuming that legal services are available)" (Newham Rights Centre, 1975:42). This more overtly political strategy—the effort to develop or strengthen community groups—has been part of the NLF arsenal since the OEO program began in the United States, but it has only recently emerged, particularly in England, as a realistic challenger of the law reform and individual service functions as the major strategy for NLFs seeking to effect social change.

A. Group Representation and Organization in the NLF Movement

In the Cahns' original proposal for a neighborhood law firm in the United States, they noted the importance of helping to form associations of tenants, welfare recipients, local consumers, and the like (Cahn and Cahn, 1964). The OEO guidelines similarly referred to group representation as an essential NLF activity,[7] and the pamphlet *Legal Services in Action*, published in 1967, included examples of lawyers taking the initiative in organizing groups (Office of Economic Opportunity, 1967).

Nevertheless, for a variety of reasons, services to groups were not emphasized in the program. The Cahns even complained as early as 1966 that "there is a pervasive absence of any relationship between legal service programs and the organization of citizen groups such as tenant councils, welfare mothers' organizations, or consumer groups" (Cahn and Cahn, 1966:928). Law reform was the chief priority aside from service work, and it has remained that way (see Johnson, 1974:128–32).[8] Empirical research conducted in late 1973, for example, found that,

> About one-half of the lawyers did no organizing at all. Lawyers were more likely to report speaking to neighborhood client groups or counseling. The average amount of time per month spent speaking was 4.1 hours; in organizing, 4.5 hours; and in counseling, 8.5 hours (Handler et al., 1978:58).

Clearly there was some group work, and certain programs may have emphasized it, but it paled in significance when compared nationally to law reform (which the Handler et al. study found took up more than fifty hours of a lawyer's monthly time (1978:58)).[9]

The Legal Services Corporation Act of 1974 actually forbade the use of LSC funds "to organize, to assist to organize, or to plan for the creation or formation of ... any organization ... or any similar entity, except for the provision of legal assistance to eligible clients...." This language was "clarified" by the 1977 amendments, which now only forbid "initiating the formation" or acting as an "organizer" of groups.[10] The change seems to make the standard more liberal, and it is sufficiently ambiguous to permit a liberal interpretation, but its existence is instructive. It is also notable that there was no published commentary on the Corporation Act which paid any attention to this prohibition. Little attention has been given to working with groups, and it follows that there has not been much concern, at least until very recently, with organizing them (see Trister, 1978).

Interestingly, however, a number of key figures in the U.S. OEO movement, including the Cahns and the founders of California Rural Legal Assistance, Gary Bellow and Jim Lorenz, did increasingly move toward a group strategy. In particular, a 1970 study based on a wide range of interviews with activist lawyers, including those named above and others who had worked or still did so with OEO, found that a "decision to go beyond test case litigation characterizes virtually all the lawyers whom we interviewed," and that "most of the lawyers ... have moved toward working with organized groups of poor people, working with organizers, and occasionally even organizing itself" (Yale Law Journal, 1970:1078–79). Yet this perspective did not permeate the legal services program to any great extent. The reasons are no doubt complex. The appeal and drama of test case litigation in the United States is one reason, but another was simply that it was considered politically unrealistic. According to Bellow, "Coalitions can be created that enable the program to survive, but a focus and emphasis on political community organizing probably can't be done with government funds at all" (Yale Law Journal, 1970:1111).

In NLF programs outside of the United States, however, the group strategy has fared better. In part, no doubt, this is because law reform through the courts is less effective in changing laws in legal cultures outside of the United States. It may also be important that these NLFs were set up after leading criticisms of test cases in the United States had been published.[11] Further, the more political, as opposed to professional, orientation of young lawyers in at least England and Holland led them to question the efficacy of a merely professional approach to reform. In any event, the emphasis on groups has gained importance and even respectability outside of the United States.

In Canada, for example, special mention of this strategy can be found in a number of major provincial policy statements. In the first report of Legal Aid Manitoba, the second priority of the community law offices, after "community legal education," was "aiding and representing groups and organizations within its community" (Legal Aid Manitoba, 1973:3). The first report in Saskatchewan stressed the strengths of community groups and noted that "A legal aid plan is in a key position to encourage the development of such groups" (Saskatchewan Community Legal Services Commission, 1975:15). And British Columbia's first report expressed the hope "that public education and community organizing will become a major role of the community offices and their lay staff in the future" (Legal Services Commission, 1976:15).

Group work is becoming the major focus of leading law shops in Holland. At the first law shop, located in Tilburg, it was decided three years ago that "the activities of the lawshop must be put at the disposal of the organisations, already existing or still to be founded, of labourers and of people who are entitled to social benefits and of tenants" (de Jong, 1977). Other law shops are following this model.

An especially strong group emphasis is developing within the English law center movement. According to the Law Centres Working Group, in their evidence to the Royal Commission on Legal Services, law centers would be pleased to see much of their individual work "go into the private sector thus liberating Law Centres' limited resources to do what we consider to be more important tasks ... under the heading of group work and community education" (Law Centres Working Group, 1978:38). Further, "Law Centres must not merely be prepared to work with existing community organizations but also to actively engage in promoting the creation of new organs of community expression" (1978:34). There are pressures, as noted, to increase their individual casework, but the group emphasis is considered basic to the work of the law centers.[12]

Unfortunately, it is difficult to quantify this enthusiasm for group work in the absence of empirical data. As with respect to law reform, caseload data does not show the commitment of time and resources to working with groups.[13] There is evidence, for example, that in British Columbia the hope expressed in the first report has not been translated into action (Morris and Stern, 1976:64). It is, in fact, difficult to know whether a continuing formal commitment to group work has led to more activism in this area than was found in the United States. Nevertheless, a number of law centers in England did report in 1975 that the "mix between individual and group work" was increasingly in favor of the latter. At least seven of ten centers

Table 9. *Group Eligibility Standards*

	Eligibility standards	Limitations on group services
United States	"Group, corporation, or association" if (1) it is primarily composed of eligible persons; (2) the "primary purpose" of the group is to further the "interests of poor persons unable to afford legal assistance"; and (3) the group provides information that it has no practical means to pay for counsel[a]	Cannot organize groups other than for "the provision of legal assistance to eligible clients"[b]
England and Wales	Informal standards	None explicitly stated
Canada		
Quebec	"A group of persons or a nonprofit corporation which does not have sufficient resources"[c]	None
Manitoba	"Such groups and organizations as is deemed advisable by the executive director"[d]	Subject to approval of the executive director[e]
Saskatchewan	"A group, organization or society the membership of which is predominantly eligible persons"[f]	None
Australia	No mention of groups in the formal eligibility criteria of the ALAO, but test cases were brought by some environmental groups[g]	
Holland	Informal eligibility criteria	None explicitly stated

(Footnotes on following page)

182

Table 10. *Who Decides if a Group is Eligible for Legal Aid?*

United States	Individual attorney, according to governing board criteria[a]
England and Wales	Individual attorney, according to management committee criteria[b]
Canada	
Quebec	General manager of one of the eleven "regional legal aid corporations" which administer the local offices[c]
Manitoba	The "executive director" of Legal Aid Manitoba (as opposed to one of the five "area directors")[d]
Saskatchewan	Individual attorneys, with review by one of the twelve "area boards"[e]
Australia	"Attorney General or his delegate"[f]
Holland	No standard method

[a] 45 CFR Part 1611.5, 1611.6.

[b] See Law Centres Working Group, *Evidence to the Royal Commission on Legal Services* 47 (Birmingham, Saltley Action Centre, 1978).

[c] Regulations Under the Legal Aid Act (Quebec), §3.11.

[d] Regulation Under the Legal Aid Services Society of Manitoba Act, §53(c).

[e] Regulations Made Under the Community Legal Services (Saskatchewan) Act, 1974, §2.

[f] See Harkins, "Federal Legal Aid in Australia," at 15–18, in *Proceedings of the First International Colloquium on Legal Aid and Legal Services, London, October 25–28, 1976* (Palo Alto, International Common Law Exchange Society, 1977).

(Footnotes to Table 9)

[a] 45 CFR Part 1611.5(d).

[b] Legal Services Corporation Act of 1974, §1007(b) (6), 42 U.S.C. §2996f(b) (7), as amended by the Legal Services Act Amendments of 1977.

[c] Regulations Under the Legal Aid Act (Quebec) §3.11.

[d] Regulation Under the Legal Aid Services Society of Manitoba Act, §53(c).

[e] Id.

[f] Regulations Made Under the Community Legal Services (Saskatchewan) Act, 1974, §2(5).

[g] See Harkins, "Federal Legal Aid in Australia," at 15–18, in *Proceedings of the First International Colloquium on Legal Aid and Legal Services, London, October 25–28, 1976* (Palo Alto, International Common Law Exchange Society, 1977).

who sought to quantify this information reported over 20 percent group work, and most reported over 40 percent (Zander and Russell, 1976:210). Moreover, regardless of the exact percentages, the ideological and institutional concerns for group work no doubt affect the actions of individual NLFs (see Finman, 1972). The ideological and institutional pressures in the United States emphasize law reform while those in England strongly and increasingly favor group work. The variations between the U.S. and English approaches suggested by the limited available data no doubt reflect the underlying reality.

B. The Methods of Serving Groups

1. Eligibility Standards for Groups

The first technical problem of legal aid and advice for groups is that of eligibility. When is a group of persons qualified for legal services to the poor? What if the group contains nonpoor persons as well as poor persons? What are appropriate legal services to a group? (see generally *Report of the Task Force on Legal Aid* (Ontario), 1974:95–101).

Tables 9 and 10 summarize the two most important components of the eligibility-determination process for group representation— formal standards and who applies them (and at what level). The most discretion according to statutory criteria is in Quebec and Manitoba, but in each case the decision for eligibility must be made at a higher level than in the other programs. The U.S. and Saskatchewan programs allow low-level discretion, but the criteria seek to limit representation to groups either "primarily" (in the U.S.) or "predominantly" (Saskatchewan) composed of eligible persons. Groups organized around local issues, such as inadequate roads or schools, may not be able to meet this standard and yet may still be unable to afford the costs of assistance. In any event, only empirical study would reveal how these rather vague standards operate in practice. It is once again notable, however, that the English law centers in particular, despite their increasing central government funding, have avoided setting any formal means test. It remains to be seen whether that flexibility will survive further institutionalization, but to date it gives the centers wide flexibility to work with any community organizations felt to be advancing the interests of the underprivileged in a center's target area. Clearly group work has more potential when there is that flexibility.

2. The Importance of Paralegals as Community Workers

A strategy of working with and organizing community groups can best be implemented if local persons are recruited as "community workers." Such community workers can develop close ties with local groups and help stimulate new groups to form. Lawyers are not themselves well suited to these activities. As pointed out by the Director of the leading Ontario NLF, "Inevitably your staff lawyer, even if he moves into the community, is for economic and sociological reasons, never really going to be a part of that community" (see Penner, 1977:44). Their background sets them apart from poor persons, they may not be from the area being served, and there may be racial or language barriers between lawyers and the client community. There also may be dangers if publicly-funded lawyers identify too closely with groups. Other groups, for example, who often have no other place to turn for legal services, might feel that the lawyers' independence has been compromised (e.g., Harvard Law Review, 1967:820; Newham Rights Centre, 1975:46). For a number of reasons, lawyers' skills are better utilized in helping groups of persons find a suitable organizational form and in providing services and counseling to existing organizations.[14] Therefore, at least until the point when there is a strong network of independent community organizations with a stable relationship with NLFs, community workers are indispensable to a strong group emphasis.

In the United States this role for community workers was recognized by some NLFs. According to a detailed study of "legal paraprofessionalism" published in 1971, there were a number of "lay advocates" with legal services programs, who helped, inter alia, "in the formation of community action groups" (Brickman, 1971:1225–26). No affirmative institutional role, however, was worked out for these persons.

> The community workers attended meetings of tenants and consumers, advertised the program, and solicited clients with specified legal problems, but for the most part their activities were not integrated with those of the lawyers. Not only were they undirected, but their very whereabouts were frequently unknown to the program directors (Brickman, 1971:1249–50).

These paraprofessionals did not well fit the law reform and service work emphases of NLFs in the United States, and they were seen as a luxury when budgetary restraints hit the program after 1968. Law reform strategies and individual legal services clearly called for a lawyer-dominated program with paralegals helping principally in administrative and office tasks.

Some rough figures can give an indication of this lawyer emphasis. The total number of legal paraprofessionals or paralegals involved in legal services work in the United States is reported to be 1,500, compared to 3,700 lawyers (Legal Services Corporation, 1978:i). The

185

number of paraprofessionals is large, but the definition of "paralegal" is vague and undoubtedly includes numerous office workers.[15]

In England, where there is an emphasis on group work, paralegal community workers clearly exist in proportionately much larger numbers. According to the Law Centres Working Group, the law centers' work

> ...cannot be done by a work force dominated by those trained in law because this training leads to a narrow, precise and analytic way of thinking which (if a dominant feature of the law centre's attitude) is ill-suited to serving the expressions of communities as a whole. It is vital that those of the local community and workers skilled in community work are a strong component, numerically and ideologically in the centre ... (Law Centres Working Group, 1978:41).

Current information on law center staffs is not always given in their annual reports, but some suggestive indications can be obtained concerning the role and number of "community workers." In the Zander and Russell survey, applicable to the situation in August 1975, the reported data for thirteen law centers showed thirty-two lawyers and some sixteen community workers (Zander and Russell, 1976:726). The recent Adamsdown report indicated that the staff of eight includes "a lawyer, welfare rights officer, community worker (part-time), secretary and cleaner" (Adamsdown Community Trust, 1978:8). The Hillingdon Community Law Centre (1976:2) reported that a full-time staff of six included two community workers. Newham Rights Centre (1977:5) recently described a staff of three lawyers and two community workers; the Saltley Action Centre (1977:4) reported a staff of two community workers, one resource worker, one Asian project worker, one housing/planning worker, two secretaries, and one lawyer; and the Small Heath Community Law Centre (1977:21–24) has three lawyers, one of whom does only group and community education work, and one community worker. These data are somewhat fragmentary, but they show that community workers are utilized in at least as great a proportion as all "paraprofessionals" —most of whom probably are involved in office work—in the United States.

It is clear that the different orientations of the U.S. and English NLF movements are reflected in their methods of staffing and allocating resources. In the United States the offices are arranged and staffed to service individual cases and to encourage special units devoted to law reform. In England, the emphasis is much more on group work (and, as will be seen, community education). If there is specialization in England it is more through "community workers"

186

than "law reform units." It is indicative that U.S. specialization points away from the neighborhoods towards technical legal research, while the English counterparts point toward the community and the persons and groups that comprise it.

3. Kinds of Group Work

The idea that NLFs can concentrate on serving and even organizing groups sounds strange to a lawyer, even assuming paralegals do the real community mobilizing. It is sometimes hard even to imagine what role a lawyer can play in this apparently "political" approach. In order to clarify the practical meaning of "group work," it is helpful to specify five types of work that can be included under this heading.

First, NLFs can keep neighborhood interest groups from being crippled by the law: "nothing destroys the momentum of a militant community effort more than alleged technicalities of law or the alleged statutory inability of an official to redress a grievance" (Cahn and Cahn, 1964:1335). When a reform group is told that it cannot succeed because of the law, lawyers can, in the words of the Cahns, "detect specious claims which mask a lack of responsiveness" (Cahn and Cahn, 1964:1335). Here lawyers act defensively, helping with legal advice or action in a situation created by others. Groups are no doubt strengthened, but there is little that is objectionable or unlawyerlike about the lawyers' activities.

Similarly uncontroversial is the "corporate counsel" role, according to which lawyers advise groups on the legal implications of possible courses of action (e.g., Law Centres Working Group, 1978:39; Brent Community Law Centre, 1978:2; Penner, 1977:133). As the phrase "corporate counsel" suggests, this is the classic role of the corporate lawyer. The advice and assistance to the group might encompass a wide range of matters. The Brent Community Law Centre, for example, assists a large Federation of Tenants and Residents as follows:

> It advises on constitutional matters, problems and issues affecting tenants and residents as a group and the individual problems which tenants and residents take to their associations for help. On some occasions the Centre has been asked to advise specifically on legal matters—on others the Centre has brought matters to the attention of the Federation (Brent Community Law Centre, 1975:12).

NFLs can help social reform groups as "hired guns" just as corporate lawyers serve corporate interests.

A third type of group work is akin to the strategy of "self-help" described in the previous chapter. The idea here is for NLFs to prepare interest groups to protect their members' rights without needing to have a lawyer available (e.g., Brent Community Law Centre, 1978:2, 22). The reach of the NLF can thus be greatly increased and groups strengthened by the capacity to offer this service. Organized groups can not only conduct their own advice sessions, but also they can monitor the results of that advice. They can oversee public agencies concerned with their members' interests. The NLF can provide continuing help by keeping the group posted on current legal developments.

The obvious problem is that organized groups do not always exist for these purposes. For the group strategy to work, it is necessary sometimes for NLFs to take initiative in creating or at least stimulating the creation of new organizations. An example provided by the Law Centres Working Group is the following:

> [A] Law Centre in an area deprived of any resources will inevitably be subject to a high demand for run-of-the-mill social security advice and representation. This is work well within the capacity of a Claimants' Union. By devoting resources to the establishment of such in the short term, even though the Centre may be under intense demand from individuals for immediate help, a resource for the future can be secured which not only is capable of servicing a far larger number of people but also liberates the Centre's energies for other, analogous efforts in different areas of priority need (Law Centres Working Group, 1978:39; Penner, 1977:105).

This organizational strategy is obviously very limited in terms of its goals and its tactics.

A closely-related organizational strategy is to create groups that will be able to further the collective *legal* interests of their members in forums such as local councils and administrative agencies. This moves one more step forward toward the creation of purely political groups but it can be seen as a kind of extension of the law reform and individual advice strategies. A corporate counsel, moreover, might also encourage concerted action of this type among clients with similar interests. The emphasis of this approach is on strengthening legal rights and removing legal or institutional impediments to their enforcement.

A few examples of successful group work can help show how this latter type of organizing can take place. The first example is from the recent report of the Adamsdown Law Centre in Cardiff, Wales. The report describes a "campaign" that began when residents received a letter telling them that their neighborhood was scheduled to be included in a slum clearance program; they were told they could object at a public inquiry, but there was little likelihood that residents would have mounted any serious objections. According to the report,

188

"such a letter is experienced more as an Act of God than as an act of man" (Adamsdown Community Trust, 1978:63). The law center, however, took an interest in the problem.

Center personnel began knocking on doors to canvass neighborhood opinion. Nearly all those questioned were opposed to removal. The center then helped "the residents to· organise and mobilise themselves" (1978:65) to object at the public inquiry, although prospects for success were not too good. The Housing Act of 1974, however, became law at that time and provided new rights for residents opposed to removal, although they needed to convince the local council to declare the neighborhood a "Housing Action Area" worthy of funding to preserve it. The center sponsored (with legal aid funds obtained under the judicare system) a detailed expert report on the neighborhood, and the report, combined with the expressions of the residents, convinced the Cardiff City Council to invoke the new law and create such a Housing Action Area.

The events just described could be characterized as "law reform," in the sense that the center's activities obtained a change in public policy, but this law reform differs from a strictly technical test case or legal presentation before a legislature. First, the influence of the residents' organization might have been vital in adding depth and commitment to legal argument. Furthermore, the story must be continued to ask how the rights given by the new status were implemented to improve the area: "It is one thing to declare a Housing Action Area, it is quite another to make it work" (1978:68).

The center, building on the citizen momentum already generated, helped create a voluntary organization, the Adamsdown Housing Association, which under the 1974 Act was permitted to assume important planning functions. The Association initially depended on the center, "but within a few months the Association was employing its own officers and had set up its own offices..." (1978:68). As of 1978, the Association had used the 1974 Act to improve the neighborhood dramatically.

The Tilburg Law Shop in Holland provides another example (Knipscheer, 1977). In late 1974 several people came to the law shop complaining about the noise generated by a factory located in their neighborhood. The law shop did not immediately seek a "legal" remedy. A member of the law shop staff helped form a neighborhood committee (in which he participated). The committee then asked the local city council to do something to remedy the situation, but the council refused to take action.

Legal skills then became useful as the committee investigated the types of licenses needed by the factory and the conditions linked to

189

them. They found through an investigation by experts that the legal conditions were being violated regularly, and they brought a lawsuit to stop the violations. The lawsuit was successful and upheld on appeal, and the neighborhood group now oversees enforcement and negotiates with the factory management on behalf of residents. Moreover, the local committee became aware that "there were many more problems to solve," so the members "took the initiative to form a neighborhood council." Again, this description shows the use of lawyers and legal strategies, but the law shop's first action was not to bring a lawsuit but rather to promote an organization which *in turn* became aware of legal rights and various possibilities for action, including a lawsuit. After trying another strategy, the *group* decided to litigate, and the conclusion of the case did not mean that the group disappeared.

The examples just provided show organization above all as a means to enforce or expand *legal rights*. It should be clear that the type of group work under discussion is a rather more limited strategy than it at first glance may appear to be. A statement of the Newham Rights Centre in their influential 1975 pro-group manifesto is particularly revealing:

> The Law Centre will naturally turn to organisations which address themselves to the sort of problems with which the Centre would be dealing were it to undertake individual cases. Thus tenants associations, trades unions, claimants unions, squatters organisations, and so on naturally fall within this ambit. But what of other organisations whose purposes are just as relevant to their members but which do not deal with problems that can be seen as legal, even indirectly? *... the answer must be that it is usually outside the proper scope of the Law Centre's work to assist in the organisation of groups whose activities have no bearing on the solution of problems that can be seen as legal or susceptible to the intervention of lawyers* (Newham Rights Centre, 1975:47). (Emphasis supplied.)

These types of work are of course "political," and they may affect somewhat the balance of power in a community, but we are not talking about the creation of a political party or a broad coalition for social change. The groups being considered, at least as targets for organisation, are clearly tied to the legal issues generated by welfare state legislation.

C. Problems with Group Work

There are obvious problems with this group orientation, beginning with the question, is it "legal"? There is no problem with working with existing groups, but organizing raises real problems. Granted the virtues of organizing, should lawyers undertake the task? According

190

to Earl Johnson, Jr., justifying the U.S. emphasis on law reform, "poverty attorneys probably would have constituted the highest paid, best educated, least effective organizational force in history" (Johnson, 1974:130). This argument cannot be dismissed lightly, but it overlooks several important characteristics of group organizing by NLFs. First, community workers, not lawyers, ought to be doing any actual "organizing" that cannot be undertaken by persons outside of the NLF staff. A neighborhood law firm need not be strictly a lawyers' firm. Second, as I suggested in the preceding discussion of some examples of group work, the organization of groups is closely tied to *legal* statuses and *legal* rights. Lawyers who discern particular legal benefits that can be gained through organization are performing useful legal tasks. Their individual clients may not know of others with similar problems or of the possibilities for action.

A focus on legal rights, moreover, may help to mobilize a group, and successes in obtaining and expanding such rights can contribute to the group's continued viability. Organizations of the poor cannot easily be created and sustained: "Organizing can be very difficult and very discouraging, especially where people are exhausted by their efforts to eke out an existence, and where they are used to struggling against each other rather than working in groups to raise general standards" (Yale Law Journal, 1970:1090). One way to overcome this difficulty is by fostering knowledge of legal rights and remedies. As pointed out by Stuart Scheingold, "It is possible to capitalize on the perceptions of entitlement associated with rights to initiate and nurture political mobilization..." (Scheingold, 1974:131). Thus NLFs may have a unique capacity to disseminate legal research and expertise into the community that will facilitate organizations of tenants, welfare recipients, and the like. Thus, aside from lawyers' recognized skills in serving groups, NLFs, in contrast to what Professor Johnson asserted, may often be peculiarly suited to mobilizing groups around certain issues.

A second question, however, is whether the work of organizing the poor, even around essentially legal issues, is too "political" for government-funded lawyers to undertake without losing their support. The unique quality of lawyers is that they can advocate unpopular causes on behalf of groups without being responsible for the views or actions of the group. Lawyers who are involved in creating groups have less of a claim to professional independence. Nevertheless, as already mentioned, organizing activity by NLFs in England and Canada has been increasingly accepted. No doubt this is partly due to the recognition by governments that organizational work by NLFs is in a real sense "legal" and appropriate to make legal rights effective. It must also be mentioned, however, that "political" is a deceptive term. NLFs are political institutions regardless of what they do. The question is in what political direction they can go. What is really at stake, in other words, is whether it is too politically radical, or disruptive, to organize groups. A closer look at the effects of these organizations is accordingly required.

Organizing the poor—especially around legal issues—is not just a strategy for change. As noted for the other NLF strategies and indeed the movement as a whole, there are also more conservative dynamics at work. It can be argued from a radical point of view, for example, that organizations of such status groups as pensioners, the unemployed, and ethnic minorities, serve mainly "to discipline their members and to create integrative symbols" (Offe, 1977:46). Group leaders discourage "unrealistic" or "utopian" demands by the rank and file, and status groups ipso facto limit conflict to narrow issues flowing from that status. Such groups, in the words of the political scientist, Claus Offe, tend naturally "to exclude from the process of formation of the political will all expressions of general needs not tied to groups of status" (Offe, 1977:47).

One recent critical study by Piven and Cloward of "poor people's movements" in the United States concluded that it was not organization but "disruptive protest" that has enabled the poor to make concrete gains. They argued that, "whatever influence lower-class groups occasionally have on American politics does not result from organization, but from mass protest and disruptive consequences of protest" (Piven and Cloward, 1977:37). While, as will be explained more fully below, I do not accept this conclusion, Piven and Cloward's study substantiates an important point. The group strategy does inhibit some forms of mass protest by diverting it into more regular channels. This does not mean that the group approach does not contribute to change, but it does show that a more conservative function is also being served.

These observations suggest that the group strategy ought not to be seen as a politically radical one. Further practical limiting aspects of this strategy can also be pointed out. One can question how much reform can be accomplished by local groups of poor persons lacking any real economic and political power. Poor persons cannot succeed in making lasting gains unless they can find common ground with middle-class groups, labor unions, and the like.[16] To an extent, the English law centers (and perhaps NLFs elsewhere, depending on how tests are applied in practice) can avoid this problem since they have no means test to prevent them from aiding groups cutting across poverty lines. But one can still ask if an emphasis primarily on local legal issues will divert attention away from more important national political efforts (see, e.g., Marris and Rein, 1972:237; Leat, 1975:180–81). Finally, one must also recognize that the recurring issues of dependency and accountability are not necessarily avoided by an emphasis on groups.

D. The Need for Group Work

The group strategy is certainly not as different from the other "legal" strategies as it is often thought to be. Like the strategies of individual casework and law reform, it probably cannot realistically succeed in putting lawyers in the vanguard of national wars on poverty. Nevertheless, lowering our sights somewhat, the group strategy's advantages are substantial. It broadens the reach of NLFs and the poor's legal rights, making individual casework less of a burden on the NLF and less dependent on lawyers. Given the great number of people whose legal rights are not enforced and the evident need for organized groups to monitor institutions ostensibly created to help the disadvantaged, the encouragement and aiding of such local groups adds power to the effort to make rights effective.

Second, the encouragement of groups can add a vital new dimension to the law reform strategy, allowing for the follow-up and monitoring of law reform and adding at least some political power to the efforts of lawyers to change laws and practices. In addition, the group strategy offers the opportunity to minimize dependency on lawyers and purely legal strategies. This is especially true where lawyers work with existing community groups, but there is evidence that groups can become autonomous and self-sufficient if NLFs consciously seek to make them independent (e.g., Newham Rights Centre, 1977:29; Adamsdown Community Trust, 1978:68). Autonomous groups can then pursue a wide range of strategies, both legal and political, which they can determine for themselves. Finally, to the extent autonomous groups use legal services on their own terms, accountability problems are minimized. Lawyers can rely on the initiatives of groups responsible to their members.

If NLFs are to take even their narrow legal aims seriously, they must devote a considerable part of their energies to serving, and where necessary, creating local groups. This is the conclusion of leaders of NLFs in England, Canada, and Holland, and it was the conclusion of many leading participants in the U.S. legal services movement. Thus far, however, "group work" in the United States has not played a role comparable to that of the law reform strategy. Of course, the political system in the United States demands that test

193

cases continue to be important, but group work could increasingly supplement test cases. There are, in fact, at least some signs that changes may be on the way.

The slight relaxation in 1977 of the prohibition on group organizing is one example, especially given that it was a response to the requests of some legal services clients and attorneys.[17] The U.S. Legal Services Corporation has initiated meetings on the future of legal services. The principal discussion paper prepared thus far is by Michael Trister, entitled "Next Steps for the Legal Services Corporation" (Trister, 1978). The paper was discussed at the meeting of the Board of Directors in September 1977, and a series of task forces have been created on the basis of its proposals and suggestions. While a national discussion may not affect local priorities, the paper's conclusion shows that there is some concern with the current underemphasis on group work in the United States:

> By processing numerous similar claims, legal service projects offer an appropriate point for improving the "organizational" capacity of the poor to take advantage of the legal process. A major focus for the Legal Services Corporation should be to develop such aggregation techniques in all of the substantive areas of concern to the poor. ... [I]t might be desirable for the Corporation to allocate some money directly to client organizations that have developed programs to secure and enforce legal rights, such as a neighborhood improvement association, a tenant organization or a group concerned with specific unfair consumer practice. Also, local legal service projects could be structured to reflect organized interests within the client community and to maximize relationships between those organizations and the project. Finally the Corporation might provide seed money for the creation of organizations whose purpose is to assert the aggregate rights of its members (Trister, 1978:51–52).

The group strategy may yet find its place in the U.S. system of NLFs.

III. Community Education

Community education, the third of the major strategies for helping the poor as a class,[18] encompasses a wide variety of activities designed to make individuals and groups aware of their legal rights and obligations. It is often termed "preventive" because it may "enable people to take the steps to safeguard their positions or to exercise their rights at the appropriate time and in the appropriate manner" (Law Centres Working Group, 1978:43). Examples of community education include lectures, seminars and films at schools[19] and community organizations,[20] the holding of conferences (e.g., Brent Community Law Centre, 1978:12–13; Commission des services juridiques, 1977:19, 28), the printing of pamphlets and "do-it-yourself kits,"[21]

194

and news columns and television and radio shows (e.g., Commission des services juridiques, 1977:25; Saskatchewan Community Legal Services Commission, 1976:17). The importance of this type of work has been recognized by all NLF programs beginning with OEO Legal Services, and examples of these activities abound in the various reports and publications within the NLF movement. Everyone is generally in favor of legal education.

There is, however, evidence of differing commitments to this strategy, and education may fulfill several roles, depending on the NLF's self-image. It is helpful again to consider the important differences in emphasis between NLFs in the United States and England.

A. *Community Education in the United States and England*

The limited available evidence suggests that community education has not been undertaken to any significant degree by NLFs in the United States. One major study published in 1970 found that of all the "goal areas" of the OEO *Guidelines*, "Community education has been perhaps the most neglected ..." (Auerbach Corporation, 1970:6–7). The more recent study by Handler, Erlanger, and Hollingsworth also found a very weak commitment to community education—only 4.1 hours per month, compared to over 50 on law reform (Handler et al., 1978:58). The reason most often given for this failure is that education efforts did not generate much community interest and NLFs did not want to stimulate any more demand on their overburdened resources (e.g., Trister, 1978:49; Cappelletti et al., 1975:214–15).

In England, despite the absence of comparable data, it is clear that community education is given a higher priority. It is always given equal status with group work, and centers' reports emphasize activities carried out in the educational area. There are several reasons for this commitment, linked to the emphasis on groups and self-help. Education is not seen merely as an abstract public service activity, which may be ineffective anyway and could easily be subordinated to more pressing concerns, nor as simply a way to generate individual casework, but rather as an integral part of the effort to generate and support self-help groups to assert their interests in major community issues. According to the Law Centres Working Group, "we use posters, leaflets, and bulletins which relate to the working of the law in connection with local matters known to be of interest which can make an immediate impact" (Law Centres Working Group, 1978:43).

195

Some brief English examples can show how this community education can be integrated with other law center activities. First, speaking to local groups can be considered community education or group work. As noted in Section II of this chapter, a vital role of the center lawyers is to keep organizations informed about legal developments in order for them to advise their members and protect their legal rights. Second, also as noted before, the first step in mobilizing a part of a community may be education about a problem and the possibilities for action. For example, the Adamsdown Law Centre's "campaign" against slum clearance, discussed earlier, began with a door-to-door canvass of neighborhood residents. The Newham Rights Centre, which has a printing press to help it concentrate on group work, publishes numerous action-oriented pamphlets. One pamphlet is entitled "Organise! How to take up an issue as an organised group of people." The latest Newham report (1977:42) similarly observed that, "Our booklets on the Health and Safety at Work Act became the basis for starting a local Health and Safety at Work Committee which brought together many of the local unions." In both of these examples, education is directed toward community action against a specific problem with legal aspects.

Community education may also encourage individual self-help. The Newham Rights Centre again provides examples. It published one pamphlet with a simple form to fill out and send in to request supplementary welfare benefits for heating, blankets, and winter clothing (Newham Rights Centre, 1977:33). Another do-it-yourself kit was in preparation for tenant organizations and tenants concerned with "unfit" housing conditions (1977:35).

Educational work in England is basic to the law centers' activities with both individuals and groups. It is necessary to make the other activities successful.

B. The Purposes of Community Education

The main purposes of community education have already been indicated, and can be summarized as follows: to encourage planning on the basis of legal rights and obligations; to mobilize individuals and groups to pursue their rights; to facilitate and strengthen community organizations; and to foster self-help activities for which lawyers will not be necessary. To these can be added a more inclusive aim, expressed especially by the English law centers—the "demystification" of the law (Law Centres Working Group, 1978:43).

Demystification implies that the esoteric mysteries of the law are made comprehensible to nonlawyers. It is a central ingredient in any effort of an NLF to discourage dependency on lawyers: "Clients often accept and rely on expertise without question while the expert will get on with the solution of the problem in his own terms without explaining or discussing it" (Balham Community Law Centre, 1977:8). Dependency is the inability to evaluate or control the lawyer as much as the need to use a lawyer. Legal knowledge can help groups and individuals understand the possibilities and limits of legal action. It can combat the natural tendency of the professional to hide behind his presumed expertise in order to solve problems his own way.

There is a further reason to demystify, which goes beyond the strategies discussed so far. It may take legal sophistication to make people appreciate the *limits* of strictly legal approaches to their problem. People may believe that the lawyers' arguments will always be enough to ensure that rights are effectively vindicated. Lawyers are not the only victims of the "myth of rights," as Stuart Scheingold (1974) has called this naive belief in the efficacy of legal arguments. Accordingly, it may be necessary, as the Newham Rights Centre pointed out, for the NLF "to advise on the various nonlegal methods of tackling problems and their merits" (Newham Rights Centre, 1975:61). This may be a difficult task for lawyers to undertake, but it may be necessary if they wish to help their clients. NLFs, as one English commentator pointed out, may have to become "antilaw" centers in order to avoid "an increase in the legal profession's dependents" (Leat, 1975:181).

C. The Need for Community Education

Community education is a relatively noncontroversial strategy partly because it, too, has its socially integrative functions. Education on rights conveys also the limits of those rights and the duties that go with them. Tenants, for example, may not protest their eviction when they know their rights and duties, and welfare recipients might more easily accept inadequate benefits when they know the limits of their rights. Moreover, community legal education spreads an awareness of legal procedures and approaches to problems. In short, it may help bring "alienated" persons who represent a potential for violent protest within the legal system where protest can be moderated and kept in peaceful channels.

These observations, however, should not persuade us that an unorganized movement based on ignorance of rights should instead be supported. To the extent NLFs do seek to better the everyday lives of underprivileged groups, community education is a vital activity. It has great potential not only to inform people of rights and of

197

possibilities for effective action, but also it can serve, especially in connection with a group emphasis, to counteract tendencies of lawyers and clients to lapse into a relationship of dependency. As with group work, the U.S. approach seems thus far to have discouraged an activity that can do much to overcome the deficiencies of law reform and individual service work.

IV. The Value of the Social Change Strategies

The strategies discussed in this chapter have much to offer for disadvantaged persons. It is evident, in addition, that they can do much more for poor people than can be done through individual service work. Certainly there will be times when any NLF must take individual cases, but the effort should be to find ways to free NLFs for law reform, group work, community education, and other comparable strategies that might be developed and implemented. The overall role of these strategies, however, and the question of what "social change" they may be able to accomplish, can best wait until Part Four. It is first necessary, however, to treat a preliminary question raised by the previous two chapters. How do NLFs decide what legal needs to meet? Which social change strategies to pursue? When to bring test cases? What groups to create and support?, etc. Are these legal questions or political ones? Are lawyers with even the very best intentions capable of giving an answer that will best accord with the interests of the poor?

These questions, which concern both effectiveness and accountability, have troubled the NLF movement from the beginning. Once it is recognized that legal needs cannot simply be diagnosed and cured by legal means, criteria must be set by someone as to which legal needs should be met, and how. There has been a growing feeling that these issues are best decided locally and that the client community should be involved significantly in the decisions. The methods and approaches for doing this are the subject of the next chapter.

Notes

1. For a variety of reasons, law reform did not generally involve much legislative advocacy (see, e.g., Hazard, 1970; Karabian, 1972).

2. The thirteen centers, with their funding levels for 1976 and 1977, are as follows:

	1976	1977
1. Center for Law and Education, Inc. (Cambridge)	$419,459	$442,529
2. National Consumer Law Center, Inc. (Boston)	$425,251	$448,640
3. National Housing and Community Development Law Project (Berkeley)	$433,076	$456,895
4. National Economic Development Law Project (Berkeley)	$290,862	$306,859
5. National Health Law Program, Inc. (Santa Monica)	$382,522	$403,560
6. Center on Social Welfare Policy and Law (N.Y.)	$423,638	$446,938
7. National Senior Citizens Law Center (Los Angeles)	$392,943	$414,555
8. National Employment Law Project (N.Y.)	$241,152	$254,415
9. National Juvenile Justice Center (St. Louis)	$212,355	$224,035
10. Juvenile Rights Litigation Project–Youth Law Center (S.F.)	$108,000	$113,940
11. Migrant Legal Action Program, Inc. (Washington, D.C.)	$407,000	$429,385
12. National Social Science Law Project, Inc. (Washington, D.C.)	$224,100	$236,425
13. Indian Law Support Center, Native American Rights Fund (Boulder)	$130,000	$137,156

The 1976 figures are from Legal Services Corporation, *Annual Report 1976*, pp. 34–39 (Washington, D.C., 1976).

The 1977 figures are from Legal Services Corporation, *Annual Report 1977*, pp. 35–38 (Washington, D.C., 1978).

3. For lists of the areas in which test cases have been brought, see Johnson (1974:296) and Handler et al. (1978:56). The Handler et al. data indicate that legal services lawyers' law reform efforts in 1967 were 31.6% in housing, 20.3% in welfare, and 13.5% in consumer matters, and in 1972 the figures were 24.5%, 18.1%, and 15.1%, respectively.

4. According to Gary Bellow, one of the leading figures in the U.S. legal aid movement,

> "[T]his idea that the legal problems of the poor can and should be divided into large (political) test case claims [handled in the central office] and routine (apolitical) grievances [handled at the neighborhood offices] places a further stigma on day-to-day legal aid work, minimizing the importance of efforts on behalf of individual clients. It blurs the possibility of linking "test case" litigation to more community-based political efforts, and it justifies the limited approach to individual client grievances" (Bellow, 1977:58).

Other useful studies of this phenomenon in San Francisco are Brill (1970) and Carlin (1973).

5. One commentator favorable to test litigation has described a "cyclical pattern," found especially in welfare law.

> "Typically, a state adopts a restrictive administrative practice or regulation. Litigation is subsequently initiated against the new restriction, often proceeding

on the theory that it fails to comply with federal legislation and regulations. Successful litigation is then met with changes in the federal law that originally provided a basis for the challenge. Finally, a new round of litigation is brought, challenging the federal change and state responses, and the entire cycle may be repeated" (Capowski, 1976:664).

6. According to Selznick, referring to the test case strategy as "social advocacy,"

"[T]he demand for social change through social advocacy is heightened under two conditions: (1) the incapacity of legislative institutions to take effective action—the "deadlock of democracy," and (2) the refusal of minorities to accept repressive majority rule..." (Selznick, 1976:73).

For a balanced assessment of the test case strategy by well-informed observers, see Pye and Cochran (1969:573–79).

7. "Free legal services should be available to organizations composed primarily of residents of the areas and members of the groups served" (Office of Economic Opportunity, 1966:21).

8. It should be noted that Burt Griffin, the director who succeeded Johnson in mid-1968, did try to increase the program's concern with strengthening community groups. His emphasis was on economic development, however, and in any event he resigned after less than a year because of a tragedy in his family. The effect of his tenure was thus slight, and after his departure the "emphasis once again returned to law reform and appellate advocacy at the national level" (Pious, 1971:386).

9. According to Earl Johnson, "the use of lawyers to create organizations of poor people has seldom passed beyond the stage of theoretical discussion" (see Cappelletti et al., 1975:216).

10. Legal Services Corporation Act Amendment of 1977, Public Law No. 95–222. This change was requested by clients and project attorneys. See Memorandum from D. Miller, Project Advisory Group, to Legal Services Regulations Committee, 10 March 1978. According to the Miller Memorandum, which examines the legislative history of the change, the "clarification" can be construed to liberalize the policy regarding "concerted action."

"Legal services staff should *not* direct, head, or decide for a group. They *should*, however, be able to provide substantial encouragement and assistance to potential groups as long as it is ultimately the poor people themselves, not their legal services advocates and agents, who decide *whether* to go forward and *what* to do."

11. An article by Stephen Wexler published in 1970 (p. 1049) in the *Yale Law Journal* ("Practicing Law for Poor People") has been extremely influential in both Canada and England, yet it seems to have had little influence in the United States. Wexler, who accepted a law professorship in British Columbia, is cited extensively in the influential first report of the Newham Rights Centre in London (Newham Rights Centre, 1975). Wexler was a leading participant at the important Canadian Conference on Law and Poverty that took place in October 1971 in Ottawa (Cotter and Marx, 1977).

12. For other examples of the emphasis given to "group work," see Adamsdown Community Trust (1978: especially at 83–84); Balham Neighbourhood Law Centre

200

(1977:4); Brent Community Law Centre (1975); Holloway Neighbourhood Law Centre (1977); Newham Rights Centre (1975); Paddington Neighbourhood Advice Bureau and Law Centre (1976:13–14); Small Heath Community Law Centre (1977:7).

13. Very few institutions even attempt to measure group work. The Adamsdown Law Centre in Wales made a notable effort to describe its group work and the number of persons involved (Adamsdown Community Trust, 1978:83–84). The Newham Rights Centre in London reported that it undertook 54 cases with groups from 1 April, 1976 to 31 March, 1977, as opposed to 78 "potential test cases" (Newham Rights Centre, 1978:21). The Saskatchewan Report for 1975-76 similarly notes that the plan handled 73 matters dealing with organizational problems of groups, compared, for example, to 952 divorces (Saskatchewan Community Legal Services Commission, 1976:12–13). Unfortunately, one cannot find the extent of resources devoted to working with groups from this data, and the data in any event are bound to be incomplete and inadequate. A "group" is too abstract a term, since it can mean a paper organization or unorganized group of persons used by lawyers to bring a legal test case, or it can mean a viable autonomous organization.

14. According to Penner, based on his evaluations in Canada, lawyers can help organize by informing individuals and groups of their rights, writing manuals, training lay advocates, and "educating groups for confrontation," but "experience since 1970 suggests that while a lawyer can be a useful and in some cases indispensable resource person in all these areas, indigenous paralegals must be in the front line of this kind of service" (Penner, 1977:47).

15. It is difficult to obtain any data, but it appears that many of these paraprofessionals may help with routine divorce cases. According to Johnson, for example,

> Approximately one-third of the staff agencies in the United States have established a specialized division to process all clients who request assistance for this type of problem. Typically staffed with three or four secretaries/paraprofessionals ..., these units can process the typical divorce in a minimum time (see Cappelletti et al., 1975:153).

Other evidence can be adduced from "Project Descriptions" of twelve representative programs, published recently by the Legal Services Corporation (Legal Services Corporation, 1976:149–73). Only one of the descriptions, that of Harlem Assertion of Rights, Inc., mentions paralegals working with community groups. The two largest projects described are instructive. The Legal Aid Bureau of Baltimore, which employs in its offices some forty attorneys and twenty-nine paralegals, uses those paralegals to determine client eligibility and assist attorneys. Similarly, the Legal Aid Society of the City and County of St. Louis has a staff of thirty-three lawyers and fifteen paralegals, who are said only to help in providing legal services.

16. This is the conclusion of Edward Sparer, one of the key figures in the early history of the legal services program in the United States. He now favors representation of groups composed not of just very poor people based on single issues or areas, like welfare, but rather "multi-issue citizen's action groups" (Sparer, 1976–77:61–62). Jim Lorenz, then of CRLA, reached a similar conclusion:

201

"Our work has impact when client groups which we represent are perceived as having political power, when the cases which we handle for our clients succeed in arousing public sympathy for those clients and indignation against our opponents, and when the cases are supported by middle class groups, such as the trade unions, which do have political power" (Yale Law Journal, 1970:1085).

17. See note 10 above.

18. Another strategy, found especially in the United States, is often termed "economic development," meaning an effort to create organizations which can attract funding and capital. According to most sources, however, it has never played an important role in the U.S. legal services program.

19. Examples are in the following reports: Balham Neighbourhood Law Centre (1977:7–8); Brent Community Law Centre (1978:11–12); Camden Community Law Centre (1976:2, 30); Newham Rights Centre (1977:41); Legal Aid Services Society of Manitoba (1976:14–15); Commission des services juridiques (Quebec) (1977:30–31); Saskatchewan Community Legal Services Commission (1976:15–19).

20. Examples are in the following reports: Adamsdown Community Trust (1978:80–81); Balham Neighbourhood Law Centre (1977:7–8); Brent Community Law Centre (1978:11–12); Camden Community Law Centre (1976:30); Hillingdon Community Law Centre (1976:7); Newham Rights Centre (1977:29, 40–41); Paddington Neighbourhood Advice Bureau and Law Centre (1976:14); Saskatchewan Community Legal Services Commission (1976:17).

21. Examples are in the following reports: Adamsdown Community Trust (1978:80–81); Hillingdon Community Law Centre (1975:7); Newham Rights Centre (1977:42, 48–49); Saltley Action Centre (1977:4); Legal Aid Services Society of Manitoba (1976:14–15); Commission des services juridiques (1977:25, 28–29); Saskatchewan Community Legal Services Commission (1976:17).

202

Chapter 10

The Involvement of the Poor in NLF
Policy Making at the Local Level

The participation of the poor or local community in NLF policy
making has become an increasingly important component of the NLF
ideology. This idea began with the U.S. Legal Services Program,
which shared the emphasis of its parent agency, OEO, on ensuring
that programs would be "responsive" to concerns of the poor, but it
encountered considerable hostility in the legal profession. Many
changes have since taken place, however, and at this point few would
question the need for the strong participation of the client community
or a more broadly defined part of a local community served by an
NLF.

This chapter will examine the practical ways of ensuring such
participation, recognizing that such terms as "participation" and
"responsiveness" are extremely vague; they conceal a number of
theoretical and practical problems. In addition, the legal profession
has long argued that lay participation or especially lay control may
endanger a lawyer's independence. To what extent is this a serious
problem or merely a rationale for professional self-interest? This
question also must be dealt with here. Underlying the analysis in this
chapter, furthermore, will be the same perspective that has informed
previous chapters. In what way does this strategy help or hinder the
"social change" aims proclaimed by NLFs?

I. Methods for Providing for the Formal Participation of the Poor

A great number of methods have been devised for involving the poor
or the local community in NLFs. Local persons or clients can be made
part of the NLF staff, fulfilling such functions as that of community
worker, described in the preceding chapter. The NLF can be
required to raise a certain amount of its budget from local sources,
and "in kind" volunteer work can be used to fulfill that requirement.[1]
The hiring of lawyers from the local community can be encouraged.
Beyond these essentially ad hoc methods, however, there is a

widespread feeling that there should be formal mechanisms for local accountability. Here, too, many possibilities are available, but it is convenient to examine four basic methods found in the national or provincial schemes examined in this study. The methods can be characterized as follows: (1) control of NLFs by national or provincial governing boards, aided by local advisory committees; (2) control of NLFs by a regional board, aided by local advisory committees; (3) local board control, aided by advisory committees; and (4) local board control by a lay-dominated board. Within these models, of course, there can be many variations in client participation, and "control" is always a matter of degree; but the basic models are nevertheless useful. These models, it can also be noted, reflect the tendency to look to local "advisory committees" whenever control is not given to the local community or a representative part of it.

A. National or Provincial Control, Aided by Local Advisory Boards: Manitoba

Manitoba's six Community Law Centers have no governing board of their own. They were set up by the Board of Directors of the Legal Aid Services Society of Manitoba, and policy decisions, including the hiring and firing of personnel, are made at that level (Legal Aid Services Society of Manitoba Act, 1971 S.M. ch. 76, §19; Regulation under the Act, §§48–54, Manitoba Regulation 106/72, as amended by M.R. 12/73, 146/73, 235/73, 58/74, and 78/74). The eleven-person provincial Board must itself be composed of at least four nonlawyers, but there is no requirement that there be representatives of the poor or of poorer communities.

The effort to involve the lay public formally is made through local advisory committees linked to the Community Law Centers. These committees, composed of "residents of the community served," are appointed by the Board and must meet with the "senior attorney" of the relevant Community Law Center at least once every two months (§56(1)). In order to provide for some representativeness of the community and a certain independence from the Board, the committees must be appointed "from a list of nominees submitted by community organizations with the particular community" (§56(2)).

This method does not go very far to ensure that there will be effective community involvement. Clearly the limitation to an advisory role may discourage activism. Beyond that, however, one can question how much committees appointed by the Provincial Board will challenge that Board's decisions, and the committees do not even have direct access to the Board. They must go through an intermediary, the senior attorney, who in turn is responsible to the

Board. The role of the committee is thus a rather weak one.

According to the Executive Director this weak role does create some problems (letter from Ronald J. Meyer, 24 October 1977). While some committees have helped publicize legal aid services and made suggestions for legal actions, "a number of members feel that since all the major policy decisions of our Society are made by our Board of Directors that their input is at best nominal," Several committees have, for that reason, "remained dormant."

There may be times when these committees are active, but generally little formal involvement at the local level can be found in Manitoba. This is not to say that the legal aid system is not a very high quality one, but it does not appear to be well designed to involve the community formally in its operation.

B. Regional Control, Aided by Local Advisory Boards: Quebec

The same problem in encouraging community participation is evident in Quebec, where the system is functionally very similar. While six NLFs in Manitoba are under the provincial Board of Directors, some ninety full-time "legal aid bureaus" in Quebec are under the supervision and control of eleven regional boards which are in turn responsible to the *Commission des services juridiques* (Legal Aid Act (Quebec), §32, 1972 S.Q. ch. 14).

The "regional corporations" establish and provide for the staffing of the local legal aid bureaus (§32). The regional governing boards are composed of twelve persons appointed by the Commission for terms of three years. Four of the twelve must be lawyers, and another four must reside in the area served by the regional corporation (§35). At least four persons will therefore be residents of the relatively large regions served, but this does not necessarily connote participation by the poor. As in Manitoba, the task of involving the local community or clients is entrusted to advisory committees. The regional corporation is urged by statute to

> promote the setting up of an advisory committee of not more than twelve members or recognize such a committee to represent economically under-privileged persons at the bureau or local legal aid corporation to make representations regarding this act, advise the director of the bureau or local corporation on the needs of economically underprivileged persons and, if necessary, make recommendations to that regional corporation (§32(d)).

Unfortunately, this effort in Quebec has had even less success than the similar one in Manitoba; the committees have made almost no contribution to the legal aid system, according to a detailed study by Diane Deschamps published in Quebec's 1977 Annual Report (see

Commission des services juridiques, 1977:103–24). As of 1 May 1976, only twenty-one of the eighty-five full-time legal aid bureaus reported having or having had an advisory committee, and only six of these were considered "active" (1977:107). Of the active groups, only two "actively intervened in the internal operation of the Legal Aid Bureau and in hiring of personnel" (1977:113).

Moreover, the study showed the hostility of the NLF lawyers to the idea of an active advisory committee. The lawyers interviewed insisted that their work was purely professional and that active committees could undermine "the professional ethic" and "the responsibility of the advocates" (1977:116). This hostility, coupled with the difficulty of maintaining interest in participating in the committees, resulted in making at least this aspect of the Quebec legal aid system an "illusion." The program has not succeeded in involving the client community at the local level.

C. Local Control by Attorneys, Aided Sometimes by Local Advisory Boards: The United States

In the United States, NLF policies are primarily set at the local level, with the task entrusted to local governing boards.[2] The Legal Services Corporation has power to make or withhold grants to local projects, and under OEO the national staff sought to convert projects to a law reform strategy, but at present priorities and major decisions are entrusted to the local programs.

Individual legal services projects are not required by law or regulation to set up an advisory committee, but since the governing boards must be composed of 60 percent lawyers, such committees evidently have often been found to be desirable. There is, however, little information about the number of such advisory committees (cf. Harvard Law Review, 1967:831).

From the beginning of the OEO program, the "maximum feasible participation" of the poor was required in all projects, including legal services. The American Bar Association ensured, however, that this would be limited to require that the majority of any legal services governing board be composed of lawyers. This was not, in any event, inconsistent with the NLF philosophy prevailing in the United States, and lawyers' control has continued to be a relatively unchallenged tenet of NLF practice. As a result, as noted before, 60 percent of the members of local governing boards have been and must be lawyers (42 U.S.C. §2996f(c)). They are to be "selected from, or designated by, appropriate Bar Associations and other groups, including, but not limited to, law schools, civil rights or antipoverty organizations, and

206

organizations of eligible clients" (45 C.F.R. §1607.3(c)). Nevertheless, OEO insisted that a substantial portion of the board members be eligible clients and in practice this worked out to about one third of the board (see Cappelletti et al., 1975:100). This one-third requirement was continued in the governing regulations issued by the Legal Services Corporation, and the 1977 amendments to the Legal Services Corporation Act made this a statutory requirement. According to the regulations, these members of the governing board should "be selected from, or designated by, a variety of appropriate groups including, but not limited to, client and neighborhood associations and organizations" (45 C.F.R. §1607.3(d)).

There has been a relatively long experience, therefore, with substantial client participation on governing boards in the United States. Unfortunately, there have been few attempts to evaluate it. Considerable data, however, indicate that governing boards generally were not very active. According to a detailed study completed in 1968, "Most Boards of directors contribute little to the on-going operations of their LSP's [Legal Services Projects]. Their principal function is to select a project director and let him run the LSP, usually with minimal intervention" (Auerbach Corporation, 1970:2-8). When boards did actively intervene, it was generally because the relatively conservative lawyer members, usually appointed by the local bar association, sought to keep staff lawyers from going beyond individual service work.

The role of poor people on these boards has not been well-documented, but some relevant data are available. A study published in 1967 found that the involvement of the poor did not have a very promising beginning: "most legal services programs have approached it with indifference or reluctance, in many cases viewing the establishment of machinery for effecting participation as a necessary evil accompanying OEO funds" (Harvard Law Review, 1967:828). Later studies not surprisingly show the dominance of lawyers in board proceedings, and they indicate the problems in securing even the attendance of nonlawyers (Champagne, 1974:661; Girth, 1976:56). According to Marjorie Girth, who studied three New Jersey legal services projects in great detail, "board discussions were either so technical or so managed that the views of these representatives, if sought, mattered little. As a result, they rarely attended meetings" (Girth, 1976:56). Her conclusion, therefore, is very pessimistic:

> The role of the representatives of the poor varied little in the three local boards in this study. Each board used the presence of the representatives to justify policy decisions made by the lawyer-members of the board (or, when they abdicated, by the program director) and to give judgments about program priorities the gloss of citizen participation (1976:56).

207

Another study, however, based on a larger sample of projects but with data only from questionnaire responses, found more room for optimism. Community members of the boards questioned tended to believe that "poverty community representatives participate in discussions and have significant influence over policy outcomes..." (Champagne, 1974:663). How much credibility to give to these self-reported data, however, is hard to determine, particularly since the same representatives evidently exaggerated their own control over the projects (Champagne, 1974:663–64). The conclusion, in any event, must be that the programs for the most part have been controlled by attorneys, whether on the staff or on the governing board, even if there has been some input by the poor into board deliberations. It has been difficult to involve the poor when their power is relatively slight and they must face issues that seem to be "technical."

At least some legal services offices have created client councils, advisory committees, and the like with the specific task of setting local priorities. This method, at least as reflected in the reported examples, appears to have had some success in involving the poor in a program.[3] A recent article describes how legal aid in Hawaii was transformed by the initiation of a planning process with ultimate responsibility given to the client community (Fuller, 1977). The Board of Directors accepted the priorities set by the clients, and the client involvement created new interest in the program and a new enthusiasm on the part of program staff. The program became more controversial but, according to the article, the staff found that "the democratization process could also provide the society with its own political, grass-roots power base (the clients themselves) which would defend the program against all adversaries in the state, both public and private" (Fuller, 1977:44). Delegation to the poor of at least the general priority setting process can, as this example shows, be an important way of achieving some meaningful involvement.

Still, the U.S. model leaves ultimate power with the governing boards dominated by attorneys. Boards may differ considerably in ideology and importance, and the poor may in some programs significantly affect the conduct of a board, but the framework is local control by local attorneys, especially those beholden to local bar associations. And it is clear, as noted before, that the influence of such boards has generally been a conservative one, at least until recent years—for which no data are yet available. Local attorneys tend to be less innovative and pro-"social change" than NLF attorneys.

D. Local Control by Predominantly Lay Boards: Saskatchewan and England

The NLFs in Saskatchewan and in England are locally controlled by governing boards which need not contain a majority of lawyers. Partly for ideological and partly for practical reasons, they have chosen to take the participation of the target population one step further than advisory councils or one-third community representation.

Saskatchewan's approach is most unique. An extraordinary effort has been made to give community control over the thirteen "community law offices" which serve Saskatchewan's less than one million people. The mechanism is through "area boards" that are required "to represent fairly the interests of those persons and organizations in the area whom this Act is intended to assist" (Community Legal Services (Saskatchewan) Act, 1974 §14(4)(a)). They have the power to retain or dismiss all staff employees except solicitors,[4] for whom they must "have the prior approval of the commission or any person designated by the commission for that purpose" (§15 (f) and (h)). In implementing these measures, the Saskatchewan Community Legal Services Commission has embraced the idea of community control. Community control, of course, is not necessarily the same as control by poor persons, but it does go beyond control by lawyers.

Potential clients and other members of the local communities served were encouraged "to join and become a member of the society which elects the area board" (Community Legal Services Commission, 1975:14) *before* lawyers and staff were hired. According to the Commission's first report (1975:22), this approach was undertaken to "ensure that these boards were indeed the authoritative voice with respect to the offices set up under the plan..." The power of the local communities or boards has been strengthened in other ways. Three of the chairpersons of the area boards serve on the nine-person provincial Commission (Community Legal Services (Saskatchewan) Act, 1974, §14(c)). The area boards have themselves formed an association called the Saskatchewan Association of Community Legal Services Boards, which exchanges information and "functions as an inside critic of the ... plan" (Saskatchewan Community Legal Services Commission, 1975:8). This Association can multiply the impact of the lay perspective encouraged at the local level. It contributes further to what apparently is, as the Commission report suggests, "the first jurisdiction-wide legal aid plan where community control is a reality rather than a myth" (1975:22).

The English law centers, although not yet part of a statutory plan, are similar in their emphasis on community control. As described before, each law center has an independent management committee, and the importance of the committee in setting priorities and retaining staff is recognized by all the major interest groups. For the Law Centres Working Group, the independent committee is necessary "as a constant check that the Law Centre is remaining responsive to local need and not getting bogged down in rigid work structures as professionals left to their own devices have an inclination to do" (Law Centres Working Group, 1978:47). The Law Society, in turn, now suggests that their earlier (but not yet implemented) statutory scheme for "Section 16 Legal Aid Centres" is inadequate because, "There is no means of involving local organizations or other representatives of the community in the management of a law centre..." (Law Society, 1977:205). In the waiver agreement signed by the Law Centres Working Group and the Law Society, moreover, both sides agreed that "a majority of the voting members of the Management Committee of a salaried service should normally be able to represent the interests of the recipients of the service" ("Waivers of the Solicitors Practice Rules," 1977). This local control idea thus appears to be a lasting component of the NLF movement in England.

The methods of constituting these twelve to twenty-five member management committees vary considerably in detail, but the usual combination appears to be election plus appointments of members to represent particular groups. The local and national Law Societies, for example, are usually represented, as are often a local Citizens' Advice Bureau and the local government (when funds come from that source). As pointed out in the earlier discussion of England, the lawyers are greatly outnumbered by local citizens and members of community groups (e.g., Zander and Russell, 1976:214). Most of the citizens in the target areas, it should be remembered, are either poor or lower-middle-class. One interesting variation on this general method of election plus "co-option" is that typified by the Newham Rights Centre. The Newham Rights Centre opens its membership only to representatives of organizations whose "principal purposes ... include the improvement or protection of the working or living conditions of that organization ... as long as a substantial number of members live or work in the London Borough of Newham" (Newham Rights Centre, 1977:3). As of 1976, membership included twenty-four local organizations, two ethnic group organizations, and a number of labor unions. The center's management committee clearly is designed to complement the group emphasis in the center's day-to-day work.

Only some indication can be given as to how management committees operate in practice. In response to a survey of fifteen law centers in 1975, ten centers reported that their management committees were "important" or "quite important" (Zander and Russell, 1976:210). The Adamsdown Law Centre's 1978 report suggests what kind of involvement is in mind (Adamsdown Community Trust, 1978:61). First, it is clear that many issues for law center work are picked up through members of the management committee who are in touch with local concerns. Second, issues suggested by staff members for "campaigns" are subject to the decision of the management committees. The committee helps to decide if an issue with legal possibilities can build the local constituency deemed necessary to success. Accordingly, the concern with building and servicing groups is reinforced by the management committee structure. By way of comparison, it can be suggested that the U.S. emphasis on test cases and strictly legal strategies made it more difficult to encourage involvement in day-to-day affairs. It is suggestive that the specialized "back-up centers" in the United States have been criticized by "experienced program staff and clients" on "accountability" grounds.[5] A strictly law reform-test case approach may be hard for clients to understand, and lawyers may see no reason to involve them. Lay persons do more to contribute to group work and community education than to a strategy focused only on test cases.

This view of management committees in England, however, may exaggerate their role. The data are still fragmentary. On at least one occasion, due to an overrepresentation of Law Society representatives, the committee was very conservative (see Byles and Morris, 1977:14–20). Moreover, even the Law Centres Working Group admits that "Finding the best way to set up a Management Committee to fulfill these functions has, it must be admitted, been something of a problem in the early days of the Law Centre Movement" (Law Centres Working Group, 1978:47). Problems have been caused by the requirement of Law Society representation imposed by funding agencies, but there has also been a natural "tendency to include other professionals on the committees": "It is perhaps indicative of conditions prevailing in deprived communities that people lack confidence in their own abilities to select solutions to their problems so that they will all too readily accept the conclusion of outside professionals" (Law Centres Working Group, 1978:47). Still, the Law Centres Working Group suggests that there may be a positive evolution as law centers become established, and as independent community groups take an interest in them or spring up with their help. This hoped-for evolution may seem less appealing than Saskatchewan's aim to invoke democracy prior to the NLF's existence, but, as will be suggested below, the English approach may be more realistic.

211

II. Community Participation and Control and the "Social Change" Strategies of NLFs

A number of theoretical and practical problems are evident from the previous discussion. Many of these problems are typical of welfare state efforts to help and involve the "have nots" (cf. Gilbert and Specht, 1974:107–38; Cahn and Passet, 1971; Kramer, 1969). One problem unique to NLFs and similar institutions, however, must be examined—the question of the lawyer's professional independence.

It may be recalled that the concern for independence has been seen on at least three occasions in this study. First, the American Bar Association used the spectre of a loss of independence to insist that NLF governing boards be dominated by lawyers. Second, in the English experience, independence was manifested in a rather different way: the lay-dominated management committees were accepted by the Law Society as a means of avoiding the influence of local governments in law center activities. And third, in Australia, the law societies challenged the whole idea of federally-funded offices as a violation of professional independence. A lawyer, it was argued, could not serve two masters—the government and the client. Other examples of this concern can also be found. In fact, however, lawyers are increasingly having to submit to the scrutiny of government and the lay public, and the conservative view of independence is losing any force it might have had (see Zander, 1979). The spectre of a loss of independence through public funding or lay management is no longer compelling. It "is the red herring basis on which lawyers have demanded program control" (Ferren, 1968:285).

Independence must be taken to mean simply that the lawyer has no conflict of interest when serving a particular client. The existence of such a conflict does not depend on whether a management committee is composed of lawyers or lay persons. In either case, such a committee could not, for example, tell a lawyer to handle an individual's case in a particular way. This independence is designed to protect the client, and it is not inconsistent with priorities set by nonlawyers, including, I would submit, decisions on whether a particular case falls within those priorities.[6] Professional independence, therefore, is not a substantial rationale for denying participation or control to the client community.

Other problems, however, are more serious. It is very difficult to obtain the strong participation of members of deprived communities, particularly when all that is sought is involvement in decisions clearly made by others, either at the national, regional or local level. No one can be expected to participate actively when there is no real function to fulfill. Experience suggests that if *control* is given to the target group over at least some basic issues, most notably that of priority setting, it will be easier to spark citizen interest. Further, if the approach of the NLFs is to emphasize technical legal issues on which lay persons have little to contribute, one can expect lay interest to dwindle. Lay persons are more likely to add to group work and community education efforts than to test cases, class actions, and individual service work.

Another question concerns how best to select community representatives. General experience with participation in social welfare programs has been disappointing. According to one commentator, "Community control tends to become control of the community by some elements to the exclusion of others and does not necessarily lead to more effective service" (Weissman, quoted in Gilbert and Specht, 1974:117). A board may become a self-perpetuating minority which only appears to represent the community. An effort to represent more than just the poor or near-poor may end up with domination by just those persons the NLFs' clients are generally against.[7] Moreover, even if a way is found to obtain control by the poor, control by poor persons may still assert a conservative influence on an NLF.

The dangers of community control—even by the poor—to an innovative program can be suggested by an American example. One well-known U.S. neighborhood law firm, the San Francisco Neighborhood Legal Assistance Foundation, managed to assert the principle of community control despite the pressures from above to have lawyer-dominated governing boards (see Stanford Law Review, 1967). Representatives of the poor were very active in the setting of policies within the Foundation.[8] The experience, however, was not very successful. According to the program's coordinator, Jerome Carlin,

> The lawyer-founders had been wrong in assuming that control by the client community was a necessary condition for, let alone compatible with, a program of institutional change. We were unfortunately burdened with some romantic notions of the poor.
>
> The neighborhood leaders, particularly those identified with the poverty program, were following an old pattern fashioned by older ethnic groups as they fought their way up the power ladder. These leaders were, by and large, not out to change or seriously challenge the system; they simply wanted to be cut in (Carlin, 1973:197–98).

Community control and the goal of institutional change, in short, may conflict.

The issue may be whether to champion local democracy or the social change goals of NLFs. Put another way, given the broader substantive goals of NLFs proclaimed even by those who may overemphasize community control, the question is, in the words of the Cahns, "participation for what purpose": "What kind of participation, in what form, is necessary to perform the function which participation uniquely is required to perform?" (in Cotler and Marx, 1977:47).

Poor persons can provide expertise in their problems, decide what priorities should be undertaken, hold the NLF accountable for its methods and activities, and insulate the NLFs from attack at the community or a higher level. None of these activities need necessarily be undertaken through management committees or advisory boards. Indeed, at least one knowledgeable observer, Roland Penner, has criticized "the seeming fixation" of some Canadian NLFs "with the formal mechanisms for governing":

> It has been my observation in making these evaluations and based as well on experience with or knowledge of other legal aid plans, that the most effective involvement whether it be, generally, of the community, or somewhat more specifically of clients, is either on an ad hoc basis around particular issues or through *autonomous* community or client groups (Penner, 1977:152).

This opinion may be accurate, given the problems of assuring that community participation in formal institutions will be both representative and a help to the NLFs' activist goals.[9] Nevertheless, one should not neglect the importance of some kind of formal community control.

Ideally, perhaps, NLFs would serve autonomous groups in the way chosen by these groups. The social change orientation of the groups would create opportunities for lawyers to help; it would avoid creating dependencies and diverting reform energies towards priorities determined by lawyers attuned only to legal possibilities for action; and the professional independence of lawyers would shield them from criticism for their actions in support of groups. This ideal, however, presupposes a number of relatively strong autonomous groups. A deprived community may not have such groups—indeed an indication of deprivation may be their absence. If lawyers and NLF staff are to create or bolster particular groups or generally seek to mobilize the community around certain issues, it would be dangerous to entrust the decision only to an NLF staff or lawyer-dominated governing board. The danger, which has been noted repeatedly here, is that lawyers will mobilize communities only in relatively narrow, legalistic directions, creating counterproductive dependencies on lawyers and legal strategies. The growing concern that the poor at least set priorities for NLFs reflects an awareness of

214

this danger. An independent management committee can also help insulate proactive lawyers from the often controversial actions they may initiate.

The strategy of local control by the client community, in sum, has real dangers, but it offers possibilities that are simply unavailable to a program run from above, by the staff, or by a lawyer-dominated committee. The dilemma is how to achieve these possibilities without succumbing to a perhaps representative, but conservative committee. Put very bluntly, the aim is to find a formula for "local control" by those who will favor, even push NLFs in an activist direction.

A comparison of the Saskatchewan and English methods may show what this pragmatism could mean in practice. In Saskatchewan the paramount goal was community control, and to strengthen this aim lawyers were hired after the area boards were set up. The boards could thereby set priorities from the outset. There is little information available on how this worked in practice, but it is clear that professionals have been elected in substantial numbers to these boards (e.g., Saskatchewan Community Legal Services Commission, 1975:10).

In England, in contrast, the management committees appear to evolve toward an active role after the basic work pattern is set (e.g., Law Centres Working Group, 1978:48; Newham Rights Centre, 1975:67–71). Those who become interested in serving on management committees are generally those who find *that* work pattern worthwhile, and, in any event, law centers generally do not leave the competition for management committee places too open. The Law Centres Working Group stated this clearly in 1974:

> From our view it is the organisations of the poor people themselves, such as tenants' associations, local associations of workers in the area, old age pension clubs, etc., who, from the mere fact of being organised already have some understanding of how they can collectively tackle their collective difficulties (something of which they would be incapable individually), which should control the policies of the Law Centre. These are the organisations through which the inhabitants of "deprived areas" are best able to express their collective needs in relation to housing, development schemes, employment, etc., and it is for the Law Centre to enable them to do it better (Community Law Centres, 1974:16).

It is clear from the quoted passage that the management committees so *selected* will not change the centers' basic approach. Work with groups will continue to be emphasized, and tenants' problems will no doubt be given considerable attention. The management committee, in short, is closely linked to the law centers' self-chosen style of work. While not genuinely representative of all the community, this type of

215

committee may realistically do more for the deprived community than a more democratically selected one.

Notes

1. An OEO requirement, for example, was that local projects raise 20% of the amount given by the federal government, which in practice meant that NLFs relied on in-kind donations by lawyers, law students, and others (Huber, 1976:158).

2. According to the Legal Services Corporation Act Amendments of 1977, local programs must establish priorities regarding the relative needs of their communities, taking account of people who have special needs, such as the elderly and the handicapped. Public Law No. 95-222, 95th Cong., 2nd Sess., 1977.

3. In the example reported by Carol Silver (1969:241–43), the advisory committee "decided finally that the caseload problem could best be solved by limiting the office to cases affecting the largest groups of poor people possible." Such cases were defined as (1) representing organized groups, (2) representing unorganized groups, (3) test cases, (4) educational, and (5) development projects. According to the Legal Services Corporation (1978:12–13), an advisory committee in Kentucky "made a determination that because it was impossible to handle all the individual clients who need assistance, the staff should attempt to give major attention to cases that present significant issues to large numbers of persons." (Other examples are in Legal Services Corporation (1977b:162–67).)

4. The reasons for the different treatment of solicitors are "as a double check on quality … [and to] guard against the possibility of a board attempting to interfere, in any way, with the solicitor-client relationship" (Community Legal Services Commission, 1975:9).

5. This criticism is given in Project Advisory Group (the National Organization of U.S. Legal Services Programs), PAG 5-1977, at 6 (Cf. Carlin, 1973; Brill, 1970).

6. Ferren (1968:286) similarly supports a limitation of the notion of "professional independence" to the handling of particular cases:

> "[I]t has nothing to do with the decision *whether or not* to *accept a case*. It is the latter decision with regard to priorities of case categories under a limited budget which is crucial to the lesser public eligible for legal services; this is a political, not a legal decision, and anyone who argues that lawyers, not the client public, should control that decision is really saying that he does not trust the client public's politics."

7. According to Pauline Morris, community "representatives, whether appointed or elected, come from the ranks of those trained community 'leaders': teachers, ministers of religion, social workers and local 'worthies.' Only very rarely are unskilled factory or farm workers, status or nonstatus Indians, and welfare recipients members of such boards" (1975).

For example, the governing boards of the Community Law Offices in British Columbia were supposed to embody the principle of community control, but the definition of community was left unclear. A high percentage of local board members thus work in the "professional or managerial occupations," and the Offices have reflected that domination with a reluctance to encourage aggressive NLF activities. According to Morris and Stern, who studied the approach of the Community Law Offices,

> "[The Board Members] and the staff, are often dependent for their livelihood, and frequently their social contacts too, on those very people who may be perceived by disadvantaged clients as a cause of their problems, for example the personnel in government departments, lawyers, landlords and the police. There is, as a consequence, a very strong desire on the part of most Boards not to 'rock the boat' by involving themselves in issues which may bring them into conflict with those associates whose activities impinge on other aspects of their daily lives" (Morris and Stern, 1976:32).

8. The method of election was the following: "representatives to neighborhood councils are selected from small electoral districts, each only a few blocks square; the four neighborhood councils then selected a majority of the board for both the community action agency and the legal services program" (Harvard Law Review, 1967:832).

9. The position of a leading Dutch law shop, that of Tilburg, is similar. It is felt that the work with local groups provides sufficient community involvement (de Jong, 1977).

Chapter 11

Types of Neighborhood Law Firms

The discussion of strategies in this Part has indicated the major differences between and among NFLs in the various countries studied. This chapter will summarize the previous three by enumerating briefly the major types of NLFs that have been examined or could be created (see, e.g., Hazard, 1969; Byles and Morris, 1977:57; Newham Rights Centre, 1975:24–51). These types can be called (1) the "legal needs" model; (2) the "professional" model; (3) the "therapeutic" model; (4) the "community control" model; and (5) the "social reform through groups" model. Needless to say, none of these models exists in pure form, but at least a few of the models are close to those which now exist. The contrast between the professional model found generally in the United States and the social reform/ group model in England is especially notable.

I. The Legal Needs Model

The theme of "unmet legal need" has had a powerful influence on NLFs, as has repeatedly been noted. It will suffice here to say that the focus of the pure "legal needs" model of NLFs would be on individual cases. The assumption of such an approach is that there is a *need for lawyers* which, because of economic, geographical, social, and psychological barriers to access, is not being met. The remedy for the gap is accessible lawyers, located as close as possible to poor people's residences. The goal is to get lawyers to the poor.

This model has not worked very well even on its own terms. NLFs in every country studied have been flooded with individual cases, and increases in the number of lawyers available to the poor still cannot handle the demand. There are simply too many potential legal problems. In addition, many of these problems can be handled at the individual level without NLFs. The kind of problems that gave rise to the concept of unmet need—welfare problems, consumer matters, landlord–tenant disputes—may even be handled better at the individual level without lawyers, through new dispute-processing institutions; and other types of problems, particularly divorce and criminal defense, can be dealt with adequately by a judicare system.

Finally, the legal problems of the poor must be seen as problems of a group or class, not simply as an array of disparate individual problems. Many poor consumers may be cheated by the same bank or department store; a welfare office may deprive thousands of recipients of their supplementary benefits; or a slum clearance program may threaten an entire neighborhood. Most NLFs therefore at least attempt to go beyond individual needs. The legal need model joins with another. The task is made simpler, of course, if there are alternatives available for individual cases, such as private, subsidized lawyers, effective small claims courts, and citizens' advice bureaus.

II. The Professional Model

The professional model of an NLF is best represented historically by the NLF system in the United States and perhaps also by that in Quebec. It goes further than the previous one in the application of legal skills. The aim is to give the poor high-quality professional advocates who can handle individual cases, use their skills to aggregate claims (e.g., class actions), and bring test actions to reform laws that are unfair to the poor. The Chairman of the Board of Directors of the U.S. Legal Services Corporation expressed this approach as follows:

> The legal services program is set on a road that emphasizes professional quality, and the board intends to provide the leadership necessary to ensure that the poor receive the same quality and range of service that is provided to the rich (Crampton, 1975:1342).

The problems of the poor are treated in only their legal dimension, and the remedy for these problems is sought in legal arguments and actions.

The organization of legal services in the United States reflects this approach. Most important NLFs are divided into units providing service work and specialists in "impact work," and the latter is usually meant to be law reform advocacy in the courts, administrative agencies, or (to a lesser extent) legislatures. Work with groups is given a low priority, especially organizing activities, which are considered political, not legal. Community education takes place in only very small amounts, since its only role is the rather abstract one of conveying general information. Further, there is little place for the participation of the poor in any continuing manner, since lawyers are involved primarily with legal doctrines and arguments. The poor are generally not capable of evaluating or contributing to such work.

219

The principal virtue of the professional approach is that it can pretend to be "nonpolitical." Lawyers for the poor are simply doing the same thing as lawyers for the rich; the professional responsibility of lawyers in fact requires zealous advocacy of the rights of clients.

The problems with this approach begin with the recognition that legal arguments and test cases are only a partial strategy for helping the poor. The weaknesses of law reform have been amply documented. The results of test cases may be only symbolic victories which assuage dissent without leading to concrete gains on behalf of very many poor persons. Moreover, a purely "professional" approach encourages lawyers to think only in terms of legal rights and remedies. A critic of the U.S. approach recently made the following observation:

> Legal aid lawyers unwilling or unable to respond to client concerns in ways that link them to a larger vision of social justice can easily become the purveyors of resignation and acquiescence in existing social arrangements. Clients can literally be taught that their situations are natural, inevitable, or their own fault, and that they themselves are ultimately dependent on professional advice and guidance (Bellow, 1977:60).

NLFs are inevitably involved in politics, and to rely only on a professionally-oriented theory of action—the likely result if lawyers are left to themselves—is to hinder other courses of action and undermine the lawyers' own reform efforts. An uneasiness with leaving decisions to lawyers is certainly evident in the United States and Quebec, but the move toward a different style of advocacy has not yet taken place.

III. The Therapeutic Model

While not explicitly mentioned before, a therapeutic model of an NLF can be suggested on the basis of NLF aims and strategies. The aim is to use NLFs to "cure" personal defects of the underprivileged which allegedly prevent their advancement. The approach is not just legal, but multidisciplinary:

> [It] is argued that if lawyers, social workers, and community workers would only pool their resources, the problems faced by the underprivileged would be viewed from a wider perspective, legal services would no longer be isolated and community action programs could be initiated (Byles and Morris, 1977:56).

The group models found in England have tendencies in this direction. "Community action" can be considered (as it once was also in the United States) not as an effort to build community power, but rather as one of "breaking the cycle of poverty" to allow people to take advantage of laws and programs supposed to help them (see, e.g., Johnson, 1974:25–27, 34–35). Of course, a group may move beyond the role assigned to it by its founders, but the element of therapy, undertaken by a team of professionals, can be seen as a separate emphasis of a group strategy.

This therapeutic strategy has an obvious limitation. The problems of the poor may relate to individual deficiencies of poor individuals, but they also stem from the actions of others, particularly institutions and organizations such as corporations, banks, welfare departments, and landlords. It is not enough simply to change the poor.

IV. The Community Control Model

One of the criticisms of the previous three models is that they leave "need" to be defined primarily by professionals. This is said to be paternalism and, even worse, tends to create stultifying dependencies on lawyers and legal strategies. One remedy is to take the power from the professionals and place it in the hands of the community being served. The community then will have a tool, the NLF, which it can use to improve its position. Saskatchewan's legal aid plan, under which the lay-elected governing boards were given the basic power at the outset, comes closest to this model.

Problems with this model, despite the appeal of community participation and control, were discussed in the previous chapter. The appropriate "community" is not always easy to define. Finding mechanisms to insure that the community, or the poorer part of it, is effectively represented in a governing board may also be difficult. And the representatives of the community might even work against, not for, the "social change" goals of NLFs.

Community control, therefore, should not be romanticized. When an NLF goes into a poor community, it may be too much to expect the community to suddenly wake up to the potential of the NLF. The poor may also have traditional ideas of what constitutes legal service, and they may, in any event, defer to others with traditional opinions. Accordingly, community control is probably best seen as a strategy for giving a "consumer perspective" to NLFs already oriented in a certain direction. This, it was suggested, is what has apparently happened with the English law centers.

V. The Social-Reform-through-Groups Model

The previous four models may all be considered "social reform" models by their proponents. Meeting legal needs, for example, gives

221

benefits and rights to underprivileged people. The professional model can result in the same improvements as well as important changes in the law and legal practices affecting the poor. The therapeutic model, in turn, may prepare individuals and groups to help themselves advance out of poverty or at least take advantage of opportunities available to them. Finally, community control can give the poor community a weapon which it can utilize to improve the position of its inhabitants. Each can be seen as a way for NLFs to make "social change."

Each of these models, however, suffers from a limiting frame of reference. The goals are given, respectively, as (1) providing accessible lawyers to poor individuals, (2) providing high-quality legal services to the poor, (3) preparing the poor to utilize available services, and (4) promoting community participation or control. A realistic political perspective, I think, can see the limitations of these various goals, not to mention the strategies chosen to pursue the goals. Most NLFs are a combination of these various models, and are not content with any of the above statements of goals. They want to make real social change on behalf of the poor, and they recognize that this is a political and not merely legal problem. Nevertheless, the "professional model" continues to be the prevailing one in at least the United States, and this limits the program's utility as a force for social change through NLF activities.

The continuing appeal of this strict professionalism in the United States is somewhat surprising in view of developments elsewhere. Even a leading U.S. liberal periodical, *The New Republic*, has printed an article denouncing the "intellectual poverty of legal services": "The legal services program ... rests on the ... premise that what really separates the poor from the upper-middle-classes is that they can't afford as much legal advice" (Chapman, 1977:9–10). There is some truth to the charge.

Such an assumption no longer characterizes an increasing number of the English, Dutch, and Canadian NLFs. The reasons for this evident naiveté in the United States or, if one prefers, realism elsewhere, are no doubt complex. A paper by R.I. Martin, entitled, "The Philosophy of Law Centres," may provide some illumination (Martin, 1975-76). Martin, a participant in the law center movement in England and Wales, develops a pattern for the de-professionalization of the law center lawyer in England. We can use his evolutionary scheme to ask what happens to U.S. lawyers. According to his analysis, law center experience anywhere produces a tension in lawyers. They are forced to examine "the relevance of the legal ideal of equal justice to social goals of political and economical equality"

222

(1975-76:45). Litigation—"the one locus in which the law would be given an opportunity to produce social change"—does not produce that change. Equal justice—lawyers for everyone—does not make social justice. An inescapable tension is created in a lawyer between "the strictures of his professional socialisation and the perceived need for politically effective tactics" (1975-76:51), i.e., professionalism vs. politics.

In resolving this tension, the lawyer is influenced by several factors. "Community workers," according to Martin, push the lawyer away from his faith in the "autonomy of the law" and toward a recognition that law is "one of several interconnecting systems of relationships, legal, economic and political" (1975-76:52). "Equal justice" is no longer a sufficient goal for the lawyer; "he is drawn to the values of his new reference group, law centre colleagues and clients, and their interpretation of 'justice'" (1975-76:56). The lawyer is pulled in an openly political direction.

The problem may finally be resolved, according to Martin, through a "median path" between legalism (or professionalism) and politicization. This median path is in fact the approach increasingly taken by the law centers, which I have called the "social-reform-through-groups" model of NLFs. It is an effort to use legal skills in a broader, more political effort to help the poor.

This evolutionary scheme is necessarily oversimplified, but it is a plausible one. The lawyer seeking social change should realize that changes in the law are not sufficient to obtain what is an undeniably political goal. Why this realization in lawyers has not yet taken place, or if so, had any significant impact on the U.S. program could be explained by comparing the United States and England. First, law reform is more effective in the United States than in England or elsewhere. Lawyers might stay persuaded that this "equal justice" can make "social justice." Second, the organization of legal services projects in the United States into service and law reform units may have discouraged work which is somewhere in between law reform and service work. Those in the service units, for example, could assume that since "impact work"—law reform—was beyond their competence, they should not attempt to transcend their limited role. Third, the influence of politically-oriented community workers has largely been absent in the United States. And, fourth, and perhaps most importantly, the organized bar in the United States has had enough power and influence to prevent this evidently political work from taking place. The English Law Society had less influence in the formative years of English law centers.

It should be recognized that this social-reform-through-groups model of change, no less than the others, rests on assumptions about causes of poverty, possible remedies, and how lawyers can contribute to those remedies. In particular, the paradigm of reform is that political change, at either the local or national level, is made and enforced by organized pressure groups. Since lawyers advocating reforms either in courts or before other decision-making bodies cannot substitute effectively for such groups, it is necessary for lawyers to help create groups and support existing ones (e.g., Trubek, 1977).

The social-reform-through-groups approach implies that rights proclaimed by the law are used, with the help of community workers, to mobilize groups to organize and take action on behalf of their members and others who are similarly situated. Test cases and law reform are very much part of this model, but it is considered useful— even essential—for organized groups to play the major role in changing and enforcing the law. Community education is also assigned considerable importance. NLFs can "demystify" the law, build group autonomy, and show groups both the possibilities and the limits of legal strategies. Ideally, the organizations will be able to decide themselves when to bring legal actions, when to seek legislative or administrative changes through lobbying, when to build coalitions with other groups, and in general how best to pursue the interests of their members. In addition, at least as envisioned in the evolving English model, an independent management committee, composed largely of representatives of local groups, has the task of welding the group strategy to a solid, activist community network and keeping it responsible to that network.

The group orientation, in addition, implies a great reduction in individual casework. It is indicative that the report on the annual conference of the Law Centres Working Group in 1977 noted "the desire of more and more centres to move towards a 'closed door' policy" (Brindmann, 1977). No longer is it considered desirable to serve all comers. The Brent Community Law Centre, for example, provides individual advice mainly to persons referred to the center from community organizations: "The function of the Centre is to provide legal back-up to 'frontline' organizations and agencies..." (Brent Community Law Centre, 1978:22).

A high degree of selectivity, necessary also for a pure law reform strategy, is only possible, of course, if clients are turned away or referred elsewhere. The possibility for referrals, as noted before, is enhanced greatly by the existence of complementary judicare schemes. Other advice centers such as the English Citizens' Advice Bureaus may also be of notable value in allowing a selective strategy. The Newham Rights Centre in London even runs free evening advice sessions at eight locations in its borough (Newham Rights Centre, 1978:7–13). The sessions are staffed by volunteer lawyers and local organizations. This type of advice session—which frees law centers for nonindividual work—could also be adopted where there is no judicare system, but the possibility of referrals from the sessions to private attorneys is certainly helpful to the success of advice sessions such as these.

The social-reform-through-groups NLF model does not create the drama of highly-publicized class actions and test cases brought one after another, and it reduces somewhat the premium put on clever legal arguments and prestigious appellate advocacy, but it seems to offer the best chance of winning lasting benefits on behalf of the poor. From my viewpoint, there is no doubt that NLFs in the United States will and should continue to emphasize test cases more than is done in other countries, but the program suffers to the extent that it is unable or unwilling to move one more step in a political direction. Hopefully the present planning process will lead to some change.

It should be clear by now, however, that this model NLF is still limited in what it can do to remedy social problems. We are, after all, dealing with the law, legal strategies, and organizations of persons based primarily on statuses that assume great inequalities of wealth and power. The contribution that NLFs ultimately can make to social change is difficult to assess, given these institutional dilemmas, but some further suggestions can be made in the next chapter.

Part Four

Conclusion

This comparative study has covered a lot of ground, beginning with a discussion of "legal needs," going through the history of neighborhood law firms, and ending with a comparative discussion of the strategies and tactics of NLFs. I have been concerned throughout, at least implicity, with the question of how much lawyers and legal strategies, as implemented through NLFs, can contribute to "social change." That has not been this study's only concern, of course, but it is an issue which must be addressed, given the NLF ideology. NLFs have been created ostensibly to effect change on behalf of the poor; many within the NLF movement have taken that mandate seriously, and some have claimed that NLFs have succeeded in this clearly novel role for lawyers and the law. In this concluding chapter, I will summarize the threads of the NLF story that relate to this theme.

The following questions, in my opinion, must be answered before even a tentative conclusion can be reached: Is the novel role of lawyers for social change one that can be expected to last? And if so, will the lawyers develop strategies which can maximize their social change impact? Can lawyers politically adopt those strategies? Even if lawyers do adopt those strategies, how much "social change," as opposed simply to "social control," can be expected to result?

Chapter 12

Neighborhood Law Firms, the Legal Needs of the Poor, and Social Change

I. The Changing Professional Role of Lawyers

Part Two was essentially a study in the development and institutionalization of new roles for legal aid lawyers. It traced the conditions which nourished the NLF idea, the emergence of that idea, and how it gained—and is gaining—strength in numerous modern, "welfare state," countries, beginning in the United States and extending even to non-English-speaking, non-common law countries such as Holland, Belgium, Norway, and France. Results strongly suggest that, despite some hostility in the legal profession and among political conservatives, the peculiar nature of NLF constituencies and welfare state political requirements promotes the institutionalization of NLFs—at least as a complement to judicare systems of legal aid. Without repeating those observations, detailed in Chapter 7, a few more generalizations can be made.

The institutionalization of NLFs has broader implications than are at first apparent. Further change in the legal profession is promoted in several ways, each with potentially important ramifications. First, the notion of professional responsibility for enforcing "legal needs" is continuing to develop beyond simply calling for legal services for the poor. Public interest law firms, for example, followed the legal services movement in the United States (e.g., Council for Public Interest Law, 1976), and have recently been called for by the influential Society of Labour Lawyers in England (1978). The right of public interest lawyers to solicit clients, proclaimed recently by the U.S. Supreme Court, epitomizes the importance attributed to the profession's "law enforcement" responsibilities (*In re Primus*, 436 U.S. 412 (1978)). We can expect countries where NLFs get a later start to evince similar movements in their legal professions (see Denti, 1978).

Second, the institutionalization of NLFs provides an ongoing way to mobilize lawyers to become active on behalf of the under-privileged. Lawyers who might have gravitated to traditional legal

228

practices are "saved" by the existence of employment alternatives in the poverty or public interest sectors. Howard Erlanger, for example, suggested on the basis of his data that "lawyers joined the [poverty] program for a variety of reasons and that many, perhaps most, would not have been active on their own, even though they may have felt that there ought to be broader access to legal representation" (Erlanger, 1978:269). The result of this is not only the obvious one of filling staff positions for poverty lawyers, but also there tends to be a filtering out into the community of lawyers who in effect do their apprenticeship with a government program. Jack Katz, for example, found,

> that at least 40 percent of the 102 staff lawyers who left the major Legal Services Program in Chicago between 1965 and 1974 subsequently entered other Legal Services Programs, administrative jobs in Legal Services, "radical" private law practices, law teaching in clinical legal aid settings, public interest law firms, or government jobs enforcing civil rights (Katz, 1978:287).

It is likely, therefore, that many persons who are attracted to the legal services programs and subsequently leave them continue the kind of legal activism developed in the programs. The institutionalization of NLFs accordingly accelerates the momentum for change in the profession (see also Bruinsma, 1976).

The next issue, of course, is how that kind of legal activism will be implemented. Part Three of this study concluded that a "group"- and community-oriented strategy is indispensable to effective "social change" advocacy. The problem is adapting NLFs to such an approach, since it is obvious that a traditional lawyer will generally be unlikely to adopt such seemingly political tactics. Are lawyers congenitally doomed to rely only on less "political," more "professional" strategies? Two questions are involved. First is whether lawyers *can* in a real sense overcome their parochial view of legal reform and actively pursue group work. It is no doubt very difficult, but, as was suggested before, an idealistic lawyer may—indeed should—realize the limits of a purely "legal" approach of service work and law reform and move to the more "political" position of the lawyers exemplified especially by some Canadian NLFs, the law centers in England, and the law shops in Holland.

Thus far the legal service program in the U.S.—partly because of structural features, including the division of projects into "service" and "litigation" units—has not evolved appreciably in that direction, but the evidence from other countries suggests that such a professional evolution is at least possible. The profession in the United States is not so different from that in the other countries examined in this study.

229

Moreover, it appears that many in the U.S. legal services movement, as well as in the U.S. public interest movement, have recognized the necessity of group-oriented strategies (e.g., Trubek, 1977b; Nader, 1976). To date, unfortunately, they have evidently felt unable to encourage such strategies within the government legal aid program. Very recently, however, there have been signs that reformers well-placed in the Legal Services Corporation do now recognize the need to go beyond the law reform–service work paradigm (see Trister, 1978). I would suggest, therefore, that the evolving U.S. recognition bolsters the data from other countries. Lawyers, this study suggests, are *capable* of transcending their professional orientation, at least to the extent of promoting the organization of groups affected by a given legal rule or policy.

But the second question in examining the limits of legal activism is whether governments will *allow* such a movement, given that a lawyer's "professional independence" is his most persuasive means of avoiding the controversy caused by siding with the "have-nots" against the "haves." This is a difficult problem and one on which knowledgeable persons disagree. Comparative study, however, suggests that governments will not automatically reject such a "political" approach; the approach is not necessarily inconsistent with the "legal needs" diagnosis which has proved so powerful with welfare state governments. Governments also no doubt recognize the pacifying effects of an organizational strategy. That strategy is the most controversial—at least when first adopted—of the NLF strategies, but it has gained increasing legitimacy in a number of NLF programs, especially in England, Canada, and Holland. In short, the group strategy is not, I think, so different from other NLF activities that it *necessarily* will not be allowed. As with the other NLF strategies examined in this study, the group strategy tends to be legitimated by its close ties to legal rights and remedies.

This study suggests, therefore, that (1) the NLF movement in the legal profession is capable of finding a permanent institutional form consistent with a new, socially-oriented professional role, and (2) lawyers can evolve beyond a strictly professional approach to the problems of the poor. It is, of course, never certain that either of these developments will take place, but it is important to recognize that the forces behind the NLF movement seem to favor such an evolution. Within the framework of welfare state politics, at least, there are grounds for some optimism generally about the future of legal aid and comparable reforms. Lawyers for social change are not simply dying off with the exhaustion of the student movements of the 1960s.

230

II. The Legal Profession as a Force for Social Change

Assuming NLFs can evolve toward the kind of legal aid agency that will maximize "social change," what can we realistically hope for in the way of such change? This topic was addressed throughout Part Three, but here we can more explicitly confront the problem and its implications for the NLF experiment.

Social change can be defined in terms of the benefits that accrue to the "have-nots" or the relative balance of power between "haves" and "have-nots," however such classes are defined. The term social change could also be reserved for a more dramatic societal transformation, for example the abolition of poverty or the effecting of a fundamental redistribution of income. It should be clear that NLFs are institutions for social change in a relatively limited sense. NLFs and complementary "rights" strategies serve three basic "offensive" functions within wars on poverty: (1) they and institutions such as reformed small claims courts may lead individuals and groups to enforce legal rights, thereby helping translate the promises of the welfare state into real gains for the poor; (2) they may promote law reform, through litigation, negotiation, or lobbying, thereby extending the welfare state rights of the poor; or (3) they may help mobilize and sustain community groups whose roles are essentially those listed in (1) and (2).

These are important functions, but they clearly are not substitutes for broader-based political movements. They are inherently limited to groups of the poor or near poor, and the legal rights which are promoted and used to foster organization tend to confine debate and limit action to a relatively narrow range of political tactics and ends. We are dealing with an effort primarily to ameliorate the conditions of inherently underprivileged statuses—the poor, tenants, consumers, and the like. This is not an effort to attack the existence of such inferior statuses.

NLF reformers, it is true, have worked out a variety of methods for coping with the ambiguities of building a movement on the concept of "legal need." The group strategy, the effort to promote self-help, and the fostering of community control all help avoid these problems. Ultimately, however, we are left with a localized, technical effort to meet the unmet need defined by lawyers and welfare state legislation. The problem of dependency on lawyers and legal strategies can be dealt with, at least to an extent, but the NLF movement (and its analogues) is incapable of transcending the welfare state categories which erected it. Put starkly, if we want to do more than ameliorate the inherently inferior statuses of the poor, tenants, consumers, employees, etc., we need to look toward more traditional forms of broad-based political action.

Still, there is no reason to ignore the possibilities of NLFs, even if they and similar reforms are unlikely to eliminate fundamental societal inequalities (see Trubek, 1979). Because of the institutional characteristics of NLFs and their ability to attract young members of the legal profession, they do have a proven potential to mobilize people to pursue their rights and receive at least some welfare state entitlements. It is generally easier to organize around welfare state rights than around more abstract issues such as "equality," or "social justice," or "socialism," and lawyers able to see through and dramatize the laws' promises may be more effective than overtly political agencies. Those who choose to wait for broader movements based on abstract concerns—especially persons who can wait from a position of relative comfort—have, to my mind, a very heavy burden to bear. Moreover, the movements within welfare state categories may ultimately unleash forces promoting broader political approaches. It may be that only repeated efforts to realize the promises of the welfare state will permit the development of different approaches to problems such as poverty and unemployment. (This is the hope of Harrington, 1976.)

In short, aside from the last rather speculative possibility, we must accept the limitations of NLFs in wars on poverty and other inequalities. Obviously they have a more modest but important role to play—helping to make effective the rights given in recent decades to the underprivileged.

III. Preserving and Extending the Best Qualities of NLFs

My own vision of the appropriate strategies and aims of NLFs was spelled out in the previous chapter and in sections of this chapter. Clearly this study's assessment of the comparative data leads me to favor NLFs that can mobilize groups, minimize dependence, and move beyond Pyrrhic victories achieved through unenforced test case decisions and legislative changes. I would like to conclude with a few other practical insights which have emerged from this study.

First, the necessity of a certain degree of independence from the government, the organized legal profession, and short-term, especially local, funding requirements can be emphasized. In virtually every setting where NLFs have been created, legal activists have found a certain degree of independence essential to the kind of work NLFs can best do. There is no doubt a strong trend to set up quasi-independent legal services corporations with long-term funding, evident especially in the United States and Canada, where reforms have already been implemented. But it must be recognized that much work will be required before this trend is translated into statutory changes in such places as Belgium, England, and Holland.

Second, virtually all NLFs have had to face the difficult choices between "individual" strategies and "impact" strategies designed to help groups or classes of persons. Clearly the "unmet need" is too great for NLFs to meet. Helping the poor requires careful assessment and control of NLF caseloads and more attention to strategies going beyond individual casework. Here, too, a trend is apparent. Virtually all person associated with NLFs urge a focus away from individual casework. For many NLFs, however, it is simply too agonizing to cut caseloads and have to tell needy people that they must go without legal assistance. This problem is true of all NLFs, but its magnitude depends on the availability of alternative means for enforcing legal claims. The importance of alternatives, in fact, must be seen as a basic conclusion of this study.

The reform potential of NLFs, other things being equal, is clearly maximized by what have been termed combined models of legal aid. Two such "combined models" have been discussed, and each has the virtue of allowing an easing of the individual caseload burden. The NLF–judicare combined model is especially well suited to free NLFs from getting bogged down in divorce and criminal work, and the possibility of referrals generally facilitates caseload reduction in favor of other strategies. Also, this combined model can promote new institutions with great potential, such as the lawyers' collectives in Holland. These legal aid lawyers can pursue their social change ends at the same time they survive on *judicare* income. This may further insulate them from political pressure since their income is protected by the power of the profession *as a whole* to the extent that it profits from judicare subsidies. The second combined model discussed here was one involving new or revitalized dispute processing institutions also able to relieve NLFs of their caseload burden while avoiding dependence on lawyers and promoting "self-help" strategies. As demonstrated by other studies within the framework of the Florence Access-to-Justice Project, there is a vast, largely unexplored potential for enforcing rights through these mechanisms.

Finally, the importance of building constituencies ought to be stressed once more. In many ways the key to NLF survival and effectiveness is success in building constituencies. This generally means working with local community groups, but it should include not only mobilizing the poor, but also facilitating alliances and communication with groups not strictly composed of poor persons.

233

This latter strategy has not been implemented to a great extent to date, but its virtues are obvious. If the group strategy is indispensable to effective NLF advocacy, groups with more political power than organizations strictly of the poor will especially serve that strategy well.

My last two points perhaps reveal my inevitable national bias as an American. Both points, which I think are amply documented by comparative study, correspond to continuing remedial weaknesses in the U.S. NLF program, now under the Legal Services Corporation. The NLF–judicare debate in the United States is still being conducted as if the two systems were necessarily opposites, rather than *complementary*, and the group strategy is still generally thought to be too political. Americans can be proud that their innovative NLF model has spread to many other countries, but it is time for Americans to look abroad to see what they can learn from the institution in its transplanted form.

BIBLIOGRAPHY

The following bibliography lists the sources used to document this study. For convenience they are grouped by country and type of work. This should facilitate easier access to the literature, even if it means that it will be necessary to ascertain the correct subdivision in order to trace the sources cited by author and year in the text. The subdivision should in virtually all cases be clear from the context in which the source is used.

Bibliographical Sources for Further Research

I. *General*

M. Cappelletti, J. Gordley, and E. Johnson, Jr., *Toward Equal Justice: A Comparative Study of Legal Aid in Modern Societies* 927–43 (Milan/Dobbs Ferry, N.Y., Giuffre/Oceana, 1975).

K. Schuyt, K. Groenendyk, and B. Sloot, *De Weg Naar Het Recht* 347–57 (Deventer, Kluwer, 1976).

II. *Canada*

J. Reid, *Bibliography on Legal Aid in Canada* (Montreal, National Legal Aid Research Centre, 1978).

III. *England*

M. Partington, J. Hull, and S. Knight, *Welfare Rights: A Bibliography on Law and the Poor*, 1970–1975 (London, Frances Pinter Ltd., 1976).

IV. *United States*

R. Abel, The Legal Profession (Syllabus and annotated bibliography for course taught at U.C.L.A. School of Law, Spring 1977).

Brickman, "Legal Delivery Systems—A Bibliography," 4 *Toledo Law Review* 456 (1973).

Huber, "Thou Shalt Not Ration Justice: A History and Bibliography of Legal Aid in America," 44 *George Washington Law Review* 754 (1976).

E. Johnson, *Justice and Reform: The Formative Years of the OEO Legal Services Program* 389–402 (N.Y., Russell Sage Foundation, 1974).

Works Cited in This Study

I. General or Comparative

Books

T. Bottomore, *Sociology as Social Criticism* (New York, William Morrow and Co., Inc. 1976).

M. Cappelletti and B. Garth, *Access to Justice: A World Survey* (Leyden, London, Boston/Milan, Sijthoff/Guiffrè, 1978).

M. Cappelletti and B. Garth, *Access to Justice: Emerging Issues and Perspectives* (Leyden, London, Boston/Milan, Sijthoff/Guiffrè, 1979).

L. Friedman, *The Legal System: A Social Science Perspective* (New York, Russell Sage Foundation, 1975).

N. Gilbert and H. Specht, *Dimensions of Social Welfare Policy* (Englewood Cliffs, N.J., Prentice-Hall, Inc., 1974).

I. Illich, I. Zola, J. McKnight, J. Kaplan, and H. Shaiken, *Disabling Professions* (London, Marion Boyers, 1976).

M. Janowitz, *Social Control of the Welfare State* (New York/Amsterdam, Elsevier, 1976).

D. MacCormick, ed., *Lawyers in their Social Setting* (Edinburgh, W. Green and Son Ltd., 1976).

P. Marris and M. Rein, *Dilemmas of Social Reform* (Harmondsworth, Penguin Books, 1972).

C. Offe, *Lo Stato nel Capitalismo Maturo* (Milan, Etas Libri, 1977).

W. Pfennigstorf, *Legal Expense Insurance* (Chicago, American Bar Foundation, 1975).

D. Rueschmeyer, *Lawyers and Their Societies* (Cambridge, Mass., Harvard University Press, 1973).

R. Unger, *Law in Modern Society* (New York, The Free Press, 1976).

M. Weber, *Law in Economy and Society* (Cambridge, Mass., Harvard University Press, M. Rheinstein, ed., 1954).

Articles

Denti, "L'avvocato e la difesa di interessi collettive," [1978] *Foro Ital.* IV 111.

Luhman, "The Legal Profession: Comments on the Situation in the Federal Republic," in *Lawyers in their Social Setting* 98 (Edinburgh, W. Green and Son, Ltd., D. MacCormick, ed., 1976).

II. Comparative Legal Aid

Books

M. Cappelletti, J. Gordley, and E. Johnson, Jr., *Toward Equal Justice: A Comparative Study of Legal Aid in Modern Societies* (Milan/Dobbs Ferry, N.Y., Guiffrè/Oceana, 1975).

Council of Europe, *Legal Services for Deprived Persons, Particularly in Urban Areas. Proceedings of the Sixth Colloquy on European Law, May 11–13, 1976* (Strasbourg, Council of Europe, 1976).

236

Council of Europe, *Replies Made by Governments to the Questionnaire on Legal Aid and Advice* (Strasbourg, Council of Europe, 1977).

Nations Unies, *Etude sur l'égalité dans l'administration de la justice* (New York, United Nations, 1972).

Proceedings of the First International Colloquium on Legal Aid and Legal Services, 25–28 October 1976, London (Palo Alto, International Common Law Exchange Society, 1977).

Articles

Berney and Pierce, "An Evaluative Framework of Legal Aid Models," 1975 *Washington University Law Quarterly* 5.

Cappelletti, "Legal Aid in Europe: A Turmoil," 60 *American Bar Association* 206 (1974).

Magavern, Thomas, and Stuart, "Law, Urban Development and the Poor in Developing Countries," 1975 *Washington University Law Quarterly* 45.

III. United States

Books and Reports

American Assembly, *Law and the American Future* (Englewood Cliffs, N.J., Prentice-Hall, M. Schwartz, ed., 1976).

American Bar Association, *The Corporation for Legal Services: A Study* (Chicago, ABA, 1971).

Auerbach Corporation, Office of Legal Services, *Individual Project Evaluations: Final Report* (Washington, D.C., Auerbach Corporation, 1970).

J. Auerbach, *Unequal Justice: Lawyers and Social Change in Modern America* (New York, Oxford University Press, 1976).

D. Bell, *The End of Ideology* (New York, Collier Books, 1961).

E. Brownell, *Legal Aid in the United States* (Rochester, Lawyers Cooperative Publishing Co., 1951).

E. Cahn and B. Passet, eds., *Citizen Participation: Effecting Community Change* (New York, Praeger, 1971).

Council for Public Interest Law, *Balancing the Scales of Justice: Financing Public Interest Law in America* (Washington, D.C., Council for Public Interest Law, 1976).

B. Curran, *The Legal Needs of the Public: The Final Report of a National Survey* (Chicago, American Bar Foundation, 1977).

M. Girth, *Poor People's Lawyers* (Hicksville, N.Y., Exposition Press, 1976).

J. Handler, E. Hollingsworth, and H. Erlanger, *Lawyers and the Pursuit of Rights* (New York, Academic Press, 1978).

J. Handler, *Social Movements and the Legal System* (New York, Academic Press, 1978).

M. Harrington, *The Other America: Poverty in the United States* (New York, MacMillan, 1962).

M. Harrington, *The Twilight of Capitalism* (New York, Simon and Schuster, 1976).

R. Haveman, ed., *A Decade of Federal Antipoverty Programs: Achievements, Failures, and Lessons* (New York, Academic Press, 1977).

D. Horowitz, *The Courts and Social Policy* (Washington, D.C., The Brookings Institution, 1977).

E. Johnson, Jr., *Justice and Reform: The Formative Years of the OEO Legal Services Program* (New York, Russell Sage Foundation, 1974).

R. Kramer, *Participation of the Poor: Comparative Community Case Studies in the War on Poverty* (Englewood Cliffs, N.Y., Prentice-Hall, 1969).

Legal Services Corporation, *Annual Report 1976* (Washington, D.C., Legal Services Corporation, 1977a).

Legal Services Corporation, *Annual Report 1977* (Washington, D.C., Legal Services Corporation, 1978a).

Legal Services Corporation, *Delivery Systems Study: A Research Project on the Delivery of Legal Services to the Poor* (Washington, D.C., Legal Services Corporation, 1977b).

Legal Services Corporation, *Next Steps for the Legal Services Corporation, A Set of Discussion Papers, April 1978* (Washington, D.C., Legal Services Corporation, 1978b).

R. Marks, *The Legal Needs of the Poor: A Critical Analysis* (Chicago, American Bar Foundation, 1971).

R. Murphy, *Political Entrepreneurs and Urban Poverty* (Lexington, Mass., D.C. Heath and Co., 1971).

R. Nader and M. Green, eds., *Verdicts on Lawyers* (New York, Thomas Y. Cromwell Co., 1976).

National Legal Aid and Defender Association, *1971 Statistics of Legal Assistance Work* (Chicago, NLADA, 1971).

Office of Economic Opportunity, *Guidelines for Legal Services Programs* (Washington, D.C., OEO, 1966).

Office of Economic Opportunity, *Legal Services in Action* (Washington, D.C., OEO, 1967).

F. Piven and R. Cloward, *Poor People's Movements: Why They Succeed, How They Fail* (New York, Pantheon, 1977).

F. Piven and R. Cloward, *Regulating the Poor: The Functions of Public Welfare* (London, Tavistock, 1972).

Report of the National Advisory Commission on Civil Disorders (New York, Bantam, 1968).

S. Schiengold, *The Politics of Rights: Lawyers, Public Policy, and Political Change* (New Haven, Yale University Press, 1974).

R. Smith, *Justice and the Poor* (New York, Carnegie Foundation, 1919).

H. Stumpf, *Community Politics and Legal Services: The Other Side of the Law* (Beverly Hills/London, Sage Publications, 1975).

U.S Dept. of Health, Education, and Welfare, *Conference Proceedings, The Extension of Legal Services for the Poor, November 12–14, 1964* (Washington, D.C., Gov't Printing Office, 1964).

P. Wald, *Law and Poverty* (Working Paper for National Conference on Law and Poverty, Washington, D.C., 23–25 June, 1965).

H. Weissman, *Community Councils and Community Control* (Pittsburgh, University of Pittsburgh Press, 1970).

Articles

Abel, "Socializing the Legal Profession: Can Redistributing Lawyers' Services Achieve Social Justice?" 1 *Law and Policy Quarterly* 5 (1979).

Abrahams, "The Neighborhood Law Office Plan," 1949 *Wisconsin Law Review* 634.

238

Abrahams, "Twenty-Five Years of Service: Philadelphia's Neighborhood Law Office Plan," 50 *American Bar Association Journal* 728 (1964).

Agnew, "What's Wrong with the Legal Services Program?", 58 *American Bar Association Journal* 930 (1972).

Arnold, "And Finally, 342 Days Later...," *Juris Doctor*, September 1975, at 32.

Arnold, "The Knockdown, Drag-Out Battle Over Legal Services," *Juris Doctor*, April 1973, at 4.

Bamberger, "The American Approach: Public Funding, Law Reform, and Staff Attorneys," 10 *Cornell International Law Journal* 207 (1977).

Bamberger, "Basic Principles," 1966 *California State Bar Journal* 224 (1966a).

Bamberger, "The Legal Services Program of the Office of Economic Opportunity," 41 *Notre Dame Lawyer* 847 (1966b).

Bellow, "The Legal Aid Puzzle: Turning Solutions into Problems," *Working Papers*, Spring 1977, at 52.

Bellow, "Which Lawyers Win?", *Working Papers*, Fall 1976, at 4.

Black, "The Mobilization of Law," 2 *Journal of Legal Studies* 125 (1973).

Breger, "The Legal Services Corporation: A Report to the Bar," 1976 *Texas Bar Journal* 423.

Brakel, "Styles of Delivery of Legal Services to the Poor: A Review Article," 1977 *American Bar Foundation Research Journal* 219.

Brickman, "Expansion of the Lawyering Process Through a New Delivery System: The Emergence and State of Legal Paraprofessionalism," 71 *Columbia Law Review* 1153 (1971).

Brill, "The Uses and Abuses of Legal Assistance," 31 *The Public Interest* 58 (1970).

Cahn and Cahn, "The War on Poverty: A Civilian Perspective," 73 *Yale Law Journal* 1317 (1964).

Cahn and Cahn, "What Price Justice?" The Civilian Perspective Revisited," 41 *Notre Dame Lawyer* 927 (1966).

Carlin, "Store Front Lawyers in San Francisco," in *The Scales of Justice* 173 (New Brunswick, N.J., Transaction Books, A. Blumberg, ed., 2nd ed. 1973).

Carlin and Howard, "Legal Representation and Class Justice," 12 *U.C.L.A. Law Review* 381 (1965).

Carlin, Howard, and Messinger, "Civil Justice and the Poor," 1 *Law and Society Review* 9 (1966).

Capowski, "Introduction to the Welfare Law Issue," 61 *Cornell Law Review* 663 (1976).

Champagne, "The Internal Operation of OEO Legal Services Projects," 51 *Journal of Urban Law* 649 (1974).

Champagne, "Lawyers and Government Funded Legal Services," 21 *Villanova Law Review* 860 (1975–76).

Chapman, "The Rich Get Rich, and the Poor Get Lawyers," *The New Republic*, 4 Sept., 1977, at 9.

Comment, "Participation of the Poor: Section 202(a) (3) Organizations Under the Economic Opportunity Act of 1964," 75 *Yale Law Journal* 599 (1966).

Crampton, "Promise and Reality in Legal Services," 61 *Cornell Law Review* 670 (1976).

Crampton, "The Task Ahead in Legal Services," 61 *American Bar Association Journal* 1339 (1975).

Drinan, "Reflections on the Struggle," 33 *NLADA Briefcase* 51 (1976).

Ehrlich, "A Year in the Life ... The Legal Services Corporation," 34 *NLADA Briefcase* 63 (1976–77).

Ehrlich, "Decent Legal Care" (Remarks before the Conference on Legal Needs, Northwestern School of Law, Chicago, Illinois, 11 June, 1977).

Erlanger, "Lawyers and Neighborhood Legal Services, Social Background and the Impetus for Reform," 12 *Law and Society Review* 189 (1978).

Falk and Pollak, "Political Interference with Publicly Funded Lawyers: The CRLA Controversy and the Future of Legal Services," 24 *Hastings Law Journal* 599 (1973).

Falk and Pollak, "What's Wrong with Attacks on the Legal Services Program," 58 *American Bar Association Journal* 1287 (1972).

Fendler, "Utilization of Legal Manpower to Assist the Poor (Legal Aid)," 25 *Arkansas Law Review* 203 (1971).

Ferren, "Preliminary Thoughts about Public Decision Making and Legal Aid: The Prospects for Legitimacy," 1 *Connecticut Law Review* 263 (1968).

Finman, "OEO Legal Service Programs and the Pursuit of Social Change: The Relationship Between Program Ideology and Program Performance," 1971 *Wisconsin Law Review* 1001.

Francis, "Legal Aid: The Demise of Idealism," 23 *Wayne Law Review* 1261 (1977).

Friedman, "The Social and Political Context of the War on Poverty: An Overview," in *A Decade of Federal Antipoverty Programs: Achievements, Failures, and Lessons* 21 (New York, Academic Press, R. Haveman, ed., 1977).

Fuller, "A Long Road to the Luau or, the Democratization of Legal Aid in Hawaii," 34 *NLADA Briefcase* 41 (1976–77).

Galanter, "Why the Haves Come Out Ahead: Speculations on the Limits of Legal Change," 9 *Law and Society Review* 95 (1974).

Galanter, "Afterword: Explaining Litigation," 9 *Law and Society Review* 347 (1975).

George, "Development of the Legal Services Corporation," 61 *Cornell Law Review* 681 (1976).

Handler, "Public Interest Law: Problems and Prospects," in American Assembly, *Law and the American Future* (Englewood Cliffs, N.J., Prentice-Hall, M. Schwartz, ed., 1976).

Hannon, "From Politics to Reality: An Historical Perspective of the Legal Services Corporation," 25 *Emory Law Journal* 639 (1976).

Hannon, "Law Reform Enforcement at the Local Level: A Legal Services Case Study," 19 *Journal of Public Law* 23 (1970).

Hannon, "The Leadership Problem in the Legal Services Program," 4 *Law and Society Review* 235 (1969a).

Hannon, "National Policy Versus Local Control: The Legal Services Dilemma," 5 *California Western Law Review* 223 (1969b).

Hazard, "Law Reforming in the Antipoverty Effort," 37 *University of Chicago Law Review* 242 (1970).

Hollingsworth, "Ten Years of Legal Services for the Poor," in *A Decade of Federal Antipoverty Programs: Achievements, Failures, and Lessons* 285 (New York, Academic Press, R. Haveman, ed., 1977).

Huber, "Thou Shalt Not Ration Justice: A History and Bibliography of Legal Aid in America," 44 *George Washington Law Review* 754 (1976).

240

Johnson, "Discussion," in *A Decade of Federal Antipoverty Programs: Achievements, Failures, and Lessons* 316 (New York, Academic Press, R. Haveman, ed., 1977).

Johnson et al., "Access to Justice in the United States," in *Access to Justice: A World Survey* 913 (Leyden and London/Milan, Sijthoff/Giuffre, M. Cappelletti and B. Garth, eds., 1978).

Karabian, "Legal Services for the Poor: Some Political Observations," 6 *University of San Francisco Law Review* 253 (1973).

Katz, "Lawyers for the Poor in Transition: Involvement, Reform, and the Turnover Problem in the Legal Services Program," 12 *Law and Society Review* 275 (1978).

Klaus, "Civil Legal Services for the Poor," in The American Assembly, *Law and the American Future* (Englewood Cliffe, N.J., Prentice-Hall, M. Schwartz, ed., 1976).

Klaus, "Legal Services Program: Reply to President Agnew," 58 *American Bar Association Journal* 1178 (1972).

Lempert, "Mobilizing Private Law: An Introductory Essay," 11 *Law and Society Review* 173 (1976).

Levi, "Focal Leverage Points in Problems Relating to Real Property," 66 *Columbia Law Review* 275 (1966).

Levine and Preston, "Community Resource Orientation Among Low Income Groups," 1970 *Wisconsin Law Review* 80.

Llewelyn, "The Bar's Troubles, and Poultices—and Cures?", 5 *Law and Contemporary Problems* 104 (1938).

Lochner, "The No Fee and Low Fee Practice of Private Attorneys," 9 *Law and Society Review* 431 (1975).

Marden, "Introduction," 41 *Notre Dame Lawyer* 843 (1966).

Marks, "Some Research Perspectives for Looking at Legal Need and Legal Services Delivery Systems: Old Forms or New?", 11 *Law and Society Review* 191 (1977).

Mayhew, "Institutions of Legal Representation: Civil Justice and the Public," 9 *Law and Society Review* 401 (1975).

Mayhew and Reiss, "The Social Organization of Legal Contacts," 34 *American Sociological Review* 309 (1969).

McCalpin, "The Bar Faces Forward," 51 *American Bar Association Journal* 548 (1965).

Note, "Competition in Legal Services Under the War on Poverty," 19 *Stanford Law Review* 579 (1967).

Note, "Depoliticizing Legal Aid: A Constitutional Analysis of the Legal Services Corporation Act," 61 *Cornell Law Review* 734 (1976).

Note, "The Legal Services Corporation: Curtailing Political Interference," 81 *Yale Law Journal* 231 (1971).

Note, "Legal Services—Past and Present," 59 *Cornell Law Review* 960 (1974).

Note, "Neighborhood Law Offices: The New Wave in Legal Services for the Poor," 80 *Harvard Law Review* 805 (1967).

Note, "The New Public Interest Lawyers," 79 *Yale Law Journal* 1069 (1970).

Parker, "The Impact of Federal Funding on Legal Aid," 10 *California Western Law Review* 503 (1974).

Pearson, "To Protect the Rights of the Poor: The Legal Services Corporation Act of 1971," 19 *Kansas Law Review* 641 (1974).

Pelletier, "English Legal Aid: The Successful Experiment in Judicare," 40 *University of Colorado Law Review* 10 (1967).

Pious, "Congress, The Organized Bar, and the Legal Services Program" 1972 *Wisconsin Law Review* 418.

Pious, "Policy and Public Administration: The Legal Services Program in the War on Poverty," 1 *Politics and Society* 365 (1971).

Powell, "The State of the Legal Profession," 51 *American Bar Association Journal* 823 (1965).

Pye, "The Role of Legal Services in the Antipoverty Program," 31 *Law and Contemporary Problems* 211 (1966).

Pye and Cochran, "Legal Aid—A Proposal," 47 *North Carolina Law Review* 528 (1969).

Pye and Garraty, "The Involvement of the Bar in the War Against Poverty," 41 *Notre Dame Lawyer* 860 (1966).

Rabin, "Lawyers for Social Change: Perspectives on Public Interest Law," 28 *Stanford Law Review* 207 (1976).

Robb, "Controversial Cases and the Legal Services Program," 56 *American Bar Association Journal* 329 (1970).

Robb, "New Niche for Legal Services," 59 *American Bar Association Journal* 557 (1971a).

Robb, "Poverty Lawyers' Independence—Battle Cry for Justice," 1 *New Mexico Law Review* 215 (1971b).

Rothstein, "The Myth of Sisyphus: Legal Services Efforts on Behalf of the Poor," 7 *Journal of Law Reform* 493 (1974).

Schwartz, "Foreward: Group Legal Services in Perspective," 12 *U.C.L.A. Law Review* 279 (1965).

Selznick, "Social Advocacy and the Legal Profession in the U.S.A.," in *Lawyers in their Social Setting* (Edinburgh, W. Green and Co., D. MacCormick ed., 1976).

Shriver, "The OEO and Legal Services," 51 *American Bar Association Journal* 1064 (1965).

Silver, "The Imminent Failure of Legal Services for the Poor: Why and How to Limit Caseload?", 46 *Journal of Urban Law* 217 (1969).

Sparer, "Legal Services and Social Change: The Uneasy Question and the Missing Perspective," 34 *NLADA Briefcase* 58 (1976–77).

Sullivan, "Law Reform and the Legal Services Crisis," 59 *California Law Review* 1 (1971).

Sykes, "Legal Needs of the Poor in the City of Denver," 4 *Law and Society Review* 255 (1969).

Thompson, "Constitutional Theory and Political Action," 31 *Journal of Politics* 655 (1969).

Thurman, "The Legal Services Corporation," 1976 *Utah Law Review* 103.

Trister, "Next Steps for the Legal Services Corporation," in Legal Services Corporation, *Next Steps for the Legal Services Corporation, A Set of Discussion Papers, April 1978* (Washington, D.C., Legal Services Corporation, 1978).

Trubek, "Complexity and Contradiction in the Legal Order: Balbus and the Challenge of Critical Social Thought About Law," 11 *Law and Society Review* 529 (1977a).

Trubek, "Review of Balancing the Scales of Justice: Financing Public Interest Law in America," 1977b *Wisconsin Law Review* 303.

242

Trubek, "Public Advocacy: Administrative Government and the Representation of Diffuse Interests," in *Access to Justice: Emerging Issues and Perspectives* 445 (Leyden and London/Milan, Sijthoff/Giuffrè, M. Cappelletti and B. Garth, eds., 1979).

Tushnet, "Perspectives on the Development of American Law," 1977 *Wisconsin Law Review* 81.

Ventantonio, "Equal Justice Under the Law: The Evolution of a National Commitment to Legal Services for the Poor and A Study of its Impact on New Jersey Landlord–Tenant Law," 7 *Seton Hall Law Review* 233 (1976).

Voorhees, "The OEO Legal Services Program: Should the Bar Support It?", 53 *American Bar Association Journal* 23 (1967).

Wexler, "Practicing Law for Poor People," 79 *Yale Law Journal* 1049 (1970).

Yngvesson and Hennessey, "Small Claims, Complex Disputes: A Review of the Small Claims Literature," 9 *Law and Society Review* 219 (1974).

IV. England and Wales

Books

B. Abel-Smith and R. Stevens, *Lawyers and the Courts: A Sociological Study of the English Legal System 1750–1965* (London, Heineman, 1967).

B. Abel-Smith and P. Townsend, *The Poor and the Poorest* (London, Bell, 1965).

B. Abel-Smith, M. Zander, and R. Brooke, *Legal Problems and The Citizen* (London, Heineman, 1973).

L. Bridges, B. Sufrin, J. Whetton, and R. White, *Legal Services in Birmingham* (Birmingham, Institute for Judicial Administration, 1975).

R. Brooke, ed., *Advice Services in Welfare Rights* (London, Fabian Society, 1976).

A. Byles and P. Morris, *Unmet Need: The Case of the Neighbourhood Law Centre* (London, Routledge Kegan Paul, 1977).

Community Law Centres, *Towards Equal Justice* (London, Law Centres Working Group, 1974).

M. Freeman, *The Legal Structure* (London, Greene, Ltd., 1974).

Haldane Society of Socialist Lawyers, *Evidence to the Royal Commission on Legal Services* (London, Haldane Society, 1977).

R. Hill, *Democratic Theory and Local Government* (London, George Allen Unwin Ltd., 1974).

Home Office Community Development Project, *Limits of the Law* (London, CDP Inter-Project Editorial Team, 1977).

R. Jackson, *The Machinery of Justice in England* (Cambridge, Cambridge University Press, 1977).

Law Centres Working Group, *Evidence to the Royal Commission on Legal Services* (Birmingham, Saltley Action Centre, 1978).

The Law Society, *Memorandum No. 3: Replies by the Council of the Law Society to the Request for Evidence from the Law Society by the Royal Commission, Part I* (London, The Law Society, 1977).

The Law Society, *Memorandum on Legal Advice and Assistance, Feb. 1968* (London, The Law Society, 1968).

The Law Society, *Memorandum on Legal Advice and Assistance, August 1969* (London, The Law Society, 1969).

Legal Action Group, *Directory of Legal Advice and Law Centres* (London, Legal Action Group, 1977a).

Legal Action Group, *Legal Advice Centres—An Explosion?* (London, Legal Action Group, 1972).

Legal Action Group, *Legal Services: A Blueprint for the Future: Evidence of the Legal Action Group to the Royal Commission on Legal Services* (London, Legal Action Group, 1977b).

Legal Action Group, *Legal Services for the Future: Towards a New Framework for Legal Services* (London, Legal Action Group, 1974).

Lord Chancellor's Office, *Legal Aid and Advice 1965–66 [Sixteenth Report]* (London, H.M.S.O., 1967).

Lord Chancellor's Office, *Legal Aid and Advice 1971–72 [Twenty-second Report]* (London, H.M.S.O., 1972).

Lord Chancellor's Office, *Legal Aid and Advice 1972–73 [Twenty-third Report]* (London, H.M.S.O., 1973).

Lord Chancellor's Office, *Legal Aid and Advice 1973–74 [Twenty-fourth Report]* (London, H.M.S.O., 1974).

Lord Chancellor's Office, *25th Legal Aid Annual Reports [1974–75]* (London, H.M.S.O., 1975).

Lord Chancellor's Office, *26th Legal Aid Annual Reports [1975–76]* (London, H.M.S.O., 1976).

Lord Chancellor's Office, *27th Legal Aid Annual Reports [1976–77]* (London, H.M.S.O., 1978).

Memorandum of Evidence of the Young Solicitors Group of the Law Society (London, The Law Society, 1977).

P. Morris, R. White, and P. Lewis, *Social Needs and Legal Action* (London, Martin Robertson and Company, Ltd., 1973).

F. Morrison, *Courts and the Political Process in England* (Beverly Hills/London, Sage Publications, 1973).

National Consumer Council, *The Fourth Right of Citizenship: A Review of Civil Legal Advice Services* (London, National Consumer Council, 1977).

M. Partington, *Recent Development in Legal Services for the Poor: Some Reflections on the Experience in Coventry* (London, CDP Occasional Paper N. 13, 1975).

S. Pollock, *Legal Aid—The First 25 Years* (London, Oyez, 1974).

Report of the Advisory Committee on the Better Provision of Legal Advice and Assistance, Cmnd. 4249 (London, H.M.S.O., 1970).

Report of the Committee on Legal Aid and Advice in England and Wales, Cmd. 6641 (London, H.M.S.O., 1945).

Report of the Committee on Local Authority and Allied Personal Social Services, Cmnd. 3703 (London, H.M.S.O., 1968).

Royal Commission on Legal Services, *Report on Progress April 1977, Cmnd. 6770* (London, H.M.S.O., 1977).

Society of Conservative Lawyers, *Rough Justice* (London, Conservative Political Centre, 1968).

Society of Labour Lawyers, *Justice for All* (London, Fabian Society, 1968).

Society of Labour Lawyers, *Legal Services for All* (London, Fabian Society, 1978).

University of Birmingham, Institute for Judicial Administration, *Priorities in Legal Services* (Birmingham, Institute for Judicial Administration, 1974).

M. Zander, *Cases and Materials on the English Legal System* (London, Weidenfeld and Nicolson, 2d ed., 1976).

M. Zander, *Legal Services for the Community* (London, Temple Smith, 1978).

Reports of Law Centers

Adamsdown Community Trust, *Community Need and Law Centre Practice; An Empirical Assessment* (Adamsdown, Cardiff, 1978).

Balham Neighbourhood Law Centre, *Into the Community: Annual Report April 1976— March 1977* (London, 1977).

Brent Community Law Centre, *First Report* (London, 1975).

Brent Community Law Centre, *Report* (London, 1976).

Brent Community Law Centre, *Report 1978* (London, 1978).

Camden Community Law Centre, *Annual Report 1975–76* (London, 1976).

Camden Community Law Centre, *Annual Report 1976–77* (London, 1977).

Camden Community Law Centre, *Annual Report 1977–78 and 5 Year Review* (London, 1978).

Hackney Advice Bureau and Law Centre, *Annual Report* (London, 1977).

Hillingdon Community Law Centre, *Annual Report 1975–76* (London, 1976).

Holloway Neighbourhood Law Centre, *Report 1971–74* (London, 1974).

Holloway Neighbourhood Law Centre, *Report 1975–76* (London, 1977).

Islington Community Law Centre, *Report '74* (London, 1975).

Newham Rights Centre, *Report and Analysis of a Community Law Centre 1974–75* (London, 1975).

Newham Rights Centre, *Two Years Work, 1975–77: Lousy Houses and Dole Queues* (London, 1977).

North Kensington Law Centre, *Annual Report May 1974* (London, 1974).

North Kensington Law Centre, *Annual Report 1975* (London, 1976).

Paddington Neighbourhood Advice Bureau and Law Centre, *Annual Report 1975* (London, 1975).

Paddington Neighbourhood Advice Bureau and Law Centre, *Annual Report 1976* (London, 1976).

Saltley Action Centre, *The Future* (Birmingham, 1977).

South Wales Anti-Poverty Action Centre, *Progress Report Part II* (1976).

Small Heath Community Law Centre, *First Annual Report 1976–77* (Birmingham, 1977).

Vauxhall Community Law Centre, *June 1975–June 1976, Third Annual Report* (Liverpool, 1976).

Articles

Alcock, "Legal Aid: Whose Problem?", 3 *British Journal of Law and Society* 151 (1976).

Brindmann, "LCWG Annual Conference," *LAG Bulletin*, November 1977, at 252.

Campbell, "Legal Thought and Juristic Values," 1 *British Journal of Law and Society* 13 (1974).

Dworkin, "The Progress and Future of Legal Aid in Civil Litigation," 28 *Modern Law Review* 432 (1965).

Foster, "The Location of Solicitors," 36 *Modern Law Review* 153 (1973).

Glasgow East End Legal Group, "Lawyers and Social Work," 2 *Law and State*, No. 2, at 37 (1977).

Green and Green, "The Legal Profession and the Process of Social Change: Legal Services in England and the United States," 21 *Hastings Law Journal* 563 (1970).

Leach, "Legal Advice Centres and Neighbourhood Law Centres," 71 *Law Society's Gazette* 726 (1974).

Leat, "The Rise and Role of the Poor Man's Lawyer," 2 *British Journal of Law and Society* 166 (1975).

Lill, "Why Not Neighbourhood Law Offices?", 111 *Solicitors' Journal* 763 (1967).

Local Government Group of the Law Society, "Royal Commission on Legal Services: Law Centres Background Paper," 76 *Law Society's Gazette* 330 (1977).

Lord Chancellor, "Law Reform and Legal Services: The Lord Chancellor's Address," [1975] *New Zealand Law Journal* 312.

Lydiate, "What is a Neighbourhood Law Centre?", 1975 *LAG Bulletin* 92.

Martin, "The Philosophy of the Law Centres" (unpublished, Faculty of Law, University of Sheffield, 1975–76).

Morris, Cooper, and Byles, "Public Attitudes to Problem Definition and Problem Solving: A Pilot Study," 3 *British Journal of Social Work* 301 (1973).

"No Joy for Law Centres?", *Law Centres News*, Summer 1979, at 1.

Partington, "Legal Services for the Poor in Britain: Current Pressures for Reform," (British National Report for International Congress on the Law of Civil Procedure, Ghent, Aug. 28–Sept. 4, 1977).

Partington, "Some Thoughts on a 'Test-Case Strategy'," 124 New Law Journal 236 (1974).

"Public Legal Services Threatened," 1977 *LAG Bulletin* 150.

Tiplady, "British and American Legal Aid: A Comparison," 129 *New Law Journal* 724 (1979).

"Tom Thumb," 123 *New Law Journal* 1147 (1973).

"Waivers of the Solicitors Practice Rules 1936–72 for Law Centres and Similar Organizations," 76 *Law Society's Gazette* 698 (1977).

Wegg-Prosser, "North Kensington Law Centre," 71 *Law Society's Gazette* 875 (1974).

Wegg-Prosser, "The North Kensington Neighbourhood Law Centre," 67 *Law Society's Gazette* 634 (1970).

Wegg-Prosser, "Political Action Against Law Centres," 75 *Law Society's Gazette* 578 (1978).

Zander, "English Legal Aid System at the Crossroads," 59 *American Bar Association Journal* 368 (1973).

Zander, "Poverty and the Law," 1966 *Socialist Commentary* 13.

Zander, "Waivers—The End of a Long Story?", 127 *New Law Journal* 1236 (1977).

Zander, "Who Should Manage Legal Services?", in *Access to Justice: Emerging Issues and Perspectives* 389 (Leyden and London/Milan, Sijthoff/Giuffrè, M. Cappelletti and B. Garth, eds., 1979).

Zander and Russell, "Law Centres Survey," 73 *Law Society's Gazette* 726 (1976).

V. Canada

Books and Reports

British Columbia Legal Services Commission, *First Report*, March 1976 (Vancouver, 1976).

Canadian Council on Social Development, *Access to Justice: Report on the Conference on Legal Aid, 1975* (Ottawa, Canadian Council on Social Development, 1976).

Canadian Council on Social Development, *Conference on Legal Aid: Report and Proceedings* (Ottawa, Canadian Council on Social Development, 1975).

Clinique juridique communautaire de Point St. Charles et Petite Bourgogne, Inc., *Travail Communautaire de 1970 a 1977* (Montreal, 1977).

Commission des services juridiques, *4th Annual Report* 31 March 1976 (Montreal, 1976).

Commission des services juridiques, *5th Annual Report* 31 March 1977 (Montreal, 1977).

Commission des services juridiques, *6th Annual Report* 31 March 1978 (Montreal, 1978).

I. Cotler and H. Marx, eds., *The Law and the Poor in Canada* (Montreal, Black Rose Books/Les Editions Themes, 1977).

Department of Justice, *The Delivery of Legal Services in Canada: Part One: Provincial-Territorial Legal Aid* (Ottawa, Department of Justice, 1974).

C. Harvey, ed., *The Law Society of Manitoba 1877–1977* (Winnipeg, Peguis Publishers, Ltd,, 1977).

Justice Development Commission, Delivery of Legal Services Project, *Interim Report No. 2: Systems of Delivery* (Vancouver, Justice Development Commission, 1974).

Legal Aid Manitoba, *Fiscal Year Ending March 31st, 1973: First Annual Report* (Winnipeg, 1973).

Legal Aid Service Society of Manitoba, *Annual Report 1974* (Winnipeg, 1974).

Legal Aid Service Society of Manitoba, *Annual Report 1976* (Winnipeg, 1976).

D. Lowry, *Report '71, DAL Legal Aid* (Halifax, 1971).

D. Lowry, *Social Justice Through Law*, A Brief Presented to the Attorney General's Committee on Legal Aid in Nova Scotia (Halifax, 1970).

I. McDougal, *Brief to the Special Senate Committee on Poverty: Legal Assistance of the Poor and the Principle of Equality Under the Law* (Toronto, 1971).

C. Messier, *Les Mains de la loi: Une problematique des besoins juridiques des économiquements faibles du québec* (Montreal, Commission des services juridiques, 1975).

P. Morris and R. Stern, *Cui Bono? A Study of Community Law Offices and Legal Aid Society Offices in British Columbia* (Vancouver, Ministry of the Attorney General, 1976).

Nova Scotia Legal Aid, *Annual Report 1976–77* (New Glasgow, 1977).

R. Penner, *The Development of Community Legal Services in Canada: An Evaluation of Parkdale Community Legal Services in Toronto, Dalhousie Legal Aid Service in Halifax, and Community Legal Service, Inc., in Point St. Charles, Montreal* (Manuscript, August 1977, prepared for the Canadian Department of Health and Welfare).

Report of the Advisory Committee on Legal Aid in Nova Scotia (Halifax, 1971).

Report of the Committee for the Study of Legal Aid in Nova Scotia (Halifax, 1971).

Report of the Task Force on Legal Aid, Part I (Toronto, Ministry of the Attorney General, 1974).

Saskatchewan Community Legal Services Commission, *The First Annual Report: Our Legal Aid Plan* (Saskatoon, 1975).

Saskatchewan Community Legal Services Commission, *Second Annual Report 1975–1976* (Saskatoon, 1976).

L. Taman, *The Legal Services Controversy: An Examination of the Evidence* (Toronto, National Council Welfare, 1971).

Articles

Bowlby, "The Canadian Judicare Plan," in *Proceedings of the First International Colloquium on Legal Aid and Delivery of Legal Services, London, Oct. 25–28, 1976* (Palo Alto, International Common Law Exchange Society, 1977).

Brooke, "Legal Services in Canada," 40 *Modern Law Review* 533 (1977).

Cooper and Kastner, "Access to Justice in Canada," in *Access to Justice: A World Survey* 247 (Leyden and London/Milan, Sijthoff/Guiffrè, M. Cappelletti and B. Garth, eds., 1978).

Gold, "The Law Centre: Victoria, B.C.," *New Directions* May–June 1977, at 88.

Gold, "Some Current Issues in the Delivery of Legal Service," 3 *Canadian Legal Aid Bulletin* 143 (1979).

Jabour, "From the Chairman," *Legal Services Commission Newsletter*, Vol. 1, No. 3, at 3 (1977).

Larsen, "Legal Aid in Manitoba," in *The Law Society of Manitoba 1877–1977*, at 158 (Winnipeg, Peguis Publishers Ltd., C. Harvey, ed., 1977).

Morris, "Decentralization: Some Issues Arising" (unpublished, 1975).

Morris, "The Grass is Always Greener," 42 *Modern Law Review* 291 (1979).

Saint-Cyr, "Legal Aid Services in Canada (1976)," in *Proceedings of the First International Colloquium on Legal Aid and Delivery of Legal Services, 25–28 Oct. 1976* (Palo Alto, International Common Law Exchange Society, 1977).

Sauve, "Legal Aid: Staff Lawyers and Private Practicioners," in *Proceedings of the First International Colloquium on Legal Aid and Delivery of Legal Services, London 25–28 Oct. 1976* (Palo Alto, International Common Law Exchange Society, 1977).

Taman, "Legal Aid in Ontario: More of the Same?", 22 *McGill Law Journal* 369 (1976).

Taman and Zemans, "The Future of Legal Services in Canada," 51 *Canadian Bar Review* 32 (1973).

Wakeling, "A Case for the Neighbourhood Legal Assistance Clinic," 3 *Queens Law Journal* 99 (1976).

Zemans, "Canadian National Report on Legal Aid and Legal Advice," (prepared for International Congress on the Law of Civil Procedure, Ghent, 28 Aug.–4 Sept. 1977).

Zemans, "Legal Aid and Legal Advice in Canada," 16 *Osgoode Hall Law Journal* 663 (1978).

VI. Australia

Books

M. Cass and R. Sackville, *Legal Needs of the Poor* (Canberra, Australian Government Publishing Service, 1975).

J. Disney, J. Basten, P. Redmond, and S. Ross, *Lawyers* (Sydney, Law Book Company, Ltd., 1977).

R. Sackville, *Commission of Inquiry into Poverty, Second Main Report: Law and Poverty in Australia* (Canberra, Australian Government Publishing Service, 1975a).

R. Sackville, *Legal Aid in Australia* (Canberra, Australian Government Publishing Service, 1975b).

R. Tomasic, *Australian Legal Aid: Policy Advisors and Governmental Initiative* (St. Leonard, New South Wales, Law Foundation of New South Wales, 1976a).

R. Tomasic, *Law, Lawyers, and the Community* (Sydney, Law Foundation of New South Wales, 1976b).

Articles

Bayne, "Special Benefits for Migrants: A Fitzroy Legal Service Case-Study," 2 *Legal Service Bulletin* 372 (1977).

Epstein, "Accessibility of Legal Proceedings for the Underprivileged: Legal Aid and Advice" (Australian Report for the International Congress on the Law of Civil Procedure, Ghent, 28 Aug.–4 Sept. 1977a).

Epstein, "Future of Legal Aid, Legal Profession's Second Thought," 2 *Legal Service Bulletin* 250 (1977b).

Fitzroy Legal Service, "Future of Legal Aid (1)—The Fitzroy Submission," 2 *Legal Service Bulletin* 245 (1977).

Harkins, "Federal Legal Aid in Australia," in *Proceedings of the First International Colloquium on Legal Aid and Delivery of Legal Services, London, 25–28 Oct. 1976* (Palo Alto, International Common Law Exchange Society, 1977).

Hermandad, "Legal Services Commission of New South Wales," 3 *Legal Service Bulletin* 74 (1978).

Khan and Hacket, "Legal Aid: The West Australian Commission," 2 *Legal Service Bulletin* 274 (1977).

"Legal Aid—A Meaner Means Test," 2 *Legal Service Bulletin* 405 (1977).

"Legal Aid in the A.C.T.," 3 *Legal Service Bulletin* 74 (1978).

O'Connor, "Salaried Legal Service: The Professional Relationship with the Client," 12 *University of West Australia Law Review* 199 (1975).

Purcell, "Legal Aid Developments in Australia," in *Proceedings of First International Colloquium on Legal Aid and Delivery of Legal Services, London, 25–28 Oct. 1976* (Palo Alto, International Common Law Exchange Society, 1977).

"Redfern Legal Centre," 2 *Legal Service Bulletin* 263 (1977).

Ross and Mossman, "Legal Aid in New South Wales—Politics and Policies," 47 *Australian Quarterly* 6 (1975).

Sexton, "South Australia Moves Into Line," 2 *Legal Service Bulletin* 262 (1977).

VII. Holland

Books

K. Schuyt, K. Groenendyk, and B. Sloot, *De Weg Naar Het Recht* (Deventer, Kluwer, 1976).

Articles

Boer, "Going Dutch on Legal Aid," *3 Legal Service Bulletin* 19 (1978).

Bruinsma, "Les boutiques de droit aux Pays-Bas" (unpublished, April–May 1976).

de Jong, "The origin of the Tilburg lawship and the fields it is involved in" (speech delivered at Tilburg, 9 June, 1977).

Garth, "Legal Aid at the Local Level in the Netherlands and Norway: Report to the Florence Access-to-Justice Project" (unpublished, 4 July 1977).

Griffiths, "The Distribution of Legal Services in the Netherlands—Book Review of 'De Weg Naar Het Recht,'" 4 *British Journal of Law and Society* 260 (1977).

Houtappel, "Access to Justice in Holland," in *Access to Justice: A World Survey* 579 (Leyden and London/Milan, Sijthoff/Guiffrè, M. Cappelletti and B. Garth, eds., 1978).

Knipscheer, "Structural Legal Aid, Legal Aid to Groups, Collective Legal Aid, Neighbourhood Action" (speech delivered at Tilburg, 9 June 1977).

Schuyt, Groenendyk, and Sloot, "Access to the Legal System and Legal Services Research," in *European Yearbook in Law and Sociology* 98 (The Hague, Nijhoff, B. Blegvad, C. Campbell, and K. Schuyt, eds., 1977).

VIII. Belgium

Books

J. Godding, *Le consommateur de justice: questions sur l'acces au droit et a la justice* (Louvain, Catholic University of Louvain, 1975).

S. Pelgrims, *Le bureau de consultation et de defense et la boutique de droit, deux acces a la justice* (Brussels, Free University of Brussels, 1977).

Articles

Panier, "Les boutiques de droit: reflexions sur une experience," 33 *La revue nouvelle* 148 (1977).

Pelgrims, "L'aide juridique en Belgique," 2 *Canadian Legal Aid Bulletin* 348 (1978).

Van de Heuvel, Le point de vue barreau concernant le probleme de l'accès a la justice," (translated by Cristiane Colinet from the article in Flemish in 1976 *Jura Falconis*).

IX. France

Books

R. Dumas, *Les Avocats* (Paris, B. Grasset, 1977).

Boutiques de Droit (Paris, Solon, 1978).

N. Poulantzas, ed., *La crise de l'Etat* (Paris, Presses Universitaires de France, 1976).

M. Valetas, *Aide judiciaire et accès a la justice* (Paris, CREDOC, 1976).

Articles

Hartman, "Permanences juridiques, consultation, et boutiques de droit" (unpublished, European University Institute, Florence, Law Department, April 1978).

"Une ideologie en declin: le droit," Actes, Sept.–Oct. 1974, at 21.

X. Sweden

Hellners, "Legal Services in Sweden for Deprived Persons," in Council of Europe, *Legal Services for Deprived Persons, Particularly in Urban Areas* 84 (Strasbourg, Council of Europe, 1976).

Muther, "The Reform of Legal Aid in Sweden," 9 *International Lawyer* 475 (1975).

INDEX

ABOUT THE AUTHOR

Bryant G. Garth is at present assistant professor of law at the Indiana University School of Law, and prior to this he was Research Associate at the European University Institute in Florence (1975–78). Professor Garth has co-edited with Mauro Cappelletti two other books, Access to Justice: A World Survey (1978) and Access to Justice: Emerging Issues and Perspective (1979) and both were published by Sijthoff & Noordhoff.

Colophon

letter: Baskerville 11/12, 9/11
setter: H. Charlesworth bv
printer: Samsom Sijthoff Grafische Bedrijven
binder: Callenbach
cover-design: Bram de Blécourt